Artificial Intelligence for Big Data

Complete guide to automating Big Data solutions using
Artificial Intelligence techniques

Anand Deshpande
Manish Kumar

BIRMINGHAM - MUMBAI

Artificial Intelligence for Big Data

Commissioning Editor: Sunith Shetty
Acquisition Editor: Tushar Gupta
Content Development Editor: Tejas Limkar
Technical Editor: Dinesh Chaudhary
Copy Editor: Safis Editing
Project Coordinator: Manthan Patel
Proofreader: Safis Editing
Indexer: Priyanka Dhadke
Graphics: Tania Dutta
Production Coordinator: Aparna Bhagat

First published: May 2018

Production reference: 1170518

Published by Packt Publishing Ltd.
Livery Place
35 Livery Street
Birmingham
B3 2PB, UK.

ISBN 978-1-78847-217-3

www.packtpub.com

`mapt.io`

Mapt is an online digital library that gives you full access to over 5,000 books and videos, as well as industry leading tools to help you plan your personal development and advance your career. For more information, please visit our website.

Why subscribe?

- Spend less time learning and more time coding with practical eBooks and Videos from over 4,000 industry professionals

- Improve your learning with Skill Plans built especially for you

- Get a free eBook or video every month

- Mapt is fully searchable

- Copy and paste, print, and bookmark content

PacktPub.com

Did you know that Packt offers eBook versions of every book published, with PDF and ePub files available? You can upgrade to the eBook version at `www.PacktPub.com` and as a print book customer, you are entitled to a discount on the eBook copy. Get in touch with us at `service@packtpub.com` for more details.

At `www.PacktPub.com`, you can also read a collection of free technical articles, sign up for a range of free newsletters, and receive exclusive discounts and offers on Packt books and eBooks.

Contributors

About the authors

Anand Deshpande is the Director of big data delivery at Datametica Solutions. He is responsible for partnering with clients on their data strategies and helps them become data-driven. He has extensive experience with big data ecosystem technologies. He has developed a special interest in data science, cognitive intelligence, and an algorithmic approach to data management and analytics. He is a regular speaker on data science and big data at various events.

> *This book and anything worthwhile in my life is possible only with the blessings of my spiritual Guru, parents, and in-laws; and with unconditional support and love from my wife, Mugdha, and daughters, Devyani and Sharvari. Thank you to my co-author, Manish Kumar, for his cooperation. Many thanks to Mr. Rajiv Gupta and Mr. Sunil Kakade for their support and mentoring.*

Manish Kumar is a Senior Technical Architect at Datametica Solutions. He has more than 11 years of industry experience in data management as a data, solutions, and product architect. He has extensive experience in building effective ETL pipelines, implementing security over Hadoop, implementing real-time data analytics solutions, and providing innovative and best possible solutions to data science problems. He is a regular speaker on big data and data science.

> *I would like to thank my parents, Dr. N.K. Singh and Dr. Rambha Singh, for their blessings. The time spent on this book has taken some precious time from my wife, Mrs. Swati Singh, and my adorable son, Lakshya Singh. I do not have enough words to thank my co-author and friend, Mr. Anand Deshpande. Niraj Kumar and Rajiv Gupta have my gratitude too.*

About the reviewers

Albenzo Coletta is a senior software and system engineer in robotics, defense, avionics, and telecoms. He has a master's in computational robotics. He was an industrial researcher in AI, a designer for a robotic communications system for COMAU, and a business analyst. He designed a neuro-fuzzy system for financial problems (with Sannio University) and also designed a recommender system for a few key Italian editorial groups. He was also a consultant at UCID (Ministry of Economics and Finance). He developed a mobile human robotic interaction system.

Giancarlo Zaccone has more than 10 years, experience in managing research projects in scientific and industrial areas. He has worked as a researcher at the CNR, the National Research Council, in projects on parallel numerical computing, and in scientific visualization.

He is a senior software engineer at a consulting company, developing and testing software systems for space and defense applications. He holds a master's in physics from University of Naples Federico II and a 2nd-level PG master's in scientific computing from La Sapienza of Rome.

Packt is searching for authors like you

If you're interested in becoming an author for Packt, please visit `authors.packtpub.com` and apply today. We have worked with thousands of developers and tech professionals, just like you, to help them share their insight with the global tech community. You can make a general application, apply for a specific hot topic that we are recruiting an author for, or submit your own idea.

Table of Contents

Index

Preface

We are at an interesting juncture in the evolution of the digital age, where there is an enormous amount of computing power and data in the hands of everyone. There has been an exponential growth in the amount of data we now have in digital form. While being associated with data-related technologies for more than 6 years, we have seen a rapid shift towards enterprises that are willing to leverage data assets initially for insights and eventually for advanced analytics. What sounded like hype initially has become a reality in a very short period of time. Most companies have realized that data is the most important asset needed to stay relevant. As practitioners in the big data analytics industry, we have seen this shift very closely by working with many clients of various sizes, across regions and functional domains. There is a common theme evolving toward open distributed open source computing to store data assets and perform advanced analytics to predict future trends and risks for businesses.

This book is an attempt to share the knowledge we have acquired over time to help new entrants in the big data space to learn from our experience. We realize that the field of artificial intelligence is vast and it is just the beginning of a revolution in the history of mankind. We are going to see AI becoming mainstream in everyone's life and complementing human capabilities to solve some of the problems that have troubled us for a long time. This book takes a holistic approach into the theory of machine learning and AI, starting from the very basics to building applications with cognitive intelligence. We have taken a simple approach to illustrate the core concepts and theory, supplemented by illustrative diagrams and examples.

It will be encouraging for us for readers to benefit from the book and fast-track their learning and innovation into one of the most exciting fields of computing so they can create a truly intelligent system that will augment our abilities to the next level.

Who this book is for

This book is for anyone with a curious mind who is exploring the fields of machine learning, artificial intelligence, and big data analytics. This book does not assume that you have in-depth knowledge of statistics, probability, or mathematics. The concepts are illustrated with easy-to-follow examples. A basic understanding of the Java programming language and the concepts of distributed computing frameworks (Hadoop/Spark) will be an added advantage. This book will be useful for data scientists, members of technical staff in IT products and service companies, technical project managers, architects, business analysts, and anyone who deals with data assets.

What this book covers

Chapter 1, *Big Data and Artificial Intelligence Systems*, will set the context for the convergence of human intelligence and machine intelligence at the onset of a data revolution. We have the ability to consume and process volumes of data that were never possible before. We will understand how our quality of life is the result of our decisive power and actions and how it translates into the machine world. We will understand the paradigm of big data along with its core attributes before diving into the basics of AI. We will conceptualize the big data frameworks and see how they can be leveraged for building intelligence into machines. The chapter will end with some of the exciting applications of Big Data and AI.

Chapter 2, *Ontology for Big Data*, introduces semantic representation of data into knowledge assets. A semantic and standardized view of the world is essential if we want to implement artificial intelligence, which fundamentally derives knowledge from data and utilizes contextual knowledge for insights and meaningful actions in order to augment human capabilities. This semantic view of the world is expressed as ontologies.

Chapter 3, *Learning from Big Data*, shows broad categories of machine learning as supervised and unsupervised learning, and we understand some of the fundamental algorithms that are very widely used. In the end, we will have an overview of the Spark programming model and Spark's **Machine Learning library** (Spark **MLlib**).

Chapter 4, *Neural Networks for Big Data*, explores neural networks and how they have evolved with the increase in computing power with distributed computing frameworks. Neural networks get their inspiration from the human brain and help us solve some very complex problems that are not feasible with traditional mathematical models.

Chapter 5, *Deep Big Data Analytics*, takes our understanding of neural networks to the next level by exploring deep neural networks and the building blocks of deep learning: gradient descent and backpropagation. We will review how to build data preparation pipelines, the implementation of neural network architectures, and hyperparameter tuning. We will also explore distributed computing for deep neural networks with examples using the DL4J library.

Chapter 6, *Natural Language Processing*, introduces some of the fundamentals of **Natural Language Processing** (**NLP**). As we build intelligent machines, it is imperative that the interface with the machines should be as natural as possible, like day-to-day human interactions. NLP is one of the important steps towards that. We will be learning about text preprocessing, techniques for extraction of relevant features from natural language text, application of NLP techniques, and the implementation of sentiment analysis with NLP.

Chapter 7, *Fuzzy Systems*, explains that a level of fuzziness is essential if we want to build intelligent machines. In the real-world scenarios, we cannot depend on exact mathematical and quantitative inputs for our systems to work with, although our models (deep neural networks, for example) require actual inputs. The uncertainties are more frequent and, due to the nature of real-world scenarios, are amplified by incompleteness of contextual information, characteristic randomness, and ignorance of data. Human reasoning are capable enough to deal with these attributes of the real world. A similar level of fuzziness is essential for building intelligent machines that can complement human capabilities in a real sense. In this chapter, we are going to understand the fundamentals of fuzzy logic, its mathematical representation, and some practical implementations of fuzzy systems.

Chapter 8, *Genetic Programming*, big data mining tools need to be empowered by computationally efficient techniques to increase the degree of efficiency. Genetic algorithms over data mining create great, robust, computationally efficient, and adaptive systems. In fact, with the exponential explosion of data, data analytics techniques go on to take more time and inversely affect the throughput. Also due to their static nature, complex hidden patterns are often left out. In this chapter, we want to show how to use genes to mine data with great efficiency. To achieve this objective, we'll introduce the basics of genetic programming and the fundamental algorithms.

Chapter 9, *Swarm Intelligence*, analyzes the potential of swarm intelligence for solving big data analytics problems. Based on the combination of swarm intelligence and data mining techniques, we can have a better understanding of the big data analytics problems and design more effective algorithms to solve real-world big data analytics problems. In this chapter, we'll show how to use these algorithms in big data applications. The basic theory and some programming frameworks will be also explained.

Chapter 10, *Reinforcement Learning*, covers reinforcement learning as one of the categories of machine learning. With reinforcement learning, the intelligent agent learns the right behavior based on the reward it receives as per the actions it takes within a specific environmental context. We will understand the fundamentals of reinforcement learning, along with mathematical theory and some of the commonly used techniques for reinforcement learning.

Chapter 11, *Cyber Security*, analyzes the cybersecurity problem for critical infrastructure. Data centers, data base factories, and information system factories are continuously under attack. Online analysis can detect potential attacks to ensure infrastructure security. This chapter also explains **Security Information and Event Management** (**SIEM**). It emphasizes the importance of managing log files and explains how they can bring benefits. Subsequently, Splunk and ArcSight ESM systems are introduced.

Chapter 12, *Cognitive Computing*, introduces cognitive computing as the next level in the development of artificial intelligence. By leveraging the five primary human senses along with mind as the sixth sense, a new era of cognitive systems can begin. We will see the stages of AI and the natural progression towards strong AI, along with the key enablers for achieving strong AI. We will take a look at the history of cognitive systems and see how that growth is accelerated with the availability of big data, which brings large data volumes and processing power in a distributed computing framework.

To get the most out of this book

The chapters in this book are sequenced in such a way that the reader can progressively learn about *Artificial Intelligence for Big Data* starting from the fundamentals and eventually move towards cognitive intelligence. Chapter 1, *Big Data and Artificial Intelligence Systems*, to Chapter 5, *Deep Big Data Analytics*, cover the basic theory of machine learning and establish the foundation for practical approaches to AI. Starting from Chapter 6, *Natural Language Processing*, we conceptualize theory into practical implementations and possible use cases. To get the most out of this book, it is recommended that the first five chapters are read in order. From Chapter 6, *Natural Language Processing*, onward, the reader can choose any topic of interest and read in whatever sequence they prefer.

Download the example code files

You can download the example code files for this book from your account at `www.packtpub.com`. If you purchased this book elsewhere, you can visit `www.packtpub.com/support` and register to have the files emailed directly to you.

You can download the code files by following these steps:

1. Log in or register at `www.packtpub.com`.
2. Select the **SUPPORT** tab.
3. Click on **Code Downloads & Errata**.
4. Enter the name of the book in the **Search** box and follow the onscreen instructions.

Once the file is downloaded, please make sure that you unzip or extract the folder using the latest version of:

- WinRAR/7-Zip for Windows
- Zipeg/iZip/UnRarX for Mac
- 7-Zip/PeaZip for Linux

The code bundle for the book is also hosted on GitHub at `https://github.com/PacktPublishing/Artificial-Intelligence-for-Big-Data`. We also have other code bundles from our rich catalog of books and videos available at `https://github.com/PacktPublishing/`. Check them out!

Download the color images

We also provide a PDF file that has color images of the screenshots/diagrams used in this book. You can download it here: `http://www.packtpub.com/sites/default/files/downloads/ArtificialIntelligenceforBigData_ColorImages.pdf`.

Conventions used

There are a number of text conventions used throughout this book.

`CodeInText`: Indicates code words in text, database table names, folder names, filenames, file extensions, pathnames, dummy URLs, user input, and Twitter handles. Here is an example: "Mount the downloaded `WebStorm-10*.dmg` disk image file as another disk in your system."

A block of code is set as follows:

```
StopWordsRemover remover = new StopWordsRemover()
  .setInputCol("raw")
  .setOutputCol("filtered");
```

Any command-line input or output is written as follows:

```
$ mkdir css
$ cd css
```

Bold: Indicates a new term, an important word, or words that you see onscreen. For example, words in menus or dialog boxes appear in the text like this. Here is an example: "Select **System info** from the **Administration** panel."

Warnings or important notes appear like this.

Tips and tricks appear like this.

Get in touch

Feedback from our readers is always welcome.

General feedback: Email feedback@packtpub.com and mention the book title in the subject of your message. If you have questions about any aspect of this book, please email us at questions@packtpub.com.

Errata: Although we have taken every care to ensure the accuracy of our content, mistakes do happen. If you have found a mistake in this book, we would be grateful if you would report this to us. Please visit www.packtpub.com/submit-errata, selecting your book, clicking on the Errata Submission Form link, and entering the details.

Piracy: If you come across any illegal copies of our works in any form on the Internet, we would be grateful if you would provide us with the location address or website name. Please contact us at copyright@packtpub.com with a link to the material.

If you are interested in becoming an author: If there is a topic that you have expertise in and you are interested in either writing or contributing to a book, please visit authors.packtpub.com.

Reviews

Please leave a review. Once you have read and used this book, why not leave a review on the site that you purchased it from? Potential readers can then see and use your unbiased opinion to make purchase decisions, we at Packt can understand what you think about our products, and our authors can see your feedback on their book. Thank you!

For more information about Packt, please visit packtpub.com.

Big Data and Artificial Intelligence Systems

The human brain is one of the most sophisticated machines in the universe. It has evolved for thousands of years to its current state. As a result of continuous evolution, we are able to make sense of nature's inherent processes and understand cause and effect relationships. Based on this understanding, we are able to learn from nature and devise similar machines and mechanisms to constantly evolve and improve our lives. For example, the video cameras we use derived from the understanding of the human eye.

Fundamentally, human intelligence works on the paradigm of *sense*, *store*, *process*, and *act*. Through the sensory organs, we gather information about our surroundings, store the information (memory), process the information to form our beliefs/patterns/links, and use the information to act based on the situational context and stimulus.

Currently, we are at a very interesting juncture of evolution where the human race has found a way to store information in an electronic format. We are also trying to devise machines that imitate the human brain to be able to sense, store, and process information to make meaningful decisions and complement human abilities.

This introductory chapter will set the context for the convergence of human intelligence and machine intelligence at the onset of a data revolution. We have the ability to consume and process volumes of data that were never possible before. We will understand how our quality of life is the result of our decisive power and actions and how it translates to the machine world. We will understand the paradigm of Big Data along with its core attributes before diving into **artificial intelligence** (**AI**) and its basic fundamentals. We will conceptualize the Big Data frameworks and how those can be leveraged for building intelligence into machines. The chapter will end with some of the exciting applications of Big Data and AI.

We will cover the following topics in the chapter:

- Results pyramid
- Comparing the human and the electronic brain
- Overview of Big Data

Results pyramid

The quality of human life is a factor of all the decisions we make. According to Partners in Leadership, the results we get (positive, negative, good, or bad) are a result of our actions, our actions are a result of the beliefs we hold, and the beliefs we hold are a result of our experiences. This is represented as a results pyramid as follows:

At the core of the results pyramid theory is the fact that it is certain that we cannot achieve better or different results with the same actions. Take an example of an organization that is unable to meets its goals and has diverted from its vision for a few quarters. This is a result of certain actions that the management and employees are taking. If the team continues to have same beliefs, which translate to similar actions, the company cannot see noticeable changes in its outcomes. In order to achieve the set goals, there needs to be a fundamental change in day-to-day actions for the team, which is only possible with a new set of beliefs. This means a cultural overhaul for the organization.

Similarly, at the core of computing evolution, man-made machines cannot evolve to be more effective and useful with the same outcomes (actions), models (beliefs), and data (experiences) that we have access to traditionally. We can evolve for the better if human intelligence and machine power start complementing each other.

What the human brain does best

While the machines are catching up fast in the quest for intelligence, nothing can come close to some of the capabilities that the human brain has.

Sensory input

The human brain has an incredible capability to gather sensory input using all the senses in parallel. We can see, hear, touch, taste, and smell at the same time, and process the input in real time. In terms of computer terminology, these are various data sources that stream information, and the brain has the capacity to process the data and convert it into information and knowledge. There is a level of sophistication and intelligence within the human brain to generate different responses to this input based on the situational context.

For example, if the outside temperature is very high and it is sensed by the skin, the brain generates triggers within the lymphatic system to generate sweat and bring the body temperature under control. Many of these responses are triggered in real time and without the need for conscious action.

Storage

The information collected from the sensory organs is stored consciously and subconsciously. The brain is very efficient at filtering out the information that is non-critical for survival. Although there is no confirmed value of the storage capacity in the human brain, it is believed that the storage capacity is similar to terabytes in computers. The brain's information retrieval mechanism is also highly sophisticated and efficient. The brain can retrieve relevant and related information based on context. It is understood that the brain stores information in the form of linked lists, where the objects are linked to each other by a relationship, which is one of the reasons for the availability of data as information and knowledge, to be used as and when required.

Processing power

The human brain can read sensory input, use previously stored information, and make decisions within a fraction of a millisecond. This is possible due to a network of neurons and their interconnections. The human brain possesses about 100 billion neurons with one quadrillion connections known as synapses wiring these cells together. It coordinates hundreds of thousands of the body's internal and external processes in response to contextual information.

Low energy consumption

The human brain requires far less energy for sensing, storing, and processing information. The power requirement in calories (or watts) is insignificant compared to the equivalent power requirements for electronic machines. With growing amounts of data, along with the increasing requirement of processing power for artificial machines, we need to consider modeling energy utilization on the human brain. The computational model needs to fundamentally change towards quantum computing and eventually to bio-computing.

What the electronic brain does best

As the processing power increases with computers, the electronic brain—or computers—are much better when compared to the human brain in some aspects, as we will explore in the following sections.

Speed information storage

The electronic brain (computers) can read and store high volumes of information at enormous speeds. Storage capacity is exponentially increasing. The information is easily replicated and transmitted from one place to another. The more information we have at our disposal for analysis, pattern, and model formation, the more accurate our predictions will be, and the machines will be much more intelligent. Information storage speed is consistent across machines when all factors are constant. However, in the case of the human brain, storage and processing capacities vary based on individuals.

Processing by brute force

The electronic brain can process information using brute force. A distributed computing system can scan/sort/calculate and run various types of compute on very large volumes of data within milliseconds. The human brain cannot match the brute force of computers.

Computers are very easy to network and collaborate with in order to increase collective storage and processing power. The collective storage can collaborate in real time to produce intended outcomes. While human brains can collaborate, they cannot match the electronic brain in this aspect.

Best of both worlds

AI is finding and taking advantage of the best of both worlds in order to augment human capabilities. The sophistication and efficiency of the human brain and the brute force of computers combined together can result in intelligent machines that can solve some of the most challenging problems faced by human beings. At that point, the AI will complement human capabilities and will be a step closer to social inclusion and equanimity by facilitating collective intelligence. Examples include epidemic predictions, disease prevention based on DNA sampling and analysis, self driving cars, robots that work in hazardous conditions, and machine assistants for differently able people.

Taking a statistical and algorithmic approach to data in machine learning and AI has been popular for quite some time now. However, the capabilities and use cases were limited until the availability of large volumes of data along with massive processing speeds, which is called Big Data. We will understand some of the Big Data basics in the next section. The availability of Big Data has accelerated the growth and evolution of AI and machine learning applications. Here is a quick comparison of AI before and with with Big Data:

AI before Big Data	AI with Big Data
Availability of limited data sets (MBs)	Availability of ever increasing data sets (TBs)
Limited Sample Sizes	Massive Sample Sizes resulting in increased model accuracy
Inability to analyze large data in milliseconds	Large data analysis in milliseconds
Batch oriented	Real-time
Slow learning curve	Accelerated learning curve
Limited Data Sources	Heterogeneous and multiple data sources
Based on mostly structured data sets	Based on Structured / unstructured and semi-structured data

The primary goal of AI is to implement human-like intelligence in machines and to create systems that gather data, process it to create models (hypothesis), predict or influence outcomes, and ultimately improve human life. With Big Data at the core of the pyramid, we have the availability of massive datasets from heterogeneous sources in real time. This promises to be a great foundation for an AI that really augments human existence:

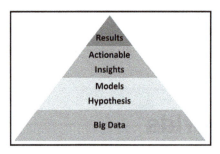

Big Data

"We don't have better algorithms, We just have more data."

- Peter Norvig, Research Director, Google

Data in dictionary terms is defined as *facts and statistics collected together for reference or analysis*. Storage mechanisms have greatly evolved with human evolution—sculptures, handwritten texts on leaves, punch cards, magnetic tapes, hard drives, floppy disks, CDs, DVDs, SSDs, human DNA, and more. With each new medium, we are able to store more and more data in less space; it's a transition in the right direction. With the advent of the internet and the **Internet of Things** (**IoT**), data volumes have been growing exponentially.

 Data volumes are exploding; more data has been created in the past two years than in the entire history of the human race.

The term Big Data was coined to represent growing volumes of data. Along with volume, the term also incorporates three more attributes, velocity, variety, and value, as follows:

- **Volume**: This represents the ever increasing and exponentially growing amount of data. We are now collecting data through more and more interfaces between man-made and natural objects. For example, a patient's routine visit to a clinic now generates electronic data in the tune of megabytes. An average smartphone user generates a data footprint of at least a few GB per day. A flight traveling from one point to another generates half a terabyte of data.

- **Velocity**: This represents the amount of data generated with respect to time and a need to analyze that data in near-real time for some mission critical operations. There are sensors that collect data from natural phenomenon, and the data is then processed to predict hurricanes/earthquakes. Healthcare is a great example of the velocity of the data generation; analysis and action is mission critical:

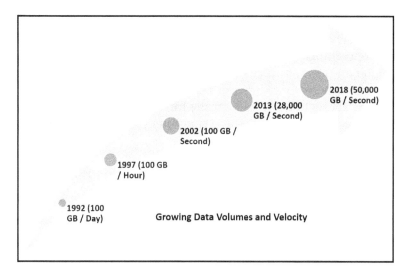

- **Variety**: This represents variety in data formats. Historically, most electronic datasets were structured and fit into database tables (columns and rows). However, more than 80% of the electronic data we now generate is not in structured format, for example, images, video files, and voice data files. With Big Data, we are in a position to analyze the vast majority of structured/unstructured and semi-structured datasets.

- **Value**: This is the most important aspect of Big Data. The data is only as valuable as its utilization in the generation of actionable insight. Remember the results pyramid where actions lead to results. There is no disagreement that data holds the key to actionable insight; however, systems need to evolve quickly to be able to analyze the data, understand the patterns within the data, and, based on the contextual details, provide solutions that ultimately create value.

Evolution from dumb to intelligent machines

The machines and mechanisms that store and process these huge amounts of data have evolved greatly over a period of time. Let us briefly look at the evolution of machines (for simplicity's sake, computers). For a major portion of their evolution, computers were dumb machines instead of intelligent machines. The basic building blocks of a computer are the **CPU** (**Central Processing Unit**), the RAM (temporary memory), and the disk (persistent storage). One of the core components of a CPU is an **ALU** (**Arithmetic and Logic Unit**). This is the component that is capable of performing the basic steps of mathematical calculations along with logical operations. With these basic capabilities in place, traditional computers evolved with greater and higher processing power. However, they were still dumb machines without any inherent intelligence. These computers were extremely good at following predefined instructions by using brute force and throwing errors or exceptions for scenarios that were not predefined. These computer programs could only answer *specific* questions they were meant to solve.

Although these machines could process lots of data and perform computationally heavy jobs, they would be always limited to what they were programmed to do. This is extremely limiting if we take the example of a self driving car. With a computer program working on predefined instructions, it would be nearly impossible to program the car to handle all situations, and the programming would take forever if we wanted to drive the car on ALL roads and in all situations.

This limitation of traditional computers to respond to unknown or non-programmed situations leads to the question: Can a machine be developed to *think* and evolve as humans do? Remember, when we learn to drive a car, we just drive it in a small amount of situations and on certain roads. Our brain is very quick to learn to react to new situations and trigger various actions (apply breaks, turn, accelerate, and so on). This curiosity resulted in the evolution of traditional computers into artificially intelligent machines.

 Traditionally, AI systems have evolved based on the goal of creating *expert systems* that demonstrate intelligent behavior and learn with every interaction and outcome, similar to the human brain.

In the year 1956, the term **artificial intelligence** was coined. Although there were gradual steps and milestones on the way, the last decade of the 20th century marked remarkable advancements in AI techniques. In 1990, there were significant demonstrations of machine learning algorithms supported by case-based reasoning and natural language understanding and translations. Machine intelligence reached a major milestone when then World Chess Champion, Gary Kasparov, was beaten by Deep Blue in 1997. Ever since that remarkable feat, AI systems have greatly evolved to the extent that some experts have predicted that AI will beat humans at *everything* eventually. In this book, we are going to look at the specifics of building intelligent systems and also understand the core techniques and available technologies. Together, we are going to be part of one of the greatest revolutions in human history.

Intelligence

Fundamentally, intelligence in general, and human intelligence in particular, is a constantly evolving phenomenon. It evolves through four Ps when applied to sensory input or data assets: **Perceive**, **Process**, **Persist**, and **Perform**. In order to develop artificial intelligence, we need to also model our machines with the same cyclical approach:

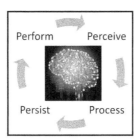

Types of intelligence

Here are some of the broad categories of human intelligence:

- **Linguistic intelligence**: Ability to associate words to objects and use language (vocabulary and grammar) to express meaning
- **Logical intelligence**: Ability to calculate, quantify, and perform mathematical operations and use basic and complex logic for inference
- **Interpersonal and emotional intelligence**: Ability to interact with other human beings and understand feelings and emotions

Intelligence tasks classification

This is how we classify intelligence tasks:

- Basic tasks:
    - Perception
    - Common sense
    - Reasoning
    - Natural language processing
- Intermediate tasks:
    - Mathematics
    - Games
- Expert tasks:
    - Financial analysis
    - Engineering
    - Scientific analysis
    - Medical analysis

The fundamental difference between human intelligence and machine intelligence is the handling of basic and expert tasks. For human intelligence, basic tasks are easy to master and they are hardwired at birth. However, for machine intelligence, perception, reasoning, and natural language processing are some of the most computationally challenging and complex tasks.

Big data frameworks

In order to derive **value** from data that is high in **volume**, **varies** in its form and structure, and is generated with ever increasing **velocity**, there are two primary categories of framework that have emerged over a period of time. These are based on the consideration of the differential time at which the event occurs (data origin) and the time at which the data is available for analysis and action.

Batch processing

Traditionally, the data processing pipeline within data warehousing systems consisted of **Extracting**, **Transforming**, and **Loading** the data for analysis and actions (**ETL**). With the new paradigm of file-based distributed computing, there has been a shift in the ETL process sequence. Now the data is **Extracted**, **Loaded**, and **Transformed** repetitively for analysis (**ELTTT**) a number of times:

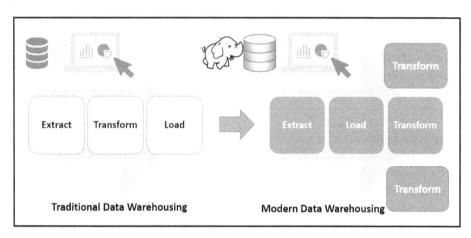

In batch processing, the data is collected from various sources in the staging areas and loaded and transformed with defined frequencies and schedules. In most use cases with batch processing, there is no critical need to process the data in real time or in near real time. As an example, the monthly report on a student's attendance data will be generated by a process (batch) at the end of a calendar month. This process will extract the data from source systems, load it, and transform it for various views and reports. One of the most popular batch processing frameworks is **Apache Hadoop**. It is a highly scalable, distributed/parallel processing framework. The primary building block of Hadoop is the **Hadoop Distributed File System**.

As the name suggests, this is a wrapper filesystem which stores the data (structured/unstructured/semi-structured) in a distributed manner on data nodes within Hadoop. The processing that is applied on the data (instead of the data that is processed) is sent to the data on various nodes. Once the compute is performed by an individual node, the results are consolidated by the master process. In this paradigm of data-compute localization, Hadoop relies heavily on intermediate I/O operations on hard drive disks. As a result, extremely large volumes of data can be processed by Hadoop in a reliable manner at the cost of processing time. This framework is very suitable for extracting value from Big Data in batch mode.

Real-time processing

While batch processing frameworks are good for most data warehousing use cases, there is a critical need for processing the data and generating actionable insight as soon as the data is available. For example, in a credit card fraud detection system, the alert should be generated as soon as the first instance of logged malicious activity. There is no value if the actionable insight (denying the transaction) is available as a result of the end-of-month batch process. The idea of a real-time processing framework is to reduce latency between **event time** and **processing time**. In an ideal system, the expectation would be zero differential between the event time and the processing time. However, the time difference is a function of the data source input, execution engine, network bandwidth, and hardware. Real-time processing frameworks achieve low latency with minimal I/O by relying on in-memory computing in a distributed manner. Some of the most popular real-time processing frameworks are:

- **Apache Spark**: This is a distributed execution engine that relies on in-memory processing based on fault tolerant data abstractions named **RDDs** (**Resilient Distributed Datasets**).
- **Apache Storm**: This is a framework for distributed real-time computation. Storm applications are designed to easily process unbounded streams, which generate event data at a very high velocity.
- **Apache Flink**: This is a framework for efficient, distributed, high volume data processing. The key feature of Flink is automatic program optimization. Flink provides native support for massively iterative, compute intensive algorithms.

As the ecosystem is evolving, there are many more frameworks available for batch and real-time processing. Going back to the machine intelligence evolution cycle (Perceive, Process, Persist, Perform), we are going to leverage these frameworks to create programs that work on Big Data, take an algorithmic approach to filter relevant data, generate models based on the patterns within the data, and derive actionable insight and predictions that ultimately lead to **value** from the data assets.

Intelligent applications with Big Data

At this juncture of technological evolution, where we have the availability of systems that gather large volumes of data from heterogeneous sources, along with systems that store these large volumes of data at ever reducing costs, we can derive value in the form of insight into the data and build intelligent machines that can trigger actions resulting in the betterment of human life. We need to use an algorithmic approach with the massive data and compute assets we have at our disposal. Leveraging a combination of human intelligence, large volumes of data, and distributed computing power, we can create expert systems which can be used as an advantage to lead the human race to a better future.

Areas of AI

While we are in the infancy of developments in AI, here are some of the basic areas in which significant research and breakthroughs are happening:

- **Natural language processing**: Facilitates interactions between computers and human languages.
- **Fuzzy logic systems**: These are based on the degrees of truth instead of programming for all situations with IF/ELSE logic. These systems can control machines and consumer products based on acceptable reasoning.
- **Intelligent robotics**: These are mechanical devices that can perform mundane or hazardous repetitive tasks.
- **Expert systems**: These are systems or applications that solve complex problems in a specific domain. They are capable of advising, diagnosing, and predicting results based on the knowledge base and models.

Frequently asked questions

Here is a small recap of what we covered in the chapter:

Q: What is a results pyramid?

A: The results we get (man or machine) are an outcome of our experiences (data), beliefs (models), and actions. If we need to change the results, we need different (better) sets of data, models, and actions.

Q: How is this paradigm applicable to AI and Big Data?

A: In order to improve our lives, we need intelligent systems. With the advent of Big Data, there has been a boost to the theory of machine learning and AI due to the availability of huge volumes of data and increasing processing power. We are on the verge of getting better results for humanity as a result of the convergence of machine intelligence and Big Data.

Q: What are the basic categories of Big Data frameworks?

A: Based on the differentials between the event time and processing time, there are two types of framework: batch processing and real-time processing.

Q: What is the goal of AI?

A: The fundamental goal of AI is to augment and complement human life.

Q: What is the difference between machine learning and AI?

A: Machine learning is a core concept which is integral to AI. In machine learning, the conceptual models are trained based on data and the models can predict outcomes for the new datasets. AI systems try to emulate human cognitive abilities and are context sensitive. Depending on the context, AI systems can change their behaviors and outcomes to best suit the decisions and actions the human brain would take.

Have a look at the following diagram for a better understanding:

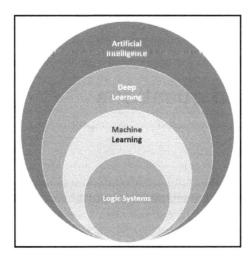

Summary

In this chapter, we understood the concept of the results pyramid, which is a model for the continuous improvement of human life and striving to get better results with an improved understanding of the world based on data (experiences), which shape our models (beliefs). With the convergence of the evolving human brain and computers, we know that the best of both worlds can really improve our lives. We have seen how computers have evolved from dumb to intelligent machines and we provided a high-level overview of intelligence and Big Data, along with types of processing frameworks.

With this introduction and context, in subsequent chapters in this book, we are going to take a deep dive into the core concepts of taking an algorithmic approach to data and the basics of machine learning with illustrative algorithms. We will implement these algorithms with available frameworks and illustrate this with code samples.

2
Ontology for Big Data

In the introductory chapter, we learned that big data has fueled rapid advances in the field of artificial intelligence. This is primarily because of the availability of extremely large datasets from heterogeneous sources and exponential growth in processing power due to distributed computing. It is extremely difficult to derive value from large data volumes if there is no standardization or a common language for interpreting data into information and converting information into knowledge. For example, two people who speak two different languages, and do not understand each other's languages, cannot get into a verbal conversation unless there is some translation mechanism in between. Translations and interpretations are possible only when there is a semantic meaning associated with a keyword and when grammatical rules are applied as conjunctions. As an example, here is a sentence in the **English** and **Spanish** languages:

English	John eats three bananas every day
Spanish	John come tres plátanos todos los días

Broadly, we can break a sentence down in the form of objects, subjects, verbs, and attributes. In this case, **John** and **bananas** are subjects. They are connected by an activity, in this case eating, and there are also attributes and contextual data—information in conjunction with the subjects and activities. Knowledge translators can be implemented in two ways:

- **All-inclusive mapping**: Maintaining a mapping between *all* sentences in one language and translations in the other language. As you can imagine, this is impossible to achieve since there are countless ways something (object, event, attributes, context) can be expressed in a language.
- **Semantic view of the world**: If we associate semantic meaning with every entity that we encounter in linguistic expression, a standardized semantic view of the world can act as a centralized dictionary for all the languages.

A semantic and standardized view of the world is essential if we want to implement artificial intelligence which fundamentally derives knowledge from data and utilizes the contextual knowledge for insight and meaningful actions in order to augment human capabilities. This semantic view of the world is expressed as **Ontologies**. In the context of this book, Ontology is defined as: a set of concepts and categories in a subject area or domain, showing their properties and the relationships between them.

In this chapter, we are going to look at the following:

- How the human brain links objects in its interpretation of the world
- The role Ontology plays in the world of Big Data
- Goals and challenges with Ontology in Big Data
- The Resource Description Framework
- The Web Ontology Language
- SPARQL, the semantic query language for the RDF
- Building Ontologies and using Ontologies to build intelligent machines
- Ontology learning

Human brain and Ontology

While there are advances in our understanding of how the human brain functions, the storage and processing mechanism of the brain is far from fully understood. We receive hundreds and thousands of sensory inputs throughout a day, and if we process and store every bit of this information, the human brain will be overwhelmed and will be unable to understand the context and respond in a meaningful way. The human brain applies filters to the sensory input it receives continuously. It is understood that there are three compartments to human memory:

- **Sensory memory**: This is the first-level memory, and the majority of the information is flushed within milliseconds. Consider, for example, when we are driving a car. We encounter thousands of objects and sounds on the way, and most of this input is utilized for the function of driving. Beyond the frame of reference in time, most of the input is forgotten and never stored in memory.

- **Short-term memory**: This is used for the information that is essential for serving a temporary purpose. Consider, for example, that you receive a call from your co-worker to remind you about an urgent meeting in room number D-1482. When you start walking from your desk to the room, the number is significant and the human brain keeps the information in short-term memory. This information may or may not be stored beyond the context time. These memories can potentially convert to long-term memory if encountered within an extreme situation.
- **Long-term memory**: This is the memory that will last for days or a lifetime. For example, we remember our name, date of birth, relatives, home location, and so many other things. The long-term memory functions on the basis of patterns and links between objects. The non-survival skills we learn and master over a period of time, for example playing a musical instrument, require the storage of connecting patterns and the coordination of reflexes within long-term memory.

Irrespective of the memory compartment, the information is stored in the form of patterns and links within the human brain. In a memory game that requires players to momentarily look at a group of 50-odd objects for a minute and write down the names on paper, the player who writes the most object names wins the game. One of the tricks of playing this game is to establish links between two objects and form a storyline. The players who try to independently memorize the objects cannot win against the players who create a linked list in their mind.

When the brain receives input from sensory organs and the information needs to be stored in the long-term memory, it is stored in the form of patterns and links to related objects or entities, resulting in mind maps. This is shown in the following figure:

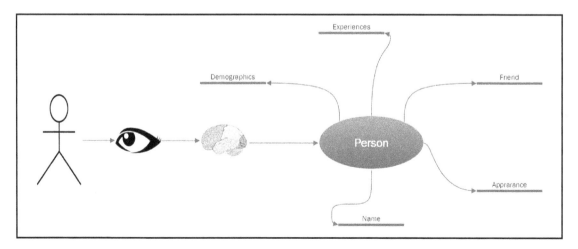

When we see a person with our eyes, the brain creates a map for the image and retrieves all the context-based information related to the person.

This forms the basis of the Ontology of information science.

Ontology of information science

Formally, the Ontology of information sciences is defined as: *A formal naming and definition of types, properties, and interrelationships of the entities that fundamentally exist for a particular domain.*

There is a fundamental difference between people and computers when it comes to dealing with information. For computers, information is available in the form of **strings** whereas for humans, the information is available in the form of **things**. Let's understand the difference between strings and things. When we add metadata to a string, it becomes a thing. Metadata is data about data (the string in this case) or contextual information about data. The idea is to convert the data into knowledge. The following illustration gives us a good idea about how to convert data into knowledge:

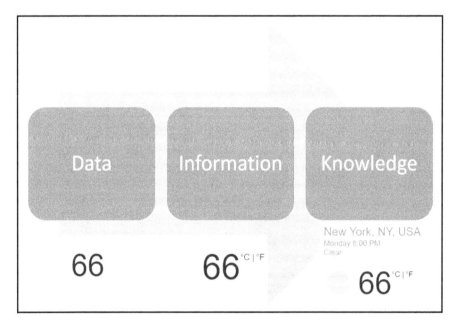

The text or the number **66** is **Data**; in itself, **66** does not convey any meaning. When we say **66⁰ F**, 66 becomes a measure of temperature and at this point it represents some **Information**. When we say **66⁰ F** in **New York** on 3rd October 2017 at **8:00 PM**, it becomes **Knowledge**. When contextual information is added to **Data** and **Information**, it becomes **Knowledge**.

In the quest to derive knowledge from data and information, Ontologies play a major role in standardizing the worldview by precisely defined terms that can be communicated between people and software applications. They create a shared understanding of objects and their relationships within and across domains. Typically, there are schematic, structural, and semantic differences, and hence conflict arises between knowledge representations. Well-defined and governed Ontologies bridge the gaps between the representations.

Ontology properties

At a high level, Ontologies should have the following properties to create a consistent view of the universe of data, information, and knowledge assets:

- The Ontologies should be complete so that all aspects of the entities are covered.
- The Ontologies should be unambiguous in order to avoid misinterpretation by people and software applications.
- The Ontologies should be consistent with the domain knowledge to which they are applicable. For example, Ontologies for medical science should adhere to the formally established terminologies and relationships in medical science.
- The Ontologies should be generic in order to be reused in different contexts.
- The Ontologies should be extensible in order to add new concepts and facilitate adherence to the new concepts, that emerge with growing knowledge in the domain.
- The Ontologies should be machine-readable and interoperable.

Here is an illustration to better explain properties of Ontologies:

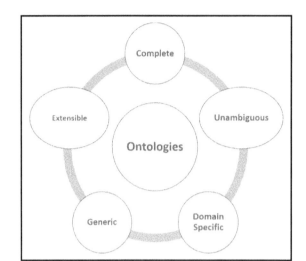

The most important advantage of Ontological representation for real-world concepts and entities is that it facilitates the study of concepts independently of programming language, platforms, and communication protocols. This enables loose coupling, and at the same time, tight integration between the concepts, which enables the software development process to reuse the software and knowledge base as modular concepts.

Advantages of Ontologies

The following are the advantages of Ontologies:

- Increased quality of entity analysis
- Increased use, reuse, and maintainability of the information systems
- Facilitation of domain knowledge sharing, with common vocabulary across independent software applications

Those who are familiar with the object-oriented programming paradigm or database design can easily relate the Ontological representation of the domain entities to classes or database schemas. The classes are generic representations of the entities that encapsulate properties and behaviors. One class can inherit behavior and properties from another class (*is-a* relationship). For example, a cat is an animal.

In this case, Animal is an abstract superclass of Cat. The Cat class inherits properties from the Animal class and adds/overrides some of the attributes and behaviors specific to a cat. This paradigm is applicable in Ontologies. Similarly, relational databases have schematic representations of the domain entities within an organization.

There are some fundamental differences between databases and Ontologies, as follows:

- Ontologies are semantically richer than the concepts represented by databases
- Information representation in an Ontology is based on semi-structured, natural language text and it is not represented in a tabular format
- The basic premise of Ontological representation is globally consistent terminology to be used for information exchange across domains and organizational boundaries
- More than defining a confined data container, Ontologies focus on generic domain knowledge representation

Components of Ontologies

The following are the components of Ontologies:

- **Concepts**: These are the general things or entities similar to classes in object-oriented programming, for example, a person, an employee, and so on.
- **Slots**: These are the properties or attributes of the entities, for example, gender, date of birth, location, and so on.
- **Relationships**: These represent interactions between concepts, or *is-a*, *has-a* relationships, for example, an employee is a person.
- **Axioms**: These are statements which are *always* true in regards to concepts, slots and relationships, for example, a person is an employee if he is employed by an employer.
- **Instances**: These are the objects of a class in object-oriented terms. For example, John is an instance of the Employee class. It is a specific representation of a concept. Ontology, along with instances, fully represents knowledge.
- **Operations**: These are the functions and rules that govern the various components of the Ontologies. In an object-oriented context, these represent methods of a class.

The following diagram explains the components of Ontologies:

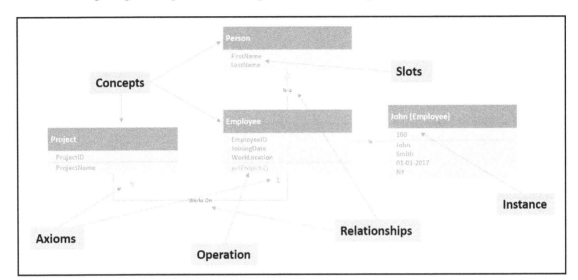

The development of Ontologies begins with defining classes in the Ontology. These classes represent real-world entities. Once the entities are clearly identified and defined, they are arranged in a taxonomic hierarchy. Once the hierarchy is defined, the Slots and Relationships are defined. Filling in the values for slots and instances completes the development of a domain-specific Ontology.

The role Ontology plays in Big Data

As we saw in the introductory chapter, data volumes are growing at a phenomenal rate and in order to derive value from the data, it is impossible to model the entire data in a traditional **Extract**, **Transform**, and **Load** (**ETL**) way. Traditionally, data sources generate the datasets in structured and unstructured formats. In order to store these data assets, we need to manually model the data based on various entities. Taking an example of Person as an entity in the relational database world, we need to create a table that represents Person. This table is linked to various entities with foreign key relationships. However, these entities are predefined and have a fixed structure. There is manual effort involved in modeling the entities and it is difficult to modify them.

In the big data world, the schema is defined at read time instead of write time. This gives us a higher degree of flexibility with the entity structure and data modeling. Even with flexibility and extensible modeling capabilities, it is very difficult to manage the data assets on an internet scale if the entities are not standardized across domains.

In order to facilitate web search, Google introduced the **knowledge graph** which changed the search from keyword statistics based on representation to knowledge modeling.

This was the introduction of the searching by things and not strings paradigm. The knowledge graph is a very large Ontology which formally describes objects in the real world. With increased data assets generated from heterogeneous sources at an accelerating pace, we are constantly headed towards increased complexity. The big data paradigm describes large and complex datasets that are not manageable with traditional applications. At a minimum, we need a way to avoid false interpretations of complex data entities. The data integration and processing frameworks can possibly be improved with methods from the field of semantic technology. With use of *things* instead of text, we can improve information systems and their interoperability by identifying the context in which they exist. Ontologies provide the semantic richness of domain-specific knowledge and its representation.

With big data assets, it is imperative that we reduce the manual effort of modeling the data into information and knowledge. This is possible if we can create a means to find the correspondence between raw entities, derive the generic schema with taxonomical representation, and map the concepts to topics in specific knowledge domains with terminological similarities and structural mappings. This implementation will facilitate automatic support for the management of big data assets and the integration of different data sources, resulting in fewer errors and speed of knowledge derivation.

We need an automated progression from **Glossary** to **Ontologies** in the following manner:

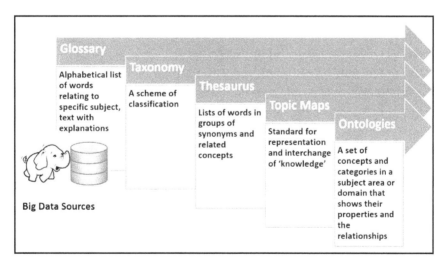

Ontology alignment

Ontology alignment or matching is a process of determining one-to-one mapping between entities from heterogeneous sources. Using this mapping, we can infer the entity types and derive meaning from the raw data sources in a consistent and semantic manner:

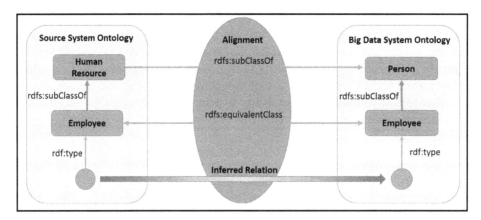

Goals of Ontology in big data

The following are the goals of Ontology in big data:

- Share a common understanding of information structures across software applications
- Make ETL faster, easier, and more accurate
- Eliminate the need for customized, situation-specific ETL pipelines
- The automatic incorporation of new data sources
- Enhance information extraction from text and convert it into knowledge assets
- Enrich existing data with structural and semantic information
- Translate business knowledge into machine-usable software
- Build once, use many times

Challenges with Ontology in Big Data

We face the following challenges when using Ontology in big data:

- Generating entities (converting strings to things)
- Managing relationships
- Handling context
- Query efficiency
- Data quality

RDF—the universal data format

With the background of Ontologies and their significance in the big data world, let us look at a universal data format that defines the schematic representations of the Ontologies. One of the most adopted and popular frameworks is the **Resource Description Framework (RDF)**. RDF has been a W3C recommendation since 2004. RDF provides a structure for describing identified things, entities, or concepts designed to be read and interpreted by computers. There is a critical need to uniquely identify an entity or concept universally. One of the most popular ways in the information science field is the use of **Universal Resource Identifiers (URIs)**. We are familiar with website addresses, which are represented as **Universal Resource Locators (URLs)**. These map to a unique IP address and hence a web domain on the internet. A URI is very similar to a URL, with the difference that the URIs may or may not represent an actual web domain. Given this distinction, the URIs that represent the real-world objects must be unambiguous. Any URI should be exclusive to either a web resource or a real-world object and should never be used to represent both at the same time, in order to avoid confusion and ambiguity:

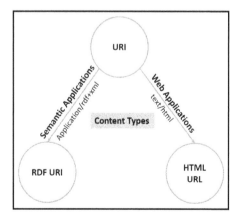

Here is a basic example that describes the `https://www.w3schools.com/rdf` resource:

```
<?xml version="1.0"?>
<RDF>
  <Description about="https://www.w3schools.com/rdf">
    <homepage>https://www.w3schools.com</homepage>
  </Description>
</RDF>
```

When defining RDFs, there are the following considerations:

- Define a simple data model
- Define formal semantics
- Use extensible URI-based vocabulary
- Preferably use an XML-based syntax

The basic building block of the RDF is a triple that consists of a **Subject**, **Predicate**, and an **Object**. The set of triples constitutes an RDF graph:

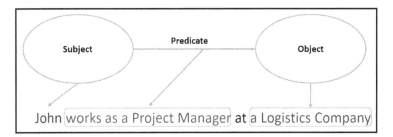

Let us look at an example of a database of books and represent it with RDF XML:

Book Name	Author	Company	Year
Hit Refresh	Satya Nadella	Microsoft	2017
Shoe Dog	Phil Knight	Nike	2016

```
<?xml version="1.0"?>

<rdf:RDF
xmlns:rdf="http://www.w3.org/1999/02/22-rdf-syntax-ns#"
xmlns:book="http://www.artificial-intelligence.big-data/book#">

<rdf:Description
rdf:about="http://www.artificial-intelligence.big-data/book/Hit-Refresh">
  <book:author>Satya Nadella</book:author>
  <book:company>Microsoft</book:company>
  <book:year>2017</book:year>
</rdf:Description>

<rdf:Description
rdf:about="http://www.artificial-intelligence.big-data/book/Shoe-Dog">
  <book:author>Phil Knight</book:author>
  <book:company>Nike</book:company>
  <book:year>2016</book:year>
</rdf:Description>
  .
  .
  .
</rdf:RDF>
```

The first line of the RDF document is the XML declaration. The XML declaration is followed by the root element of the RDF documents, `<rdf:RDF>`.

The `xmlns:rdf` namespace specifies that the elements with the `rdf` prefix are from the `http://www.w3.org/1999/02/22-rdf-syntax-ns#` namespace. The XML namespaces are used to provide uniquely named elements and attributes in an XML document.

The `xmlns:book` namespace specifies that the elements with the `book` prefix are from the – `http://www.artificial-intelligence.big-data/book#` namespace.

The `<rdf:Description>` element contains the description of the resource identified by the `rdf:about` attribute.

The elements `<book:author>`, `<book:company>`, `<book:year>`, and so on are properties of the resource.

W3C provides an online validator service (`https://www.w3.org/RDF/Validator/`), which validates the RDF in terms of its syntax and generates tabular and graphical views of the RDF document:

RDF containers

RDF containers are used to describe groups of things. Here is an example:

```
<rdf:Description
rdf:about="http://www.artificial-intelligence.big-data/book/Hit-Refresh">
  <book:author>Satya Nadella</book:author>
  <book:company>Microsoft</book:company>
  <book:year>2017</book:year>
  <book:chapters>
    <rdf:Bag>
        <rdf:li>1. From Hyderabad to Redmond</rdf:li>
        <rdf:li>2. Learning to Lead</rdf:li>
        <rdf:li>3. New Mission, New Momentum</rdf:li>
        ..
        ..
    </rdf:Bag>
  </book:chapters>
</rdf:Description>
```

The `<rdf:Bag>` element is used to describe a list of values that do not have to be in a specific order.

`<rdf:Seq>` is similar to `<rdf:Bag>`. However, the elements represent an ordered list.

`<rdf:Alt>` is used to represent a list of alternate values for the element.

RDF classes

The RDF classes are listed in the following images:

Element	Class of	Subclass of
rdfs:Class	All classes	
rdfs:Datatype	Data types	Class
rdfs:Resource	All resources	Class
rdfs:Container	Containers	Resource
rdfs:Literal	Literal values (text and numbers)	Resource
rdf:List	Lists	Resource
rdf:Property	Properties	Resource
rdf:Statement	Statements	Resource
rdf:Alt	Containers of alternatives	Container
rdf:Bag	Unordered containers	Container
rdf:Seq	Ordered containers	Container
rdfs:ContainerMembershipProperty	Container membership properties	Property
rdf:XMLLiteral	XML literal values	Literal

RDF properties

The RDF properties are listed as follows:

Element	Domain	Range	Description
rdfs:domain	Property	Class	The domain of the resource
rdfs:range	Property	Class	The range of the resource
rdfs:subPropertyOf	Property	Property	The property is a sub property of a property
rdfs:subClassOf	Class	Class	The resource is a subclass of a class
rdfs:comment	Resource	Literal	The human readable description of the resource
rdfs:label	Resource	Literal	The human readable label (name) of the resource
rdfs:isDefinedBy	Resource	Resource	The definition of the resource
rdfs:seeAlso	Resource	Resource	The additional information about the resource
rdfs:member	Resource	Resource	The member of the resource
rdf:first	List	Resource	
rdf:rest	List	List	
rdf:subject	Statement	Resource	The subject of the resource in an RDF Statement
rdf:predicate	Statement	Resource	The predicate of the resource in an RDF Statement
rdf:object	Statement	Resource	The object of the resource in an RDF Statement
rdf:value	Resource	Resource	The property used for values
rdf:type	Resource	Class	The resource is an instance of a class

RDF attributes

The various RDF attributes are listed as follows:

Attribute	Description
rdf:about	Defines the resource being described
rdf:Description	Container for the description of a resource
rdf:resource	Defines a resource to identify a property
rdf:datatype	Defines the data type of an element
rdf:ID	Defines the ID of an element
rdf:li	Defines a list
rdf:_n	Defines a node
rdf:nodeID	Defines the ID of an element node
rdf:parseType	Defines how an element should be parsed
rdf:RDF	The root of an RDF document
xml:base	Defines the XML base
xml:lang	Defines the language of the element content

Using OWL, the Web Ontology Language

While the **RDF** and **corresponding schema definitions** (**RDFS**) provide a structure for the semantic view of the information assets, there are some limitations with RDFS. RDFS cannot describe the entities in sufficient detail. There is no way to define localized ranges for the entity attributes, and the domain-specific constraints cannot be explicitly expressed. The existence or non-existence of a related entity, along with cardinality constraints (one-to-one, one-to-many, and so on), cannot be represented with RDFS. It is difficult to represent transitive, inverse, and symmetrical relationships. One of the important aspects of real-world entity relationships is logical reasoning and inferences, without explicit mention of the relationship. RDFS cannot provide reasoning support for the related entities.

The **Web Ontology Language** (**OWL**) extends and builds on top of RDF/RDFS. OWL is a family of knowledge representation languages for authoring Ontologies.

Actually, OWL is not a real acronym. The language started out as WOL. However, the working group disliked the acronym WOL. Based on conversations within the working group, OWL had just one obvious pronunciation that was easy on the ear, and it opened up great opportunities for a logo—owls are associated with wisdom!

For building intelligent systems that can communicate across domains, there is a need to overcome the limitations of RDFS and equip the machines with access to structured collections of knowledge assets and sets of inference rules that can be used for automated reasoning. OWL provides formal semantics for knowledge representation and attempts to describe the meaning of the entities and their relationships and reasoning precisely.

There are three species of OWL:

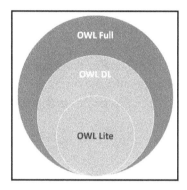

- **OWL DL**: This is used for supporting description logic. This supports maximum expressiveness and logical reasoning capabilities. This is characterized by:
    - Well-defined semantics
    - Well-understood formal properties for the entities
    - The ease of implementation of known reasoning algorithms
- **OWL Full**: This is based on RDFS-compatible semantics. It complements the predefined RDF and OWL vocabulary. However, with OWL Full, the software cannot completely reason and inference.
- **OWL Lite**: This is used for expressing taxonomy and simple constraints such as zero-to-one cardinality.

OWL represents entities as classes. For example, let's define an entity of `PlayGround` with OWL:

```
<owl:Class rdf:ID="PlayGround">
```

Now, define `FootballGround` and state that `FootballGround` is a type of `PlayGround`:

```
<owl:Class rdf:ID="FootballGround">
    <rdf:subClassOf rdf:resource="#PlayGround"/>
</owl:Class>
```

OWL provides several other mechanisms for defining classes:

- `equivalentClass`: Represents that the two classes (across Ontologies and domains) are synonymous.
- `disjointWith`: Represents that an instance of a class cannot be an instance of another class. For example, `FootballGround` and `HockyGround` are stated as disjointed classes.
- Boolean combinations:
  - `unionOf`: Represents that a class contains things that are from more than one class
  - `intersectionOf`: Represents that a class contains things that are in both one and the other
  - `complementOf`: Represents that a class contains things that are not other things

SPARQL query language

With a generic understanding of Ontologies, the RDF, and OWL, we are able to fundamentally understand how intelligent systems can communicate with each other seamlessly with a semantic view of the world. With a semantic worldview, the entities come to life by translating data assets into information and information assets into knowledge. It is imperative that there is a common language to leverage a semantic worldview so that heterogeneous systems can communicate with each other. SPARQL is a W3C standard that is attempting to be the global query language with the primary goal of interoperability. SPARQL is a recurring acronym and stands for **SPARQL Protocol and RDF Query Language**. As the name indicates, it is a query language for querying knowledge (as triples) stored in RDF format. Traditionally, we stored the information in relational databases in tabular format. The relational database view of the entities can easily be represented as triples. For example, let us once again consider the BOOK table:

Book_ID	Title	Author	Company	Year
1	Hit Refresh	Satya Nadella	Microsoft	2017
2	Shoe Dog	Phil Knight	Nike	2016

Here, the row identifier (`Book_ID` and `Title`) is the subject, the column name is the predicate, and the column value is the object. For example:

A Triple:

{1: Hit Refresh}	{Author}	{Satya Nadella}
Subject (Entity Name)	Predicate (Attribute Name)	Object (Attribute Value)

The subjects and predicates are represented using URIs which universally identify specific subjects and predicates as resources:

```
http://www.artificial-intelligence.big-data/book#
http://www.artificial-intelligence.big-data/book#author "Satya Nadella"
```

 Turtle syntax allows an RDF graph to be completely written in a compact and natural text form. It provides abbreviations for common usage patterns and datatypes. This format is compatible with the triple pattern syntax of SPARQL.

Let us use the turtle syntax to represent the `book` table in RDF format:

```
@prefix book: <http://www.artificial-intelligence.big-data/book#>

book:1 book:Title "Hit Refresh"
book:1 book:Author "Satya Nadella"
book:1 book:Company "Microsoft"
book:1 book:Year "2017"

book:2 book:Title "Shoe Dog"
book:2 book:Author "Phil Knight"
book:2 book:Company "Nike"
book:2 book:Year "2016"
```

Let us use a simple SPARQL query for getting a list of books published in the year 2017:

```
PREFIX book: <http://www.artificial-intelligence.big-data/book#>

SELECT ?books
WHERE
{
    ?books book:year "2017" .
}
```

We have the following result:

```
?books
book:1
```

Here is another SELECT query, which fetches more data elements from the dataset:

```
PREFIX book: <http://www.artificial-intelligence.big-data/book#>

SELECT ?books ?bookName ?company
WHERE
{
    ?books book:year "2017" .
    ?books book:title ?bookName .
    ?books book:company ?company .
}
```

The result is as follows:

```
?books     ?bookName      ?company
book:1     Hit Refresh    Microsoft
```

While we are discussing role of Ontologies in the context of *Artificial Intelligence for Big Data*, a complete reference to OWL and SPARQL is outside of the scope of this book. In the following subsections, we will introduce a generic SPARQL language reference, which will help us leverage Ontologies to build artificial intelligence.

Generic structure of an SPARQL query

The generic structure of SPARQL is as follows:

- PREFIX: Similar to the declaration of namespaces in the context of XML, and package in the context of Java, or any similar programming languages, PREFIX is the SPARQL equivalent, which ensures uniqueness among entity representations and eliminates the need for typing long URI patterns within SPARQL code.
- SELECT / ASK / DESCRIBE / CONSTRUCT:
  - SELECT: This is an equivalent of SQL's SELECT clause. It defines the attributes that are required to be fetched from the RDF triples that fulfill the selection criteria.
  - ASK: This returns a Boolean value of true or false depending on the availability of the RDF triples, and based on the selection criteria within the RDF knowledge base.

- DESCRIBE: This query construct returns a graph containing all the available triples from the RDF knowledge base which match the selection criteria.
- CONSTRUCT: This is very handy when creating a new RDF graph from an existing RDF based on selection criteria and filter conditions. This is the equivalent of XSLT in the context of XML. XSLT transforms XML in the intended format.

- FROM: Defines the data source of the RDF endpoint, against which the query will be run. This is the SQL equivalent of the FROM <TABLE_NAME> clause. The endpoint can be a resource on the internet or a local data store accessible to the query engine.
- WHERE: Defines the part of the RDF graph we are interested in. This is the equivalent of the WHERE SQL clause which defines filter conditions to fetch specific data from the entire dataset.

Additional SPARQL features

The additional SPARQL features are as follows:

- Optional matching: Unlike traditional relational data stores, where the database schemas and constraints are predefined for the structured representation of data, in the big data word we deal with unstructured datasets. The attributes of the two resources of the same type may be different. Optional matching comes in handy when handling heterogeneous representations of the entities. The OPTIONAL block is used to select the data elements if they exist.
- Alternative matching: Once again, considering the unstructured nature of knowledge assets, alternating matching provides a mechanism to return whichever properties are available.
- UNION: This is in contrast to the OPTIONAL pattern. In the case of UNION, at least one of the datasets must find a match given the query criteria.
- DISTINCT: This is the equivalent of the DISTINCT SQL clause, which excludes multiple occurrences of the same triple within the result.

- ORDER BY: Instructs the query to sequence results by a specific variable either in ascending or descending order. This is also equivalent to ORDER BY clause in SQL.
- FILTERS and regular expressions: SPARQL provides features to restrict the result set triples by using expressions. Along with mathematical and logical expressions, SPARQL allows for the use of regular expressions to apply filters on datasets based on textual patterns.
- GROUP BY: This allows the grouping of the resulting RDF triples based on one or more variables.
- HAVING: This facilitates a selection of the query results at the group level.
- SUM, COUNT, AVG, MIN, MAX, and so on are the functions available to be applied at the group level.

Building intelligent machines with Ontologies

In this chapter, we have looked at the role of Ontology in the management of big data assets as knowledge repositories, and understood the need for computational systems to perceive the data as things instead of strings. Although some of the big systems and web search engines use a semantic world view, the adoption of Ontology as a basis for systems is slow. The custodians of data assets (governments and everyone else) need to model knowledge assets in a consistent and standardized manner in order for us to evolve current computational systems into intelligent systems.

Let us consider a use case that leverages Ontology-based knowledge graphs in order to simplify the flight boarding process. We have all experienced a hugely manual and time-consuming process when boarding a flight. From the time we enter the airport to the time we board the flight, we go through a number of security checks and experience document verification. In a connected world where all the knowledge assets are standardized and defined as domain-specific Ontologies, it is possible to develop intelligent agents to make the flight boarding process hassle free and seamless.

Let us define the generic characteristics of an intelligent agent:

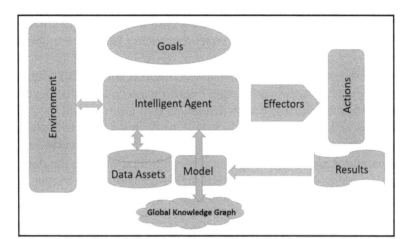

A little expansion on the characteristics is as follows:

- **Goals**: Every intelligent system should have a well defined set of goals. These goals govern the rational decisions taken by the intelligent system and drive actions and hence results. For example, in the case of an intelligent agent that is responsible for the flight boarding process, one of the goals is to restrict access to anyone who does not pass all security checks, even if the person has a valid air ticket. In defining the goals for intelligent agents, one of the prime considerations should be that the AI agent or systems should complement and augment human capabilities.

- **Environment**: The intelligent agent should operate within the context of the environment. Its decisions and actions cannot be independent of the context. In our example use case, the environment is the airport, the passenger gates, flight schedules, and so on. The agents perceive the environment with various sensors, for example video cameras.

- **Data Assets**: The intelligent agent needs access to historical data in terms of the domain and the context in which it operates. The data assets can be available locally and globally (internet endpoints). These data assets ideally should be defined as RDF schema structures with standardized representations and protocols. These data assets should be queryable with standard languages and protocols (SPARQL) in order to ensure maximum interoperability.

- **Model**: This is where the real intelligence of the agent is available as algorithms and learning systems. These models evolve continuously based on the context, historical decisions, actions, and results. As a general rule, the model should perform better (more accurately) over a period of time for similar contextual inputs.

- **Effectors**: These are the tangible aspects of the agent which facilitate actions. In the example of an airline passenger boarding agent, the effector can be an automated gate opening system which opens a gate once all the passengers are fully validated (having a valid ticket, identity, and no security check failures). The external world perceives the intelligent agent through effectors.

- **Actions and Results**: Based on the environmental context, the data assets, and the trained models, the intelligent agent makes decisions that trigger actions through the effectors. These actions provide results based on the rationality of the decision and accuracy of the trained model. The results are once again fed into model training in order to improve accuracy over a period of time.

At a high level, the method of the intelligent agent, which facilitates the flight boarding process, can be depicted as follows:

1. When a passenger walks into the airport, a video camera reads the image and matches it to the data assets available to the agent. These data assets are Ontology objects which are loosely coupled and have flexibility of structure and attributes. Some of the inferences are made at the first level of matching to correctly identify the person who has entered the airport.

2. If the person cannot be identified with the video stream, the first airport gate does not open automatically and requires a fingerprint scan from the passenger. The fingerprint scan is validated against the dataset, which is once again an Ontology object representation of the person entity. If the person is not identified at this stage, they are flagged for further manual security procedures.

3. Once the person is correctly identified, the agent scans the global active ticket directory in order to ensure that the person has a valid ticket for a flight that departs from the airport in a reasonable time window. The global ticket directory and the flight database is also available as Ontology objects for the agent to refer to in real time.

4. Once ticket validity is ensured, a boarding pass is generated and delivered to the passenger's smartphone, once again by referring to the person Ontology to derive personal details in a secure manner. The real-time instructions for directions to the gate are also sent to the device.

The agent can seamlessly guide the passenger to the appropriate boarding gate. The system can be built easily once all the heterogeneous data sources are standardized and have Ontological representation, which facilitates maximum interoperability and eliminates a need to code diverse knowledge representations. This results in an overall reduction of complexity in the agent software and an increase in efficiency.

Ontology learning

With the basic concepts on Ontologies covered in this chapter, along with their significance in building intelligent systems, it is imperative that for a seamlessly connected world, the knowledge assets are consistently represented as domain Ontologies. However, the process of manually creating domain-specific Ontologies requires lots of manual effort, validation, and approval. Ontology learning is an attempt to automate the process of the generation of Ontologies, using an algorithmic approach on the natural language text, which is available at the internet scale. There are various approaches to Ontology learning, as follows:

- **Ontology learning from text**: In this approach, the textual data is extracted from various sources in an automated manner, and keywords are extracted and classified based on their occurrence, word sequencing, and patterns.
- **Linked data mining**: In this processes, the links are identified in the published RDF graphs in order to derive Ontologies based on implicit reasoning.
- **Concept learning from OWL**: In this approach, existing domain-specific Ontologies are leveraged for expand the new domains using an algorithmic approach.
- **Crowdsourcing**: This approach combines automated Ontology extraction and discovery based on textual analysis and collaboration with domain experts to define new Ontologies. This approach works great since it combines the processing power and algorithmic approaches of machines and the domain expertise of people. This results in improved speed and accuracy.

Here are some of the challenges of Ontology learning:

- **Dealing with heterogeneous data sources**: The data sources on the internet, and within application stores, differ in their forms and representations. Ontology learning faces the challenge of knowledge extraction and consistent meaning extraction due to the heterogeneous nature of the data sources.

- **Uncertainty and lack of accuracy**: Due the the inconsistent data sources, when Ontology learning attempts to define Ontology structures, there is a level of uncertainty in terms of the intent and representation of entities and attributes. This results in a lower level of accuracy and requires human intervention from domain experts for realignment.

- **Scalability**: One of the primary sources for Ontology learning is the internet, which is an ever growing knowledge repository. The internet is also an unstructured data source for the most part and this makes it difficult to scale the Ontology learning process to cover the width of the domain from large text extracts. One of the ways to address scalability is to leverage new, open source, distributed computing frameworks (such as Hadoop).

- **Need for post-processing**: While Ontology learning is intended to be an automated process, in order to overcome quality issues, we require a level of post-processing. This process need to be planned and governed in detail in order to optimize the speed and accuracy of new Ontology definitions.

Ontology learning process

The Ontology learning process consists of six Rs:

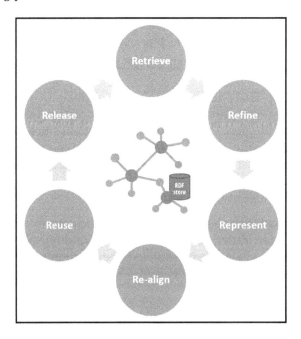

They are explained as followed:

- **Retrieve**: The knowledge assets are retrieved from the web and application sources from the domain specific stores using web crawls and protocol-based application access. The domain specific terms and axioms are extracted with a calculation of TF/IDF values and by the application of the C-Value / NC Value methods. Commonly used clustering techniques are utilized and the statistical similarity measures are applied on the extracted textual representations of the knowledge assets.

- **Refine**: The assets are cleansed and pruned to improve signal to noise ratio. Here, an algorithmic approach is taken for refinement. In the refinement step, the terms are grouped corresponding to concepts within the knowledge assets.

- **Represent**: In this step, the Ontology learning system arranges the concepts in a hierarchical structure using the unsupervised clustering method (at this point, understand this as a machine learning approach for the segmentation of the data; we will cover the details of unsupervised learning algorithms in the next chapter).

- **Re-align**: This is a type of post-processing step that involves collaboration with the domain experts. At this point, the hierarchies are realigned for accuracy. The Ontologies are aligned with instances of concepts and corresponding attributes along with cardinality constraints (one-to-one, one-to-many, and so on). The rules for defining the syntactic structure are defined in this step.

- **Reuse**: In this step, similar domain-specific Ontologies with connection endpoints are reused, and synonyms are defined in order to avoid parallel representations of the same concepts, which are finalized across other Ontology definitions.

- **Release**: In this step, the Ontologies are released for generic use and further evolution.

Frequently asked questions

Let's have a small recap of the chapter:

Q: What are Ontologies and what is their significance in intelligent systems?

A: Ontology as a generic term means the knowledge of everything that exists in this universe. As applicable to information systems, Ontologies represent a semantic and standardized view of the world's knowledge assets. They are domain-specific representations of knowledge and models related to real world entity representations. The intelligent systems that link heterogeneous knowledge domains need to have access to consistent representations of knowledge in order to interoperate and understand contextual events to make inferences and decisions, which trigger actions and hence results, in order to complement human capabilities.

Q: What are the generic properties of Ontologies?

A: Ontologies should be complete, unambiguous, domain-specific, generic, and extensible.

Q: What are the various components of Ontologies?

A: Various Ontology components are Concepts, Slots, Relationships, Axioms, Instances, and Operations.

Q: What is the significance of a universal data format in knowledge management systems?

A: The **Resource Description Format** (**RDF**) intends to be the universal format for knowledge representation, allowing heterogeneous systems to interact and integrate in a consistent and reliable manner. This forms the basis of the semantic view of the world.

Q: How is it possible to model the worldview with Ontologies? Is it possible to automate the Ontology definition process considering vast and ever-increasing knowledge stores in the universe?

A: Knowledge assets are growing exponentially in size with time. In order to create an Ontological representation of these assets, we need an automated approach, without which it will be difficult to catch up with the volume. Ontology learning takes an algorithmic approach by leveraging distributed computing frameworks to create a baseline model of the worldview. The Ontology learning process retrieves textual, unstructured data from heterogeneous sources, refines it, and represents it in a hierarchical manner. This is realigned with post-processing by reusing existing domain-specific knowledge assets, and finally released for generic consumption by intelligent agents.

Summary

In this chapter, we have explored the need for a standardized and consistent representation of the world's knowledge for the evolution of intelligent systems, and how these systems are modeled against the human brain. Ontologies, as applied to information systems, is a W3C standard that defines the generic rules for knowledge representation.

This chapter introduced the basic concepts of the RDF, OWL, and a query language to extract the knowledge representations within Ontology instances through SPARQL.

In this chapter, we have explored how to use Ontologies to build intelligent agents by looking at the generic characteristics of the intelligent agents. In the end, we learned how Ontology learning facilitates the speedy adoption of Ontologies for the worldview, with consistent knowledge assets and representations.

In the next chapter, we will get introduced to fundamental concepts of Machine Learning and how Big Data facilitates the learning process.

3
Learning from Big Data

In the first two chapters, we set the context for intelligent machines with the big data revolution and how big data is fueling rapid advances in artificial intelligence. We also emphasized the need for a global vocabulary for universal knowledge representation. We have also seen how that need is fulfilled with the use of ontologies and how ontologies help construct a semantic view of the world.

The quest is for the knowledge, which is derived from information, which is in turn derived from the vast amounts of data that we are generating. Knowledge facilitates a rational decision-making process for machines that complements and augments human capabilities. We have seen how the **Resource Description Framework (RDF)** provides the schematic backbone for the knowledge assets along with **Web Ontology Language** (OWL) fundamentals and the query language for RDFs (SPARQL).

In this chapter, we are going to look at some of the basic concepts of machine learning and take a deep dive into some of the algorithms. We will use Spark's machine learning libraries. **Spark** is one of the most popular computer frameworks for the implementation of algorithms and as a generic computation engine on big data. Spark fits into the big data ecosystem well, with a simple programming interface, and very effectively leverages the power of distributed and resilient computing frameworks. Although this chapter does not assume any background with statistics and mathematics, it will greatly help if the reader has some programming background, in order to understand the code snippets and to try and experiment with the examples.

In this chapter, we will see broad categories of machine learning in **supervised** and **unsupervised** learning, before taking a deep dive, with examples, into:

- Regression analysis
- Data clustering
- K-means

- Data dimensionality reduction
- Singular value decomposition
- Principal component analysis (PCA)

In the end, we will have an overview of the Spark programming model and **Spark's Machine Learning library** (**Spark MLlib**). With all this background knowledge at our disposal, we will implement a recommendation system to conclude this chapter.

Supervised and unsupervised machine learning

Machine learning at a broad level is categorized into two types: supervised and unsupervised learning. As the name indicates, this categorization is based on the availability of the historical data or the lack thereof. In simple terms, a supervised machine learning algorithm depends on the trending data, or version of truth. This version of truth is used for generalizing the model to make predictions on the new data points.

Let's understand this concept with the following example:

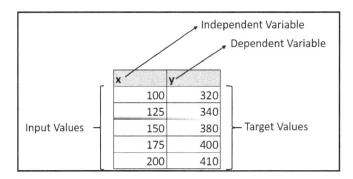

Figure 3.1 Simple training data: input (independent) and target (dependent) variables

Consider that the value of the **y** variable is dependent on the value of **x**. Based on a change in the value of **x**, there is a proportionate change in the value of **y** (think about any examples where the increase or decrease in the value of one factor proportionally changes the other).

Based on the data presented in the preceding table, it is clear that the value of **y** increases with an increase in the value of **x**. That means there is a direct relationship between **x** and **y**. In this case, **x** is called an independent, or input, variable and **y** is called a dependent, or target, variable. In this example, what will be the value of **y** when **x** is **220**? At this point, let's understand a fundamental difference between traditional computer programming and machine learning when it comes to predicting the value of the **y** variable for a specific value of **x=220**. The following diagram shows the traditional programming process:

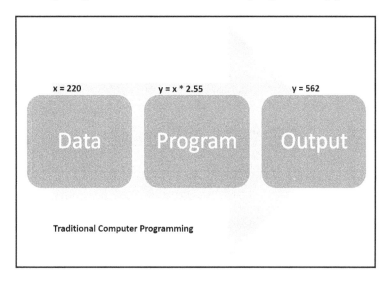

Figure 3.2 Traditional computer programming process

The traditional computer program has a predefined function that is applied on the input data to produce the output. In this example, a traditional computer program calculates the value of the (**y**) output variable as **562**.

Have a look at the following diagram:

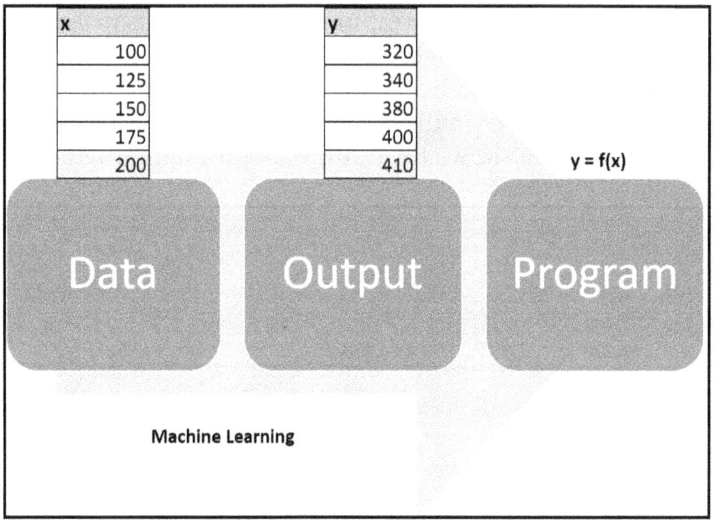

Figure 3.3 Machine learning process

In the case of supervised machine learning, the input and output data (training data) are used to create the program or the function. This is also termed the predictor function. A predictor function is used to predict the outcome of the dependent variable. In its simplest form, the process of defining the predictor function is called **model training**. Once a generalized predictor function is defined, we can predict the value of the target variable (y) corresponding to an input value (x). The goal of supervised machine learning is to develop a finely-tuned predictor function, **h(x)**, called **hypothesis**. Hypothesis is a certain function that we believe (or hope) is similar to the true function, the target function that we want to model. Let's add some more data points and plot those on a two-dimensional chart, like the following diagram:

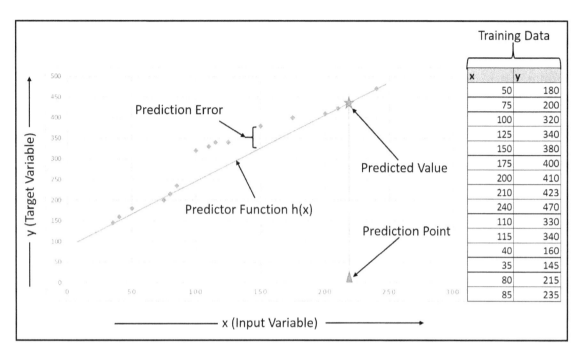

Figure 3.4 Supervised learning (linear regression)

We have plotted the input variable on the *x* axis and the target variable on the *y* axis. This is a general convention used and hence the input variable is termed *x* and the output variable is termed *y*. Once we plot the data points from the training data, we can visualize the correlation between the data points. In this case, there seems to a direct proportion between *x* and *y*. In order for us to predict the value of *y* when *x* = 220, we can draw a straight line that tries to characterize, or model, the truth (training data). The straight line represents the predictor function, which is also termed as a hypothesis.

Based on the hypothesis, in this case our model predicts that the value of *y* when *x* = 220 will be ~430. While this hypothesis predicts the value of *y* for a certain value of *x*, the line that defines the predictor function does not cover all the values of the input variable. For example, based on the training data, the value of *y* = 380 at *x* = 150. However, as per the hypothesis, the value comes out to be ~325. This differential is called prediction error (~55 units in this case). Any input variable (*x*) value that does not fall on the predictor function has some prediction error based on the derived hypothesis. The sum of errors for across all the training data is a good measure of the model's accuracy. The primary goal of any supervised learning algorithm is to minimize the error while defining a hypothesis based on the training data.

A straight-line hypothesis function is as good as an illustration. However, in reality, we will always have multiple input variables that control the output variable, and a good predictor function with minimal error will never be a straight line. When we predict the value of an output variable at a certain value of the input variable it is called **regression**. In certain cases, the historical data, or version of truth, is also used to separate data points into discrete sets (class, type, category). This is termed **classification**. For example, an email can be flagged as spam or not based on the training data. In the case of classification, the classes are known and predefined. The following image shows the classification with the **Decision Boundary**:

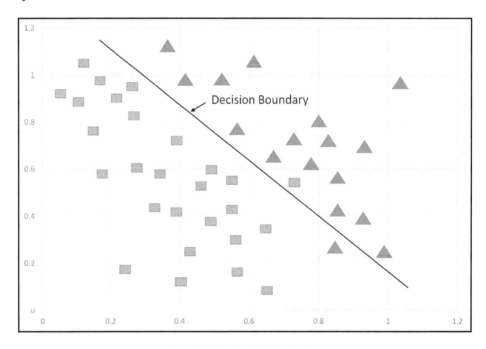

Figure 3.5 Classification with Decision Boundary

Here is a two-dimensional training dataset, where the output variables are separated by a Decision Boundary. Classification is a supervised learning technique that defines the Decision Boundary so that there is a clear separation of the output variables.

Regression and classification, as discussed in this section, require historical data to make predictions about the new data points. These represent *supervised* learning techniques. The generic process of supervised machine learning can be represented as follows:

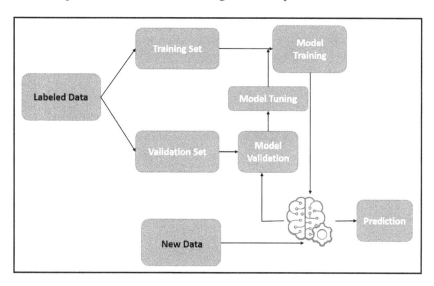

Figure 3.6 Generic supervised learning process

The labeled data, or the version of truth, is split into training and validation sets with random sampling. Typically, an 80-20 rule is followed with the split percentage of the training and validation sets. The training set is used for training the model (curve fitting) to reduce overall error of the prediction. The model is checked for accuracy with the validation set. The model is further tuned for the accuracy threshold and then utilized for the prediction of the dependent variables for the new data.

With this background in machine learning, let's take a deep dive into various techniques of supervised and unsupervised machine learning.

The Spark programming model

Before we deep dive into the Spark programming model, we should first arrive at an acceptable definition of what Spark is. We believe that it is important to understand what Spark is, and having a clear definition will help you to choose appropriate use cases where Spark is going to be useful as a technological choice.

There is no one silver bullet for all your enterprise problems. You must pick and choose the right technology from a plethora of options presented to you. With that, Spark can be defined as:

> **Spark** *is a distributed in-memory processing engine and framework that provides you with abstract APIs to process big volumes of data using an immutable distributed collection of objects called* **Resilient Distributed Datasets**. *It comes with a rich set of libraries, components, and tools, which let you write-in memory-processed distributed code in an efficient and fault-tolerant manner.*

Now that you are clear on what Spark is, let's understand how the Spark programming model works. The following diagram represents a high-level component of the Spark programming model:

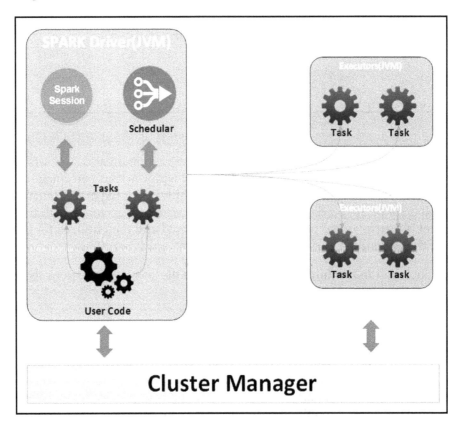

Figure 3.7 Spark programming model

As shown, all Spark applications are **Java Virtual Machine (JVM)**-based components comprising three processes: **driver**, **executor**, and **cluster manager**. The driver program runs as a separate process on a logically- or physically-segregated node and is responsible for launching the Spark application, maintaining all relevant information and configurations about launched Spark applications, executing application DAG as per user code and schedules, and distributing tasks across different available executors. Programmatically, the `main()` method of your Spark code runs as a driver. The driver program uses a `SparkContext` or `SparkSession` object created by user code to coordinate all Spark cluster activity. SparkContext or SparkSession is an entry point for executing any code using a Spark-distributed engine. To schedule any task, the driver program converts logical DAG to a physical plan and divides user code into a set of tasks. Each of those tasks are then scheduled by schedulers, running in Spark driver code, to run on executors. The driver is a central piece of any Spark application and it runs throughout the lifetime of the Spark application. If the driver fails, the entire application will fail. In that way, the driver becomes a single point of failure for the Spark application.

Spark executor processes are responsible for running the tasks assigned to it by the driver processes, storing data in in-memory data structures called RDDs, and reporting its code-execution state back to the driver processes. The key point to remember here is that, by default, executor processes are not terminated by the driver even if they are not being used or executing any tasks. This behavior can be explained with the fact that the RDDs follow a lazy evaluation design pattern. However, even if executors are killed accidentally, the Spark application does not stop and those executors can be relaunched by driver processes.

Cluster managers are processes that are responsible for physical machines and resource allocation to any Spark application. Even driver code is launched by the cluster manager processes. The cluster manager is a pluggable component and is cynical to the Spark user code, which is responsible for data processing. There are three types of cluster managers supported by the Spark processing engine: standalone, YARN, and Mesos.

> Further reference to about Spark RDDs and cluster managers can be found at the following links:
>
> - https://spark.apache.org/docs/latest/cluster-overview.html
>
> - https://spark.apache.org/docs/2.2.0/rdd-programming-guide.html#resilient-distributed-datasets-rdds

The Spark MLlib library

The **Spark MLlib** is a library of machine learning algorithms and utilities designed to make machine learning easy and run in parallel. This includes regression, collaborative filtering, classification, and clustering. Spark MLlib provides two types of API included in the packages, namely `spark.mllib` and `spark.ml`, where `spark.mllib` is built on top of RDDs and spark.ml is built on top of the DataFrame. The primary machine learning API for Spark is now the DataFrame-based API in the `spark.ml` package. Using `spark.ml` with the DataFrame API is more versatile and flexible, and we can have the benefits provided by DataFrame, such as catalyst optimizer and `spark.mllib`, which is an RDD-based API that is expected to be removed in the future.

Machine learning is applicable to various data types, including text, images, structured data, and vectors. To support these data types under a unified dataset concept, Spark ML includes the Spark SQL DataFrame. It is easy to combine various algorithms in a single workflow or pipeline.

The following sections will give you a detailed view of a few key concepts in the Spark ML API.

The transformer function

This is something that can transform one DataFrame into another. For instance, an ML model can transform a DataFrame with features into a DataFrame with predictions. A transformer contains feature transformer and learned model. This uses the `transform()` method to transform one DataFrame into another. The code for this is given for your reference:

```
import org.apache.spark.ml.feature.Tokenizer

val df = spark.createDataFrame(Seq(  ("This is the Transformer", 1.0),
("Transformer is pipeline component", 0.0))).toDF( "text", "label") val
tokenizer = new Tokenizer().setInputCol("text").setOutputCol("words") val
tokenizedDF = tokenizer.transform(df)
```

The estimator algorithm

An **estimator** is another algorithm that can produce a transformer by fitting on a DataFrame. For instance, a learning algorithm can train on a dataset and produce a model. This produces a transformer by learning an algorithm. It uses the `fit()` method to produce a transformer. For instance, the **Naïve Bayes** learning algorithm is an estimator that calls the `fit()` method and trains a Naïve Bayes model, which is a transformer. We will use the following code to train the model:

```
import org.apache.spark.ml.classification.NaiveBayes

val nb = new NaiveBayes().setModelType("multinomial")

val model = nb.fit(Training_DataDF)
```

Pipeline

`Pipeline` represents a sequence of stages, where every stage is a transformer or an estimator. All these stages run in an order and the dataset that is input is altered as it passes through every stage. For the stages of transformers, the `transform ()` method is used, while for the stages of estimators, the `fit()` method is used to create a transformer.

Every DataFrame that is output from one stage is input for the next stage. The pipeline is also an estimator. Therefore, it produces `PipelineModel` once the `fit()` method is run. `PipelineModel` is a transformer. `PipelineModel` contains the same number of stages as in the original pipeline. `PipelineModel` and pipelines make sure that the test and training data pass through similar feature-processing steps. For instance, consider a pipeline with three stages: Tokenizer, which will tokenize the sentence and convert it into a word with the use of `Tokenizer.transform()`; HashingTF, which is used to represent a string in a vector form as all ML algorithms understand only vectors and not strings and this uses the `HashingTF.transform()` method; and `NaiveBayes`, an estimator that is used for prediction.

We can save the model at `HDFSlocation` using the `save()` method, so in future we can load it using the `load` method and use it for prediction on the new dataset. This loaded model will work on the feature column of `newDataset`, and return the predicted column with this `newDataset` will also pass through all the stages of the pipeline:

```
import org.apache.spark.ml.{Pipeline, PipelineModel}
import org.apache.spark.ml.feature.{HashingTF, Tokenizer}
import org.apache.spark.ml.classification.NaiveBayes
```

```
val df = spark.createDataFrame(Seq(
  ("This is the Transformer", 1.0),
  ("Transformer is pipeline component", 0.0)
)).toDF( "text", "label")

val tokenizer = new Tokenizer().setInputCol("text").setOutputCol("words")

val
HashingTF=newHashingTF().setNumFeatures(1000).setInputCol(tokenizer.getOutp
utCol).setOutputCol("features")

val nb = new NaiveBayes().setModelType("multinomial")

val pipeline = new Pipeline().setStages(Array(tokenizer, hashingTF, nb))
val model = pipeline.fit(df)
model.save("/HDFSlocation/Path/")
val loadModel = PipelineModel.load(("/HDFSlocation/Path/")

val PredictedData = loadModel.transform(newDataset)
```

Regression analysis

Regression analysis is a statistical modeling technique that is used for predicting or forecasting the occurrence of an event or the value of a continuous variable (dependent variable), based on the value of one or many independent variables. For example, when we want to drive from one place to another, there are numerous factors that affect the amount of time it will take to reach the destination, for example, the start time, distance, real-time traffic conditions, construction activities on the road, and weather conditions. All these factors impact the actual time it will take to reach the destination. As you can imagine, some factors have more impact than the others on the value of the dependent variable. In regression analysis, we mathematically sort out which variables impact the outcome, leading us to understand which factors matter most, which ones do not impact the outcome in a meaningful way, how these factors relate to each other, and mathematically, the quantified impact of variable factors on the outcome.

Various regression techniques that are used depend on the number and distribution of values of independent variables. These variables also derive the shape of the curve that represents predictor function. There are various regression techniques, and we will learn about them in detail in the following sections.

Linear regression

With linear regression, we model the relationship between the dependent variable, y, and an explanatory variable or independent variable, x. When there is one independent variable, it is called **simple linear regression**, and in the case of multiple independent variables, the regression is called **multiple linear regression**. The predictor function in the case of linear regression is a straight line (refer to figure 4 for an illustration). The regression line defines the relationship between x and y. When the value of y increases when x increases, there is a positive relationship between x and y. Similarly, when x and y are inversely proportional, there is a negative relationship between x and y. The line should be plotted on x and y dimensions to minimize the difference between the predicted value and the actual value, called prediction error.

In its simplest form, the linear regression equation is:

$$y = a + bx$$

This is the equation of a straight line, where y is the value of dependent variable, a is the y intercept (the value of y where the regression line meets the y axis), and b is the slope of the line. Let's consider the least square method in which we can derive the regression line with minimum prediction error.

Least square method

Let's consider the same training data we referred to earlier in this chapter. We have values for the independent variable, x, and corresponding values for the dependent variable, y. These values are plotted on a two-dimensional scatter plot. The goal is to draw a regression line through the training data so as to minimize the error of our predictions. The linear regression line with minimum error always passes the mean intercept for x and y values.

The following figure shows the least square method:

x	y	x - x̄	y - ȳ	(x - x̄)²	(x - x̄) (y - ȳ)
50.00	180.00	-69.33	-123.20	4807.11	8541.87
75.00	200.00	-44.33	-103.20	1965.44	4575.20
100.00	320.00	-19.33	16.80	373.78	-324.80
125.00	340.00	5.67	36.80	32.11	208.53
150.00	380.00	30.67	76.80	940.44	2355.20
175.00	400.00	55.67	96.80	3098.78	5388.53
200.00	410.00	80.67	106.80	6507.11	8615.20
210.00	423.00	90.67	119.80	8220.44	10861.87
240.00	470.00	120.67	166.80	14560.44	20127.20
110.00	330.00	-9.33	26.80	87.11	-250.13
115.00	340.00	-4.33	36.80	18.78	-159.47
40.00	160.00	-79.33	-143.20	6293.78	11360.53
35.00	145.00	-84.33	-158.20	7112.11	13341.53
80.00	215.00	-39.33	-88.20	1547.11	3469.20
85.00	235.00	-34.33	-68.20	1178.78	2341.53
119.33	303.20			56743.33	90452.00
x̄	ȳ				

Regression Line (y = a + bx)

Slope equation

$$a = \frac{\sum(x - \bar{x})(y - \bar{y})}{\sum(x - \bar{x})^2}$$

(x:119.33,y:303.2)

y intercept (a) = 112.98

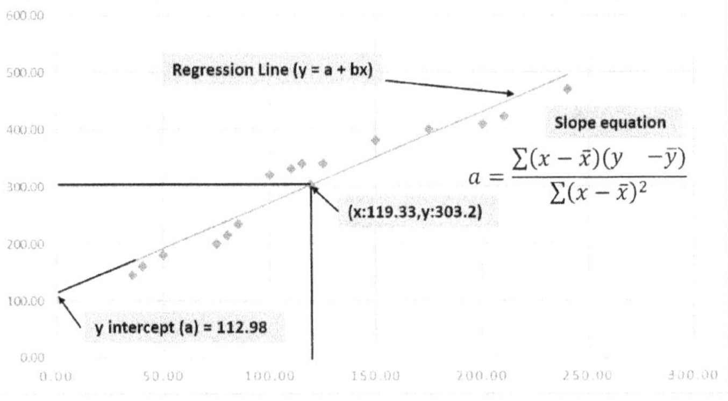

Figure 3.8 Least square method

The formula for calculating the y intercept is as follows:

$$a = \frac{\sum(x-\bar{x})(y-\bar{y})}{\sum(x-\bar{x})^2}$$

The least square method calculates the y intercept and the slope of the line with the following steps:

1. Calculate the mean of all the x values (119.33).
2. Calculate the mean of all the y values (303.20)
3. Calculate difference from the mean for all the x and y values.
4. Calculate the square of mean difference for all the x values.
5. Multiply the mean difference of x by the mean difference of y for all the combinations of x and y.
6. Calculate the sum squares of all the mean differences of the x values *(56743.33).*
7. Calculate the sum of mean difference products of the x and y values (90452.00).
8. The slope of the regression line is obtained by dividing the sum of the mean difference products of x and y by the sum of the squares of all the mean differences of the x values *(90452.00 / 56743.33 = 1.594).* In this training data, since there is direct proportion between the x and y values, the slope is positive. This is the value for b in our equation.

9. We need to calculate the value of the *y* intercept *(a)* by solving the following equation, $y = a + 1.594 * x$.

Remember, the regression line always passes through the mean intercept of the x and y values.

10. Therefore, $303.2 = a + (1.594 * 119.33)$.

11. Solving this, we get $a = 112.98$ as the *y* intercept for the regression line.

At this point, we have created our regression line with which we can predict the value of the dependent variable, *y*, for a value of *x*. We need to see how close our regression line mathematically is to the actual data points. We will use one of the most popular statistical techniques, R-squared, for this purpose. It is also called the coefficient of determination. R-squared calculates the % of response variable variation for the linear regression model we have developed. R-squared values will always be between 0% and 100%. A higher value of R-squared indicates that the model fits the training data well; generally termed the goodness of fit. The following diagram shows the calculation of R-squared with some sample data points:

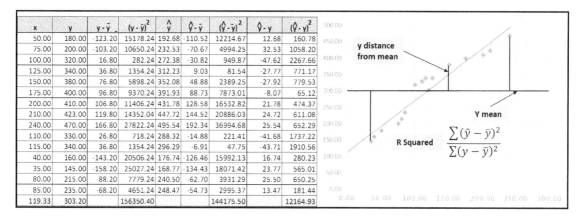

Figure 3.9 Calculation of R-squared

Let's use our training data to calculate R-squared based on the formula in the preceding image. Please refer to the diagram we just saw, in this case, R-squared = *144175.50 / 156350.40 = 0.9221*. This value is an indication that the model is fitting the training data very well. There is another parameter we can derive, called **standard error**, from the estimate. This is calculated as:

$$\sqrt{\frac{\sum(\hat{y} - y)^2}{n - 2}}$$

In this formula, *n* is the sample size or the number of observations. With our dataset, the standard error of the estimate comes out to be *30.59*.

Let's calculate the R-squared for our training dataset with the Spark machine learning library:

```
import org.apache.spark.ml.feature.LabeledPoint
import org.apache.spark.ml.linalg.Vectors
import org.apache.spark.ml.regression.LinearRegression

val linearRegrsssionSampleData =
sc.textFile("aibd/linear_regression_sample.txt")

val labeledData = linearRegrsssionSampleData.map { line =>
  val parts = line.split(',')
  LabeledPoint(parts(0).toDouble, Vectors.dense(parts(1).toDouble))
}.cache().toDF

val lr = new LinearRegression()
val model = lr.fit(labeledData)
val summary = model.summary
println("R-squared = "+ summary.r2)
```

This program produces the following output. Note the same value for R-squared:

```
scala> println("R-squared = "+ summary.r2)
R-squared = 0.9221944560356226
```

Generalized linear model

While we have tried to understand the concept of linear regression with one dependent and one independent variable, in the real world, we are always going to have multiple dependent variables that affect the output variable, termed multiple regression. In that case, our $y = a + bx$ linear equation is going to take the following form:

$$y = a_0 + b_1 x_1 + b_2 x_2 + \dots + b_k x_k$$

Once again, a_0 is the y intercept, x_1, x_2, ...x_k are the independent variables or factors, and b_1, b_2,.., b_k are the weights of the variables. They define how much the effect of a particular variable has on the outcome. With multiple regression, we can create a model for predicting a single dependent variable. This limitation is overcome by the generalized linear model. It deals with multiple dependent/response variables, along with the correlation within the predictor variables.

Logistic regression classification technique

Logistic regression is a method in which we analyze the input variables that result in the binary classification of the output variables. Even though the name suggests regression, it is a popular method to solve classification problems, for example, to detect whether an email is spam or not, or whether a transaction is a fraudulent or not. The goal of logistic regression is to find a best-fitting model that defines the class of the output variable as **0** (negative class) or **1** (positive class). As a specialized case of linear regression, logistic regression generates the coefficients of a formula to predict probability of occurrence of the dependent variable. Based on the probability, the parameters that maximize the probability of occurrence or nonoccurrence of a dependent event are selected. The probability of an event is bound between **0** and **1**. However, the linear regression model cannot guarantee the probability range of **0** to **1**.

The following diagram shows the difference between the linear regression and logistic regression models:

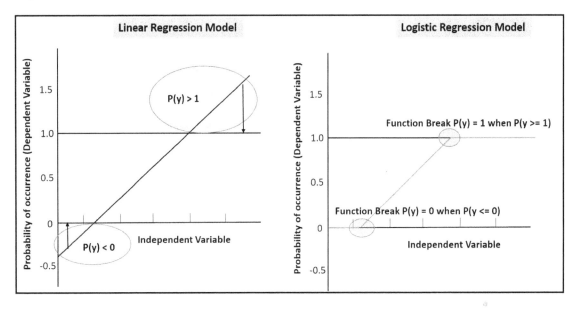

Figure 3.10 Difference between linear and logistic Regression models

There are two conditions we need to meet with regards to the probability of the intended binary outcome of the independent variable:

- **It should be positive** *(p >= 0)*: We can use an exponential function in order to ensure positivity:

$$\rho = exp(\beta0 + \beta1x) \;=\; e^{(\beta0 + \beta1x)}$$

- **It should be less than 1** *(p <=1)*: We can divide the probability exponential term with the same value, + 1, in order to ensure that the outcome probability is less than:

$$\rho = \frac{exp(\beta0 + \beta1x)}{exp(\beta0 + \beta1x) + 1} \;=\; \frac{e^{(\beta0 + \beta1x)}}{e^{(\beta0 + \beta1x)+1}}$$

Logistic regression with Spark

We progress with logistic regression with Spark as follows:

```
import org.apache.spark.ml.classification.LogisticRegression

// Load training data
val training =
spark.read.format("libsvm").load("data/mllib/sample_libsvm_data.txt")

val lr = new LogisticRegression()
  .setMaxIter(10)
  .setRegParam(0.3)
  .setElasticNetParam(0.8)

// Fit the model
val lrModel = lr.fit(training)

// Print the coefficients and intercept for logistic regression
println(s"Coefficients: ${lrModel.coefficients} Intercept:
${lrModel.intercept}")

// We can also use the multinomial family for binary classification
val mlr = new LogisticRegression()
  .setMaxIter(10)
  .setRegParam(0.3)
  .setElasticNetParam(0.8)
  .setFamily("multinomial")

val mlrModel = mlr.fit(training)

// Print the coefficients and intercepts for logistic regression with
multinomial family
println(s"Multinomial coefficients: ${mlrModel.coefficientMatrix}")
println(s"Multinomial intercepts: ${mlrModel.interceptVector}")
```

Polynomial regression

While in linear regression, the correlation between the independent and the dependent variables is best represented with a straight line, the real-life datasets are more complex and do not represent a linear relationship between cause and effect. The straight line equation does not fit the data points and hence cannot create an effective predictive model.

In such cases, we can consider using a higher-order quadratic equation for the predictor function. Given x as an independent variable and y as a dependent variable, the polynomial function takes the following forms:

$y = \beta_0 + \beta_1 x + \beta_2 x^2$	Second Order Polynomial
$y = \beta_0 + \beta_1 x + \beta_2 x^2 + \beta_3 x^3$	Third Order Polynomial

These can be visualized with a small set of sample data as follows:

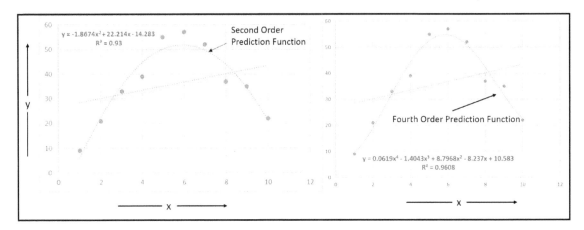

Figure 3.11 Polynomial prediction function

 Note that the straight line cannot accurately represent the relationship between x and y. As we model the prediction function with higher-order functions, R^2 is improved. This means the model is able to be more accurate.

We may think that it will be best to use the highest possible order equation for the prediction function in order to get the best fitting model. However, that is not right because as we create the regression line that goes through all the data points, the model fails to accurately predict the outcomes for any data outside of the training sample (test data). This problem is called overfitting. On the other end, we may also encounter the problem of underfitting. This is when the model does not fit the training data well and hence performs poorly with the test data.

Stepwise regression

The examples we have seen so far all had one independent and one dependent variable. This is used to illustrate the basic concepts of regression analysis. However, real-world scenarios are more complex and there are multiple factors that affect the outcome. As an example, the salary of an employee depends on multiple factors, such as skill sets, the ability to learn new tools and technologies, years of experience, past projects worked on, ability to play multiple roles, and location. As you can imagine, some of the factors contribute more than others in defining the outcome (salary, in this case).

When we do regression analysis on a dataset that contains lots of factors, the model can be accurately built if we select the factors that are more significant than others. Stepwise regression is a method by which the choice or selection of independent variables is automated.

Consider the following regression function:

$$y = \beta_0 + \beta_1 x_1 + \beta_2 x_2 + \beta_3 x_3 + \ldots + \beta_n x_n$$

There are n number of input variables, along with their weights or coefficients. The goal for stepwise regression is to shortlist the variables that are most important for building an accurate model. Stepwise regression can be done with two approaches, which will be covered in the following sections.

Forward selection

With forward selection, we start with zero or no variables in the model. One variable is added at a time, based on the chosen threshold or criteria. When adding a new variable, the improvement in the model's fit should be significant. At the point when the inclusion of a new variable does not improve the model, the process is complete.

Backward elimination

With backward elimination, we start with all the variables. Iteratively, we need to test the elimination of each of the variables. The variable, once again, is deleted with the predefined threshold or criteria. The variables that have the least significant impact on the model's accuracy are eliminated one by one in this method.

It is also possible to utilize both methods together for faster parameter tuning.

Ridge regression

With stepwise regression, we now have a set of independent variables that contribute well to the value of the dependent variable. If two or more predictors are related to each other with a near-linear relationship, we come across a problem called **multicollinearity**, for example, if we are modeling the weather data where the input data contains the altitude of the location and the average rainfall as predictor variables. These two variables are linearly related. The amount of rainfall increases with the increase in altitude. This multicollinearity leads to inaccurate estimates for the regression coefficients, leading to an increase in the standard errors, and hence degrades the model's predictability.

Multicollinearity can be corrected by gathering more data points for the related factors and ensuring that the linear relationship does not exist between the extended data points. The correction is also possible by eliminating one of the factors with lower weightage. If multicollinearity cannot be addressed with these two methods, we can use ridge regression.

LASSO regression

The term **LASSO** stands for **Least Absolute Shrinkage Selection Operator**. The coefficients that tend to zero in ridge regression are set to zero in LASSO regression, and such factors can easily be eliminated from the predictor function equation. LASSO regression is generally used when there is a very large number of variables, since LASSO automatically does the variables selection.

Data clustering

So far, we have primarily explored supervised learning methods where we have a historical trail of data that is used for training the machine learning models. However, there is a very common scenario where the machine needs to classify objects or entities into various groups based on predefined or runtime categories. For example, in the dataset that contains information about employees, we need to categorize the employees based on one or more attributes combined. With this, the goal is to group similar objects and partition the data based on similarities.

The general idea is to have a consistent attribute map within a group and distinct behaviors across the groups. Unlike the supervised learning methods, there are no dependent variables in the case of data clustering. A cluster represents various groups of entities that demonstrate similarities in attributes. At a broader level, clustering has two types:

- **Fixed clustering**: In this type of clustering, each of the data points belongs to exactly one group or cluster. The boundaries are clearly defined and clearly separate the data points.
- **Probabilistic clustering**: In this case, for each data point, the probability that the object (instance of an entity) belongs to a particular cluster. As a general rule, the cluster to which the object belongs with the highest probability takes precedence over the others.

Unlike supervised learning algorithms, the process and methods for clustering cannot be fully standardized. The outcomes differ based on the dataset and specific use cases. There are various models considered for data clustering. Based on these models, various algorithms are developed. Some of the most commonly used models are as follows:

- **Connectivity models**: These models are based on the data distance between various objects. These models take two approaches for generalization. In the first approach, all the independent data points are treated as separate clusters and as per the relative distance, the clusters are created. In the second approach, the data points are distributed in clusters and as the relative distance between the data points decreases, they are distributed into other clusters. The hierarchical clustering algorithm implements connectivity model.
- **Centroid models**: In these models, the clusters are formulated around a focal point. The number of focal points is predefined and the data points with similarities to the focal point are grouped into a cluster. In this method, the number of clusters is predefined. K-means clustering is one of the most popular implementations of the centroid model.
- **Distribution models**: In these models, the data points are categorized based on the applicability of statistical data distribution, for example, normal or Gaussian distributions. These are iterative models that calculate the maximum likelihood of entity parameters being part of the standard distribution.
- **Density models**: These are iterative models that scan the data points into multiple dimensions and create boundaries based on data point density within the data space. The regions are isolated based on the density of the data points and the isolated regions formulate the clusters.

The K-means algorithm

K-means is one of the most popular unsupervised algorithms for data clustering, which is used when we have unlabeled data without defined categories or groups. The number of clusters is represented by the k variable. This is an iterative algorithm that assigns the data points to a specific cluster based on the distance from the arbitrary centroid. During the first iteration, the centroids are randomly defined and the data points are assigned to the cluster based on the least vicinity from the centroid. Once the data points are allocated, within the subsequent iterations, the centroids are realigned to the mean of the data points and the data points are once again added to the clusters based on the least vicinity from the centroids. These steps are iterated to the point where the centroids do not change more than the set threshold. Let's illustrate the K-means algorithm with three iterations on a sample two dimensional $(x1, x2)$ dataset:

Iteration 1:

1. During the first iteration, select two centroids for the two clusters: *(C1 - 150:120)* and *(C2 - 110:100)*
2. For each data point *(x1:x2)*, calculate the ordinary straight line distance from *C1* and *C2*
3. Put the data points into *C1* or *C2* based on the minimum distance from the centroid
4. For the data points in *C1*, calculate the new *C1* as the mathematical mean of all the points *(162.50:151.67)*
5. For the data points in *C2*, calculate the new *C2* as the mathematical mean of all the points *(110:93.33)*:

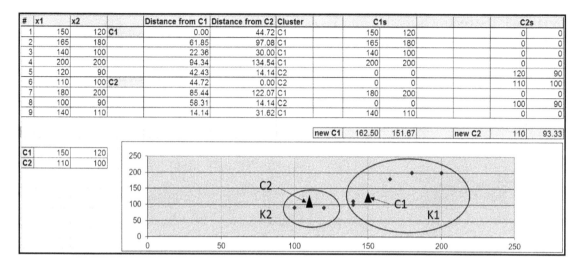

#	x1	x2		Distance from C1	Distance from C2	Cluster	C1s			C2s	
1	150	120	C1	0.00	44.72	C1	150	120		0	0
2	165	180		61.85	97.08	C1	165	180		0	0
3	140	100		22.36	30.00	C1	140	100		0	0
4	200	200		94.34	134.54	C1	200	200		0	0
5	120	90		42.43	14.14	C2	0	0		120	90
6	110	100	C2	44.72	0.00	C2	0	0		110	100
7	180	200		85.44	122.07	C1	180	200		0	0
8	100	90		58.31	14.14	C2	0	0		100	90
9	140	110		14.14	31.62	C1	140	110		0	0

new C1 | 162.50 | 151.67   new C2 | 110 | 93.33

C1	150	120
C2	110	100

Figure 3.12 Mathematical mean calculation for cluster points

Iteration 2:

For the new centroids calculated in iteration 1, realign the data points into K1 and K2 once again, based on the minimum distance from the new centroids, and repeat the process to calculate new centroids:

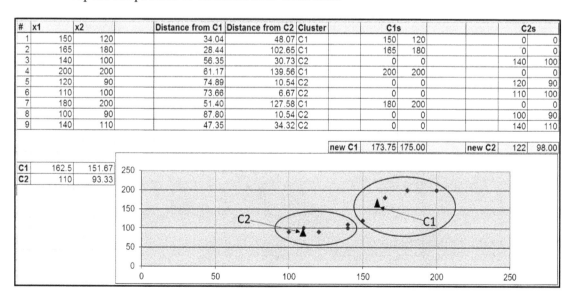

#	x1	x2	Distance from C1	Distance from C2	Cluster	C1s			C2s	
1	150	120	34.04	48.07	C1	150	120		0	0
2	165	180	28.44	102.65	C1	165	180		0	0
3	140	100	56.35	30.73	C2	0	0		140	100
4	200	200	61.17	139.56	C1	200	200		0	0
5	120	90	74.89	10.54	C2	0	0		120	90
6	110	100	73.66	6.67	C2	0	0		110	100
7	180	200	51.40	127.58	C1	180	200		0	0
8	100	90	87.80	10.54	C2	0	0		100	90
9	140	110	47.35	34.32	C2	0	0		140	110

new C1 | 173.75 | 175.00   new C2 | 122 | 98.00

C1	162.5	151.67
C2	110	93.33

Figure 3.13 K-means algorithm: iteration-2

Iteration3: The centroids for iteration 3 is as follows:

#	x1	x2	Distance from C1	Distance from C2	Cluster	C1s			C2s	
1	150	120	59.91	35.61	C2	0	0		150	120
2	165	180	10.08	92.59	C1	165	180		0	0
3	140	100	82.24	18.11	C2	0	0		140	100
4	200	200	36.25	128.41	C1	200	200		0	0
5	120	90	100.57	8.25	C2	0	0		120	90
6	110	100	98.43	12.17	C2	0	0		110	100
7	180	200	25.77	117.34	C1	180	200		0	0
8	100	90	112.53	23.41	C2	0	0		100	90
9	140	110	73.24	21.63	C2	0	0		140	110

						new C1	181.67	193.33	new C2	126.6666667	101.67

C1	173.75	175
C2	122	98

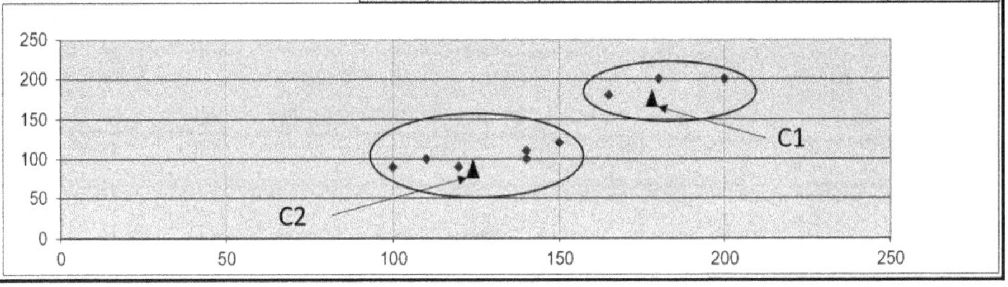

Figure 3.14 K-means algorithm: iteration-3

K-means implementation with Spark ML

We will proceed with the implementation of K-means with Spark ML as follows:

```
import org.apache.spark.ml.feature.LabeledPoint
import org.apache.spark.ml.linalg.Vectors
import org.apache.spark.ml.clustering.KMeans

val kmeansSampleData = sc.textFile("aibd/k-means-sample.txt")

val labeledData = kmeansSampleData.map { line =>
  val parts = line.split(',')
  LabeledPoint(parts(0).toDouble, Vectors.dense(parts(1).toDouble,
parts(2).toDouble))
}.cache().toDF


val kmeans = new KMeans()
.setK(2) // Setting the number of clusters
.setFeaturesCol("features")
.setMaxIter(3) // default Max Iteration is 20
.setPredictionCol("prediction")
.setSeed(1L)
```

```
val model = kmeans.fit(labeledData)

summary.predictions.show
model.clusterCenters.foreach(println)
```

The output of the code will look like the following:

```
scala> summary.predictions.show
+-----+-------------+----------+
||label|     features|prediction|
+-----+-------------+----------+
|  1.0|[150.0,120.0]|         0|
|  2.0|[165.0,180.0]|         1|
|  3.0|[140.0,100.0]|         0|
|  4.0|[200.0,200.0]|         1|
|  5.0| [120.0,90.0]|         0|
|  6.0|[110.0,100.0]|         0|
|  7.0|[180.0,200.0]|         1|
|  8.0| [100.0,90.0]|         0|
|  9.0|[140.0,110.0]|         0|
+-----+-------------+----------+

scala> model.clusterCenters.foreach(println)
[126.66666666666666,101.66666666666666]
[181.66666666666666,193.33333333333331]
```

Data dimensionality reduction

So far in this chapter, we have looked at the basic concepts of supervised and unsupervised learning with the simplest possible examples. In these examples, we have considered a limited number of factors that contribute to the outcome. However, in the real world, we have a very large number of data points that are available for analysis and model generation. Every additional factor adds one dimension within the space, and beyond the third dimension, it becomes difficult to effectively visualize the data in a conceivable form. With each new dimension, there is a performance impact on the model generation exercise.

In the world of big data, where we now have the capability to bring in data from heterogeneous data sources, which was not possible earlier, we are constantly adding more dimensions to our datasets. While it is great to have additional data points and attributes to better understand a problem, more is not always better if we consider the computational overhead due to additional dimensions in the dataset.

If we consider our datasets as rows and columns, where one row represents one instance of an entity and the columns represent the dimensions, most machine learning algorithms are implemented column-wise. These algorithms perform more and more slowly as we add more columns. Once again referring to the human brain analogy we considered in `Chapter 1`, *Big Data and Artificial Intelligence Systems*, when we drive a car, the human brain constantly receives a large number of inputs (data dimensions). Our brain can effectively consider the dimensions that are most significant, ignore some of the input, and merge other input to form a singular perception point.

We need to apply similar techniques to considering the most important dimensions that can accurately model the scenario, based on a reduced number of factors within the dataset. This process of reduction of factors is termed **Data Dimensionality Reduction (DDR)**. One of the imperatives while considering dimensionality reduction is that the model should convey the same information without any loss of insight or intelligence. Let's consider some basic techniques that can be used for DDR, before taking a deeper dive into advanced techniques such as **singular value decomposition (SVD)** and **principal component analysis (PCA)**:

- **Dimensions with missing values**: As we gather data from various sensors and data sources, it is possible that for some of the factors, there is a large number of missing observations. In such cases, we use a default value or the mean of the other observations to replace the missing values. However, if the number of missing values crosses a threshold (percentage of observations with missing values of the total number of observations), it makes sense to drop the dimension from the model since it does not contribute to the accuracy of the model.
- **Dimensions with low variance**: Within the dataset, if we have some dimensions for which the observations do not vary, or vary with a very low differential, such dimensions do not contribute to the model effectiveness. Factors with low variance across observations can be eliminated.
- **Dimensions with high correlation**: Within the dataset, if we have two or more dimensions that relate to each other, or they represent the same information in different measurement units, the factors can be ignored without any impact on the model's accuracy.

Now, let's look at the following dataset:

y	x1	x2	x3	x4	x5	x6
100	2	1	75	18	1	2
110		1	21	28	2	4
120		1	32	61	5	10
115		1	56	39	2	4
125	1	1	73	81	3	6
121	0	1	97	59	7	14

Figure 3.15 Sample dataset

In this example dataset, **x1** has a lot of missing values, **x1** has a lot of missing values, **x2** has no variance among values, and **x5** and **x6** are highly correlated, hence one of the factors can be eliminated without affecting the model's accuracy.

Singular value decomposition

As we have seen in the previous section, reducing the dimensions of the datasets increases the efficiency of the model generation, without sacrificing the amount of knowledge contained in the data. As a result, the data is compressed and easy to visualize in fewer dimensions. **SVD** is a fundamental mathematical tool that can be easily leveraged for dimensionality reduction.

Matrix theory and linear algebra overview

Before we try to understand SVD, here is a quick overview of linear algebra and matrix theory concepts. Although a comprehensive discussion on these topics is outside the scope of this book, a brief discussion is definitely in order:

- **Scalar**: A single number is termed a scalar. A scalar represents the magnitude of an entity. For example, the speed of a car is 60 miles/hour. Here, the number 60 is a scalar.
- **Vectors**: An array of multiple scalars arranged in an order is called a vector. Typically, vectors define magnitude as well as direction, and are considered points in space.

- **Matrix**: This is a two-dimensional array of scalars. Each element of a matrix is represented by a coordinate index. A matrix is denoted by a capital letter, for example A, and individual elements are denoted with subscripts, as $A_{m,n}$. A matrix can be defined as follows:

$$A = \begin{bmatrix} A_{1,1} & A_{1,2} \\ A_{2,1} & A_{2,2} \end{bmatrix}$$

Here, A_i is the ith row of A and $A_{.j}$ is the jth column of A. Matrix A has a shape of height, m, and a width of n.

- **Transpose of a matrix**: When we transpose a matrix, it results in a mirror image of the matrix structure, where the rows of the resultant matrix are the columns of the base matrix:

$$A = \begin{bmatrix} A_{1,1} & A_{1,2} & A_{1,3} \\ A_{2,1} & A_{2,2} & A_{2,3} \\ A_{3,1} & A_{3,2} & A_{3,3} \end{bmatrix} \Rightarrow A^T = \begin{bmatrix} A_{1,1} & A_{2,1} & A_{3,1} \\ A_{1,2} & A_{2,2} & A_{3,2} \\ A_{1,3} & A_{2,3} & A_{3,3} \end{bmatrix} \qquad A = \begin{bmatrix} 1 & 2 & 3 \\ 4 & 5 & 6 \\ 7 & 8 & 9 \end{bmatrix} \Rightarrow A^T = \begin{bmatrix} 1 & 4 & 7 \\ 2 & 5 & 8 \\ 3 & 6 & 9 \end{bmatrix}$$

Vectors are matrices with one column often represented as a transpose of a row matrix:

$$X = [x_1, x_2, x_3, \dots x_n]$$

- **Matrix addition**: If matrices A and B have the same shape (dimensions), with m height and n width, they can be added to form a C matrix, as follows:

$$C = A + B => C_{i,j} = A_{i,j} + B_{i,j}$$

A scalar can be added to or multiplied by a matrix, as follows:

$$D = aB + c => D_{i,j} = aB_{i,j} + c$$

- **Matrix multiplication**: In order to multiply matrix $A_{m,n}$ with matrix B, matrix B needs to have n number of rows. In that case, if A is of the shape $_{mXn}$ and B is of the shape $_{nXp}$, then C is of the shape $_{mXp}$:

$$C = AB => Ci,j = \sum A_{i,k} B_{k,j}$$

$$\begin{pmatrix} A & B \\ C & D \end{pmatrix} \times \begin{pmatrix} E & F \\ G & H \end{pmatrix} = \begin{pmatrix} AE + BG & AF + BH \\ CE + DG & CF + DH \end{pmatrix}$$

The standard product of two matrices is not just the product of individual elements with positional correspondence.

- The properties of a matrix product are:
    - **Distributability**: $A(B + C) = AB + AC$
    - **Associativity**: $A (BC) = (AB) C$
    - **Not commutative**: AB is not always equal to BA
    - $(AB)^T = B^T A^T$

- **Identity and inverse matrices**: The identity matrix is a square matrix with all the diagonals as 1 and non-diagonal elements as 0. The identity matrix does not change the value of a matrix when we multiply the matrix with the identity matrix. An n-dimensional identity matrix is denoted as I_n. The inverse of a square matrix is a matrix that, when multiplied with the original matrix, results in an identity matrix:

$$A^{-1} A = In$$

- **Diagonal matrix**: This is similar to an identity matrix. All the diagonal elements are nonzero and the non-diagonal elements are zero.
- **Symmetric matrix**: This is a square matrix that is equal to the transpose of a matrix.

- **Linear regression in matrix form**: Let's consider the simple linear regression model equation: $Y_i = \beta_0 + \beta_i x_i + \varepsilon_i \{i = 1, ..., n\}$:

$$\Rightarrow \begin{bmatrix} Y_1 = \beta_0 + \beta_1 X_1 + \varepsilon_1 \\ Y_2 = \beta_0 + \beta_1 X_2 + \varepsilon_2 \\ \vdots \\ Y_n = \beta_0 + \beta_1 X_n + \varepsilon_n \end{bmatrix}$$

Let's represent these equations in matrix form with individual matrices, as follows:

$$\mathbf{Y} = \begin{bmatrix} Y_1 \\ Y_2 \\ \vdots \\ Y_n \end{bmatrix} \qquad \mathbf{X} = \begin{bmatrix} 1 & X_1 \\ 1 & X_2 \\ \vdots & \vdots \\ 1 & X_n \end{bmatrix} \qquad \boldsymbol{\beta} = \begin{bmatrix} \beta_0 \\ \beta_1 \end{bmatrix} \qquad \boldsymbol{\varepsilon} = \begin{bmatrix} \varepsilon_1 \\ \varepsilon_2 \\ \vdots \\ \varepsilon_n \end{bmatrix}$$

With these definitions of the matrices, the linear regression can be expressed as:

$$Y = X\beta + \epsilon$$

Note the simple nature of computation of the equation when represented in matrix form.

With this background in matrix theory, it will now be easy to understand SVD as applicable to dimensionality reduction. Let's first understand how real-world entities are represented in matrix form. The columns of a matrix represent various dimensions for the individual instances, which are represented by a row. The SVD theorem says that *for any m x m matrix A, there exists an m x r orthogonal matrix U, an n x r orthogonal matrix Σ, and an r x r diagonal matrix D with nonnegative values on the diagonal so that $A = U\Sigma V^T$.* This can be represented diagrammatically as follows:

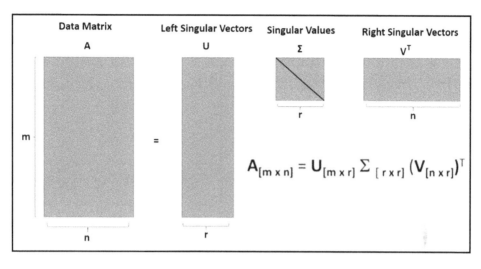

Figure 3.16 Illustration of singular value decomposition

The important properties of singular value decomposition

Now, let's take a look at some of the important properties of SVD:

- It is always possible to decompose a real matrix A into $A = U \sum VT$
- U, $\sum$, and V are unique
- U and V are orthonormal matrices:
    - $U^T U = I$ and $V^T V = I$ (I represents an identity matrix)
- $\sum$ is a diagonal matrix where the nonzero diagonal entries are positive and sorted in descending order ($\sigma_1 \geq \sigma_2 \geq \sigma_3 .... \geq \sigma_n .... > 0$)

SVD with Spark ML

Let's implement SVD code using the SparkML library:

```
import org.apache.spark.mllib.linalg.Matrix
import org.apache.spark.mllib.linalg.Vectors
import org.apache.spark.mllib.linalg.Vector
import org.apache.spark.mllib.linalg.distributed.RowMatrix
import org.apache.spark.mllib.linalg.SingularValueDecomposition
```

```
val data = Array(Vectors.dense(2.0, 1.0, 75.0, 18.0, 1.0,2),
Vectors.dense(0.0, 1.0, 21.0, 28.0, 2.0,4),
Vectors.dense(0.0, 1.0, 32.0, 61.0, 5.0,10),
Vectors.dense(0.0, 1.0, 56.0, 39.0, 2.0,4),
Vectors.dense(1.0, 1.0, 73.0, 81.0, 3.0,6),
Vectors.dense(0.0, 1.0, 97.0, 59.0, 7.0,14))

val rows = sc.parallelize(data)

val mat: RowMatrix = new RowMatrix(rows)

val svd: SingularValueDecomposition[RowMatrix, Matrix] = mat.computeSVD(3,
computeU = true)

val U: RowMatrix = svd.U // The U factor is stored as a row matrix
val s: Vector = svd.s // The sigma factor is stored as a singular vector
val V: Matrix = svd.V // The V factor is stored as a local dense matrix
```

The output of the code will look like the following:

```
scala> U.rows.foreach(println)
[-0.35299651876635013,0.6546455627747847,0.2661494440454151]
[-0.17208815312983178,-0.18242538935362893,-0.05603906415291393]
[-0.3443275098860016,0.08352969161065013,0.20707206515001908]
[-0.32130452719252234,-0.5716937426453584,-0.32950542635545377]
[-0.5430065403233052,-0.3646759753170278,0.5942645854003921]
[-0.5736941599830103,0.26713414743272607,-0.6491694948924345]

scala> s
res26: org.apache.spark.mllib.linalg.Vector = [198.18757465263172,49.70483326656433,8.7
26504121398136]

scala> V.transpose.rowIter.foreach(println)
[-0.006302108394258266,-0.01164259370611551,-0.78178708620104436,-0.61574112347255570,-0.
04358108340924147,-0.08716216681848293]
[0.01900449288636702,-0.0022831925597502443,0.6225071299227736,-0.778954235597452,-0.03
2707150050004394,-0.06541430010000879]
[0.12909676748204668,0.0037554682538526113,0.028433343688626128,0.11826121137689534,-0.
44011947285577685,-0.8802389457115537]
```

The principal component analysis method

PCA is one of the most popular methods used for dimensionality reduction. In a real-world scenario, we have thousands of dimensions in which a data point is explained. However, it is possible to reduce the number of dimensions without the loss of significant information. For example, a video camera captures the scene in three-dimensional space and it is projected onto a two-dimensional space (TV screens); despite the elimination of one dimension, we are able to perceive the scene without any problems. The data points in multidimensional space have convergence in fewer dimensions. As a technique, PCA focuses on getting a direction with the largest variance between the data points while getting to the best reconstruction of the dataset, without losing information. Let's illustrate this with a two-dimensional dataset:

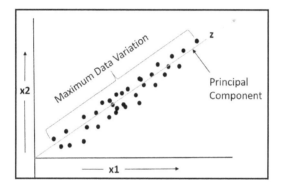

Figure 3.17 Illustration of Principal Component

This is a two-dimensional dataset where a data point is uniquely defined by $x1$ and $x2$ values. As we can see, the data is scattered linearly as a function of $x1$ and $x2$. A regression line maps all the data points and is a line that captures the maximum data variation. If we consider a new axis, which is represented by z, we can represent the dataset with a single dimension without much loss. On the new z axis, we get the minimum error while moving from two dimensions to one dimension. There is a fundamental difference between linear regression and PCA. In linear regression, we try to minimize the *vertical* distance between the data point and the point in the regression line. However, in PCA, we try to minimize the distance between the data point and the regression line in an orthogonal direction, and in PCA, there is no dependent variable to calculate.

The PCA algorithm using SVD

Now, let's look at the steps to implement the PCA algorithm using SVD. Consider the training set, $x(1), x(2), \ldots, x(m)$, with m data samples. For this dataset, we will progress with the steps as follows:

1. **Mean normalization**: Deduct the mean value of all the data points from the individual data point. With this, we increase the efficiency of model training and

$$\mu_j = \frac{1}{m} \sum_{i=1}^{m} x_i^j$$

get a better error surface shape, . Replace each $x(j)$ with $(x_{(j)} - \mu_{(j)})$.

2. **Feature scaling**: If the different features have different scales, if $x1$ is the size of a house and $x2$ is the number of bedrooms, they have different measurement scales. In that case, $x2$ will not play any role since it is orders smaller than $x1$. With normalization, we will reduce the impact of large-value features extracted on a different scale and allow small-value features to contribute to the equation.

$$\frac{1}{m} \sum_{i=1}^{m} (x^{(i)})(x^{(i)})^T$$

3. Calculate the covariance matrix sigma =

4. Apply SVD to the sigma to calculate U, Σ, and V.

5. Get the reduced matrix (UReduce) from U based on the number of dimensions to which we want to model our data. In our example, it is from two dimensions to one dimension. This is simply done by first obtaining k (number of intended dimensions) columns of the U matrix.

6. Get the z axis as $z = UReduce' (x)$.

Implementing SVD with Spark ML

It is very easy to implement the SVD algorithm explained earlier with Spark ML. The code for it is given for your reference:

```
import org.apache.spark.mllib.linalg.Matrix
import org.apache.spark.mllib.linalg.Vectors
import org.apache.spark.mllib.linalg.distributed.RowMatrix

val data = Array(Vectors.dense(2.0, 1.0, 75.0, 18.0, 1.0,2),
Vectors.dense(0.0, 1.0, 21.0, 28.0, 2.0,4),
Vectors.dense(0.0, 1.0, 32.0, 61.0, 5.0,10),
Vectors.dense(0.0, 1.0, 56.0, 39.0, 2.0,4),
Vectors.dense(1.0, 1.0, 73.0, 81.0, 3.0,6),
Vectors.dense(0.0, 1.0, 97.0, 59.0, 7.0,14))
```

```
>
val rows = sc.parallelize(data)

val mat: RowMatrix = new RowMatrix(rows)

// Principal components are stored in a local dense matrix.
val pc: Matrix = mat.computePrincipalComponents(2)

// Project the rows to the linear space spanned by the top 2 principal
components.
val projected: RowMatrix = mat.multiply(pc)

projected.rows.foreach(println)
```

Here is the program output with two principal components out of a six-dimensional dataset:

```
scala> projected.rows.foreach(println)
[-56.495425863653956,40.882009271582056]
[-101.57575183305222,39.8140203522891]
[-67.62682650712414,9.936050917628904]
[-31.51177269452176,15.871131302479899]
[-75.12738096710979,-17.497251982139915]
[-114.02568342851336,10.349201004364776]
```

Content-based recommendation systems

With the advancement of rich, performant technology and more focus on data-driven analytics, recommendation systems are gaining popularity. Recommendation systems are components that provide the most relevant information to end users based on their behavior in the past. The behavior can be defined as a user's browsing history, purchase history, recent searches, and so on. There are many different types of recommendation systems. In this section, we will keep our focus on two categories of recommendation engines: collaborative filtering and content-based recommendation.

Content-based recommendation systems are the type of recommendation engines that recommend items that are similar to items the user has liked in the past. The similarity of items is measured using features associated with an item. Similarity is basically a mathematical function that can be defined by a variety of algorithms. These types of recommendation systems match user profile attributes, such as user preferences, likes, and purchases, with attributes of an item using algorithmic functions. The best matches are presented to the user.

The following picture depicts a high-level approach to a content-based recommendation engine:

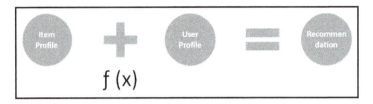

Figure 3.18 Content based recommendation

Let's now go through an example of content-based filtering. We have used movie data with this example. We will eventually use users' rating data as well. The following screenshot shows how the datasets look:

Movie Data			Users Data		
Movie	Genres		User	Movie	Ratings
Movie 1	Action,Romance		User1	Movie1	1
Movie 2	Adventure		User2	Movie1	1
Movie 3	Action,Adventure,Thriller		User1	Movie4	2
Movie 4	Romance		User1	Movie5	2
Movie 5	Romance,Thriller		User1	Movie6	2
Movie 6	Action,Romance,Thriller		User2	Movie6	2

In the movies dataset, we have the **Movie** column, which represents the movie name, and the **Genres** column, which represents the genres the movie belongs to. In the user rating dataset, we have user likes, represented by the number 1, and dislikes, represented by the number 2. No ratings have NULL or blank values.

The following Spark code can be used to load the data:

```
import org.apache.spark.ml.feature.{CountVectorizer,HashingTF, IDF,
Tokenizer}

val movieData = spark.createDataFrame(Seq(
  ("Movie1", Array("Action","Romance")),
  ("Movie2", Array("Adventure")),
  ("Movie3", Array("Action","Adventure","Thriller")),
  ("Movie4", Array("Romance")),
  ("Movie5", Array("Romance","Thriller")),
  ("Movie6", Array("Action","Romance","Thriller"))
)).toDF("Movie", "Genres")

val usersData = spark.createDataFrame(Seq(
```

```
    ("User1","Movie1",1),
    ("User2","Movie1",1),
    ("User1","Movie4",2),
    ("User2","Movie5",2),
    ("User1","Movie6",2),
    ("User2","Movie6",2)
)).toDF("User","Movie", "Ratings")
```

Now, we need to calculate the *TF-IDF* score for each of the movie's records. **TF (Term Frequency)** is the frequency of terms in a data row or document. In our example, terms would be the genres to which a movie belongs. So, for example, the *TF* for the *Action* genre for the row belonging to Movie1 would be 1. We have chosen a simple raw count for calculating *TF*. The following is an example of how *TF* calculation would look in our data sheet:

Movie Matrix (TF) Simple Count

Movie	Action	Adventure	Romance	Thriller
Movie 1	1		1	
Movie 2		1		
Movie 3	1	1		1
Movie 4			1	
Movie 5			1	1
Movie 6	1	0	1	1

> **TIP**
>
> There are many variants of *TF* calculations available. You have to choose which TF variant you want to use in your application, depending on multiple factors, such as type of data and number of records. Further details about it can be found at the following links:
>
> - https://nlp.stanford.edu/IR-book/html/htmledition/tf-idf-weighting-1.html
>
> - https://en.wikipedia.org/wiki/Tf%E2%80%93idf

The following Spark code can be used for calculating *TF*. We have used the `hashingTF` library for the process:

```
val hashingTF = new
HashingTF().setInputCol("Genres").setOutputCol("rawFeatures")
val featurizedData = hashingTF.transform(movieData)
featurizedData.show(truncate=false)
```

The following is the output of the previous code:

```
+-------+-------------------------------------+-------------------------------------------------+
|Movie  |Genres                               |rawFeatures                                      |
+-------+-------------------------------------+-------------------------------------------------+
|Movie1 |[Action, Romance]                    |(262144,[162807,188610],[1.0,1.0])               |
|Movie2 |[Adventure]                          |(262144,[86025],[1.0])                           |
|Movie3 |[Action, Adventure, Thriller]        |(262144,[1158,86025,162807],[1.0,1.0,1.0])       |
|Movie4 |[Romance]                            |(262144,[188610],[1.0])                          |
|Movie5 |[Romance, Thriller]                  |(262144,[1158,188610],[1.0,1.0])                 |
|Movie6 |[Action, Romance, Thriller]          |(262144,[1158,162807,188610],[1.0,1.0,1.0])      |
+-------+-------------------------------------+-------------------------------------------------+
```

Next, we calculate the **inverse document frequency** (**IDF**). IDF finds out whether a term is common or rare across all documents in the given corpus. It's a log-based mathematical function of the total number of documents, divided by the total number of documents in which the term has appeared. So, IDF can be calculated using the following formula (taken from Wikipedia):

$$\mathrm{idf}(t, D) = \log \frac{N}{|\{d \in D : t \in d\}|}$$

with

- N: total number of documents in the corpus $N = |D|$
- $|\{d \in D : t \in d\}|$: number of documents where the term t appears (i.e., $\mathrm{tf}(t, d) \neq 0$). If the term is not in the corpus, this will lead to a division-by-zero. It is therefore common to adjust the denominator to $1 + |\{d \in D : t \in d\}|$.

In our Excel sheet, we calculated *IDF* based on an earlier formula. Please see the following screenshot to understand how it looks in our example:

B26		f_x =LN((B27+1)/(B25+1))			
	A	B	C	D	E
13					
14					
15	Movie Matrix (TF) Simple Count				
16	Movie	Action	Adventure	Romance	Thriller
17					
18	Movie 1	1		1	
19	Movie 2		1		
20	Movie 3	1	1		1
21	Movie 4			1	
22	Movie 5			1	1
23	Movie 6	1	0	1	1
24					
25	DF	3	2	4	3
26	IDF	0.559615788	0.8472979	0.336472237	0.559615788
27	N=	6	6	6	6

After you have calculated the *IDF*, to get complete usage you need to multiply the *TF* number by the *IDF* number. Here is how the *TF*IDF* output would look in our sheet:

| Movie Matrix (TF*IDF) | | | | |
Movie	Action	Adventure	Romance	Thriller
Movie 1	0.559615788		0.336472237	
Movie 2		0.8472979		
Movie 3	0.559615788	0.8472979		0.559615788
Movie 4			0.336472237	
Movie 5			0.336472237	0.559615788
Movie 6	0.559615788		0.336472237	0.559615788

The following Spark code will calculate the *TF*IDF* score for you:

```
val idf = new IDF().setInputCol("rawFeatures").setOutputCol("features")
val idfModel = idf.fit(featurizedData)

val rescaledData = idfModel.transform(featurizedData)
rescaledData.select("Movie","rawFeatures","features").show()
```

The output of the preceding code looks as follows:

```
+------+--------------------+--------------------------------------------------------------------------+
|Movie |rawFeatures         |features                                                                  |
+------+--------------------+--------------------------------------------------------------------------+
|Movie1|(20,[3,10],[1.0,1.0])   |(20,[3,10],[0.5596157879354227,0.3364722366212129])                   |
|Movie2|(20,[13],[1.0])         |(20,[13],[0.8472978603872037])                                        |
|Movie3|(20,[3,13,14],[1.0,1.0,1.0])|(20,[3,13,14],[0.5596157879354227,0.8472978603872037,0.5596157879354227])|
|Movie4|(20,[10],[1.0])         |(20,[10],[0.3364722366212129])                                        |
|Movie5|(20,[10,14],[1.0,1.0])  |(20,[10,14],[0.3364722366212129,0.5596157879354227])                  |
|Movie6|(20,[3,10,14],[1.0,1.0,1.0])|(20,[3,10,14],[0.5596157879354227,0.3364722366212129,0.5596157879354227])|
+------+--------------------+--------------------------------------------------------------------------+
```

Now, you need to determine the user vector from user ratings. The user profile vector is calculated based on each movie genre. It is the vector dot product of all user ratings for a given genre and user ratings for all movies.

Frequently asked questions

Q: What are the two basic categories of machine learning and how do they differ from each other?

A: Machine learning can be broadly categorized into *supervised* and *unsupervised* learning. In the case of supervised learning, the model is trained based on the historical data, which is treated as the version of truth, termed training data. In the case of unsupervised learning, the algorithm derives inferences based on the input data, without labeled training data. The hidden patterns within the datasets are derived on the fly.

Q: Why is the Spark programming model suitable for machine learning with big datasets?

A: Spark is a general-purpose computation engine based on the fundamentals of distributed resilient computing. The large datasets are seamlessly distributed across cluster nodes for faster model generation and execution. Most of the underlying details are hidden from the data science engineer and hence there is a very limited learning curve involved in implementing machine learning with Spark. Spark is inherently fault-tolerant and very effectively leverages resource managers (Yarn, Mesos, and so on). It is one of the most popular Apache projects with a lot of community interest.

Q: What is the difference between regression and classification?

A: Regression is a technique that is used for predicting or forecasting the occurrence of an event or value of a continuous variable (dependent variable), based on the value of one or many independent variables. Classification is used as a grouping mechanism where the data points are tagged under a discrete category or cluster.

Q: What is dimensionality reduction and what is the basic purpose of it?

A: With the evolution of big data techniques, we are generating data from lots of heterogeneous sources. While it is true that more data is better data, modeling all the independent variables that are available requires great computational power. There are some dimensions that are redundant and some of the dimensions do not have a significant impact on the outcome. Dimensionality reduction techniques help us to reduce the number of dimensions without any loss of information by eliminating insignificant and redundant variables. This results in lowering the computational requirement, as well as easy visualization of the data within limited dimensions.

Summary

In this chapter, we were introduced to the basic concepts of machine learning algorithms and saw how the Spark programming model is an effective tool in leveraging big data assets for machine learning.

We have taken a deep dive into some of the supervised and unsupervised algorithms, and implemented those with Spark machine learning libraries. We will build on top of these fundamentals in the subsequent chapters and understand how neural networks act as the basic building blocks for creating intelligent machines.

Neural Network for Big Data

4

In the previous chapter, we established a basic foundation for our journey toward building intelligent systems. We differentiated the machine learning algorithms in two primary groups of supervised and unsupervised algorithms, and explored how the Spark programming model is a handy tool for us to implement these algorithms with a simple programming interface, along with a brief overview of the machine learning libraries available in Spark. We have also covered the fundamentals of regression analysis with a simple example and supporting code in Spark ML. The chapter showed how to cluster the data using the K-means algorithm and a deep dive into the realm of dimensionality reduction, which primarily helps us in representing the same information with fewer dimensions without any loss of information. We have formed the basis for the implementation of the recommendation engines with an understanding of principal component analysis, content-based filtering, and collaborative filtering techniques. On the way, we have also tried to understand some of the basics of matrix algebra.

In this chapter, we are going to explore the neural networks and how they have evolved with the increase in computing power with distributed computing frameworks. The neural networks take inspiration from the human brain and help us to solve some very complex problems that are not feasible with traditional mathematical models. In this chapter, we are going to cover:

- Fundamentals of neural networks and artificial neural networks
- Perceptron and linear models
- Nonlinearities model
- Feed-forward neural networks
- Gradient descent, backpropagation, and overfitting
- Recurrent neural networks

We will explain these concepts with easy-to-understand scenarios and corresponding code samples with Spark ML.

Fundamentals of neural networks and artificial neural networks

The basic algorithms and mathematical modeling concepts we covered in the last chapter are great when it comes to solving some of the structured and simpler problems. They are simpler compared to what the human brain is easily capable of doing. For instance, when a baby starts to identify objects through various senses (sight, sound, touch, and so on), it learns about those objects based on some fundamental building blocks within the human brain. There is a similar mechanism in all living beings with a difference in the level of sophistication based on the evolution cycle.

A neurological study of the brains of various animals and human beings reveals that the basic building blocks of the brain are neurons. These biological neurons are interconnected with each other and are capable of transmitting signals simultaneously to thousands of connected neurons. It is observed that in the more complex species, such as human beings, the brain contains more neurons than less-complex species. For instance, it is believed that the human brain contains 100 billion interconnected neurons. The researchers found a direct correlation between the quantity and level of interconnection between the neurons and the intelligence in various species. This has led to the development of **artificial neural networks** (**ANN**), which can solve more complex problems, such as image recognition.

ANNs offer an alternate approach to computing and the understanding of the human brain. While our understanding of the exact functioning of the human brain is limited, the application of ANNs for solving complex problems has so far shown encouraging results for primarily developing a machine that learns on its own based on the contextual inputs, unlike the traditional computing and algorithmic approach.

In our quest to developing cognitive intelligence for machines, we need to keep in mind that neural networks and algorithmic computing do not compete with each other, instead, they complement each other. There are tasks more suited to an algorithmic approach than a neural network. We need to carefully leverage both to solve specific problems. There are a lot of systems where we require a combination of both approaches.

Similar to the biological neurons, the ANNs have input and output units. A simple ANN is represented as follows:

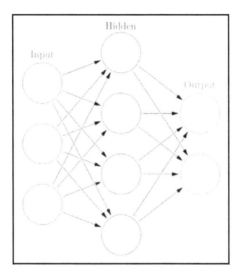

Figure 4.1 Structure of a simple ANN

An **ANN** consists of one input layer, which provides the input data to the network, one output layer, which represents the finished computation of the ANN, and one or more (depending on complexity) hidden layers, which is where actual computation and logic implementation happens.

The theory of neural networks is not new. However, at the time of its origin, the computational resources as well as datasets were limited in order to leverage the full potential of the ANNs. However, with the advent of big data technologies and massively parallel distributed computing frameworks, we are able to explore the power of ANNs for some of the innovative use cases and solving some of the most challenging problems, such as image recognition and natural language processing.

In the subsequent sections of this chapter, we will take a deep dive into the ANNs with some simple-to-understand examples.

Perceptron and linear models

Let's consider the example of a regression problem where we have two input variables and one output or dependent variable and illustrate the use of ANN for creating a model that can predict the value of the output variable for a set of input variables:

x1	x2	y
5	7	10
3	1	7
8	9	12
4	6	9
2	3	5
6	10	?

Figure 4.2 Sample training data

In this example, we have **x1** and **x2** as input variables and **y** as the output variable. The training data consists of five data points and the corresponding values of the dependent variable, **y**. The goal is to predict the value of **y** when **x1 = 6** and **x2 = 10**. Any given continuous function can be implemented exactly by a three-layer neural network with *n* neurons in the input layer, *2n + 1* neurons in the hidden layer and *m* neurons in the hidden layer. Let's represent this with a simple neural network:

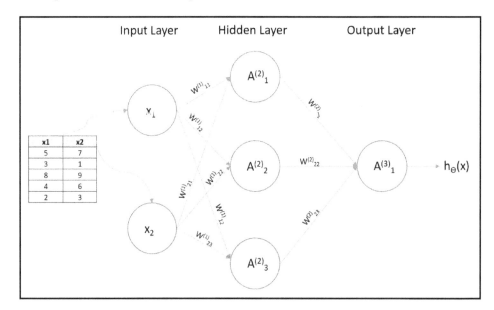

Figure 4.3 ANN notations

Component notations of the neural network

There is a standardized way in which the neural networks are denoted, as follows:

- x_1 and x_2 are inputs (It is also possible to call the activation function on the input layer)
- There are three layers in this network: the input layer, output layer, and hidden layer.
- There are two neurons in the input layer corresponding to the input variables. Remember, two neurons are used for illustration. However, in reality we are going to have hundreds of thousands of dimensions and hence input variables. The core concepts of ANN are theoretically applicable to any number of input variables.
- There are three neurons in the hidden layer (layer 2): (a^2_1, a^2_2, a^2_3).
- The neuron in the final layer produces output A^3_1.
- $a^{(j)}_i$: represents activation (the value that is computed and output by a node) of unit i in layer j. The activation function of a node defines the output of the node for a set of input. The simplest and most common activation function is a binary function representing two states of a neuron output, whether the neuron is activated (firing) or not:
    - For example, a^2_1 is the activation of the first unit in the second layer.
- $W^{(l)}_{ij}$ represents the weight on a connector, l is the layer from which a signal is moving, i represents the neuron number from which we are moving, and j represents the neuron number in the next layer to which the signal is moving. Weights are used for reducing the difference between the actual and desired output of the ANN:
    - For example, $W^{(1)}_{12}$ represents the weight for the connection between two neurons from layer **1** to layer **2** for the first neuron in the layer 1 and toward the second neuron in layer **2**.

Mathematical representation of the simple perceptron model

The output of the neural network depends on the input values, activation functions on each of the neurons, and weights on the connections. The goal is to find appropriate weights on each of the connections to accurately predict the output value. A correlation between inputs, weights, transfer, and activation functions can be visualized as follows:

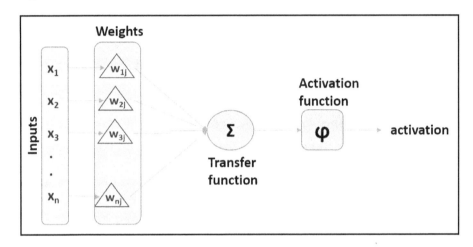

Figure 4.4 ANN components correlation

In summary, within an ANN, we do the sum of products of input *(X)* to their weights *(W)* and apply the activation function *f(x)* to get the output of a layer that is passed as input to another layer. If there is no activation function, the correlation between the input and output values will be a linear function.

 The perceptron is the simplest form of an ANN used for the classification of datasets that are linearly separable. It consists of a single neuron with varying weights and bias units.

We can represent the simple perceptron model as a dot product:

$$\varnothing\left(\sum_{i}^{n} x.w\right)$$

Since we have multiple values of x_1 and x_2 in our example, the computation is best done with a matrix multiplication so that all the transfer and activation functions can be parallely computed. The mathematical model APIs are greatly tuned to utilize the power of distributed parallel computation frameworks in order to perform the matrix multiplications. Let's now consider our example and represent it with matrix notations. The input dataset can be represented as x. In our example, this is a *(5,2)* matrix. The weights can be represented as $W^1_{(2x3)}$. The resultant matrix, (Z^2), is a 5 by 3 matrix which is the activity of the second (hidden) layer. Each row corresponds to a set of input values and each column represents the transfer function or activity on each of the nodes in the hidden layer. This can be illustrated in the following diagram:

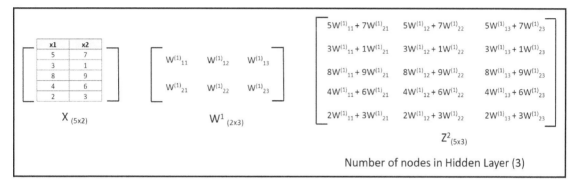

Figure 4.5: Each row corresponds to set of input values

With this, we have our first formula for the neural network. Matrix notation is really handy in this case since it allows us to perform complex computation in a single step:

$$Z^{(2)} = XW^{(1)}$$

With this formula, we are summing up the products of input and the corresponding synapse weights for each set of input. The output of a layer is obtained by applying an activation function over all the individual values for a node.

The main purpose of an activation function is to convert the input signal of a node to an output signal. As a parallel to the biological neuron, the output after application of an activation function indicates whether a neuron is fired or not. Let's quickly understand some of the most popular activation functions used within neural networks before proceeding with the next steps in our linear perceptron model.

Activation functions

Without an activation function, the output will be a linear function of the input values. A linear function is a straight line equation or a polynomial equation of the first degree. A linear equation represents the simplest form of a mathematical model and is not representative of real-world scenarios. It cannot map the correlations within complex datasets. Without an activation function, a neural network will have very limited capability to learn and model unstructured datasets such as images and videos. The difference between a linear and nonlinear function is illustrated in the following diagram:

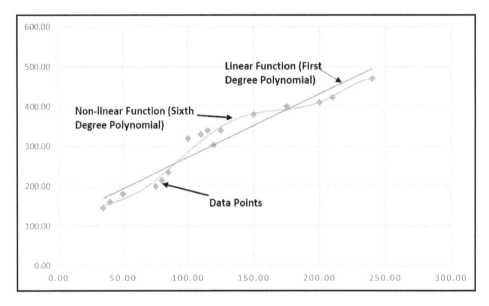

Figure 4.6: Linear versus nonlinear functions

As we can see, the linear model that we get without use of the activation function cannot accurately model the training data, whereas the multi-degree polynomial equation can accurately model the training data.

Using a nonlinear activation function, we can generate nonlinear mapping between the input and output variables and model complex real-world scenarios. There are three primary activation functions used at each neuron in the neural network:

- Sigmoid function
- Tanh function
- Rectified linear unit

Sigmoid function

The sigmoid function is one of the most popular nonlinear functions; it outputs *0* or *1* for any *x* input value between -∞ and +∞. The function can be mathematically and graphically expressed as follows:

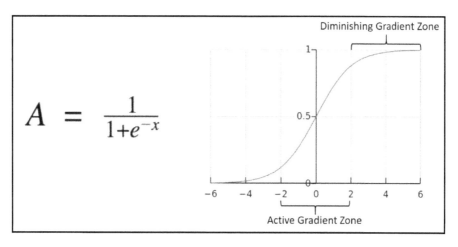

Figure 4.7: Sigmoid function

The function curve takes an *S* shape and hence the name **sigmoid**. As we can see in this example, for the values of *x* between -2 and +2, the *Y* output values are very steep. A small change in the value of *X* in this region contributes significantly to the value of the output. This can be termed as an active gradient zone. For the purpose of simplicity, let's understand this as a region on the curve with the highest slope. As the *X* values tends to be between -∞ and +∞, the curve enters into a diminishing gradient zone. In this region, a significant change in the value of *X* does not have a proportionate impact on the output value. This results in a vanishing gradient problem when the model is trying to converge. At this point, the network does not learn further or becomes extremely slow and computationally impossible to converge. The best part with the sigmoid activation function is that it always outputs *0* or *1*, regardless of the input value *X*. This makes it an ideal choice as an activation function for binary classification problems. For example, it is great for identifying a transaction as fraudulent or not. Another problem with the sigmoid function is that it is not zero-centered (*0 < Output < 1*). It is difficult to optimize the neural network computation. This drawback is overcome by the `tanh` function.

Tanh function

The **hyperbolic tangent** (**tanh**) function is a slight variation of the sigmoid function that is *0* centered. The function can be mathematically and graphically represented as follows:

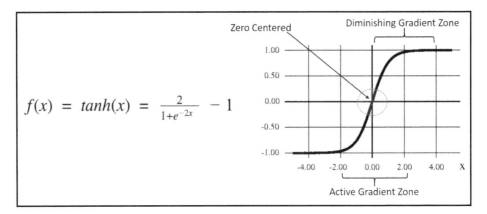

$$f(x) = tanh(x) = \frac{2}{1+e^{-2x}} - 1$$

Figure 4.8: Tanh function

The range of the `tanh` function is between *-1* and *1* and it is zero-centered; *-1 < Output < 1*. In this case, the optimization is easy and this activation function is preferred over the sigmoid function. However, the `tanh` function also suffers from a vanishing gradient problem similar to the sigmoid function. In order to overcome this limitation, the **Rectified Linear units** activation function, **ReLu**, is used.

ReLu

The ReLu function is mathematically and graphically represented as follows:

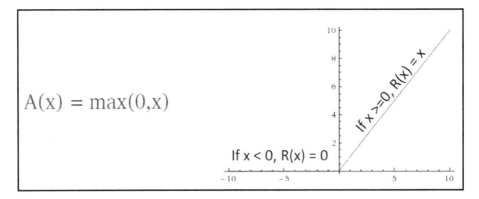

$$A(x) = \max(0,x)$$

If x < 0, R(x) = 0

If x >=0, R(x) = x

Figure 4.9 ReLu function

The mathematical form of this activation function is very simple compared to the sigmoid or `tanh` functions and it looks like a linear function. However, this is a nonlinear function that is computationally simple and efficient, hence it is deployed in deep neural networks (the neural networks with multiple hidden layers). This activation function eliminates the vanishing gradient problem. The limitation of using ReLu is that we can only use it for the hidden layers. The output layer needs to use different functions for regression and classification problems. The ReLu function simplifies and optimizes neural network computation and convergence compared to the sigmoid and `tanh` functions. In the case of the sigmoid and `tanh` functions, all the neurons within the hidden units fire during model convergence. However, in the case of ReLu, some of the neurons will be inactive (for the negative input values) and hence the activations are sparse and efficient. While the efficiency due to the horizontal activation line is desirable, it introduces a problem of dying ReLu. The neurons that go into the state due to negative x values do not respond to variations in error or input values that makes the major part of the neural network passive. This undesirable side effect of ReLu is eliminated by a slight variation of ReLu, called leaky ReLu. In the case of leaky ReLu, the horizontal line is converted into a slight sloped non-horizontal line (*0.001x* for *x < 0*), ensuring that the updates to the input values on the negative side of the spectrum are alive. The leaky ReLu is graphically represented as follows:

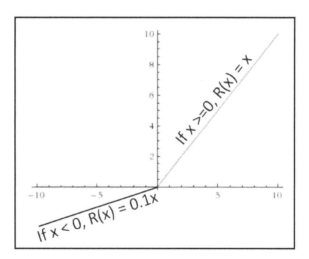

Figure 4.10: Leaky ReLu

Nonlinearities model

With the background information about the activation functions, we now understand why we need nonlinearities within the neural network. The nonlinearity is essential in order to model complex data patterns that solve regression and classification problems with accuracy. Let's once again go back to our initial example problem where we have established the activity of the hidden layer. Let's apply the sigmoid activation function to the activity for each of the nodes in the hidden layer. This gives our second formula in the perceptron model:

- $Z^{(2)} = XW^{(1)}$
- $a^{(2)} = f(z^{(2)})$

Once we apply the activation function, f, the resultant matrix will be the same size as $z^{(2)}$. That is, *5 x 3*. The next step is to multiply the activities of the hidden layer by the weights on the synapse on the output layer. Refer to the diagram on *ANN notations*. Note that we have three weights, one for each link from the nodes in the hidden layer to the output layer. Let's call these weights $W^{(2)}$. With this, the activity for the output layer can be expressed with our third function as:

- $Z^{(3)} = a^{(2)} W^{(2)}$

As we know, $a^{(2)}$ is a *5 x 3* matrix and $W^{(2)}$ is a *3 x 1* matrix. Hence, $Z^{(3)}$ will be a *5 x 1* matrix. Each row representing an activity value corresponds to each individual entry in the training dataset.

Finally, we apply the sigmoid activation function to *Z(3)* in order to get the output value estimate based on the training dataset:

$$\hat{y} = f(Z^{(3)})$$

The application of activation functions at the hidden and output layers ensures nonlinearity in the model and we can model the nonlinear training dataset into the ANN.

Feed-forward neural networks

The ANN we have referred to so far is called a **feed-forward neural network** since the connections between the units and layers do not form a cycle and move only in one direction (from the input layer to the output layer).

Let's implement the feed-forward neural network example with simple Spark ML code:

```scala
object FeedForwardNetworkWithSpark {
def main(args:Array[String]): Unit ={
val recordReader:RecordReader = new CSVRecordReader(0,",")
val conf = new SparkConf()
.setMaster("spark://master:7077")
.setAppName("FeedForwardNetwork-Iris")
val sc = new SparkContext(conf)
val numInputs:Int = 4
val outputNum = 3
val iterations =1
val multiLayerConfig:MultiLayerConfiguration = new
  NeuralNetConfiguration.Builder()
  .seed(12345)
  .iterations(iterations)
 .optimizationAlgo(OptimizationAlgorithm
                     .STOCHASTIC_GRADIENT_DESCENT)
  .learningRate(1e-1)
  .l1(0.01).regularization(true).l2(1e-3)
  .list(3)
  .layer(0, new DenseLayer.Builder().nIn(numInputs).nOut(3)
  .activation("tanh")
  .weightInit(WeightInit.XAVIER)
  .build())
  .layer(1, new DenseLayer.Builder().nIn(3).nOut(2)
  .activation("tanh")
  .weightInit(WeightInit.XAVIER)
  .build())
  .layer(2, new
   OutputLayer.Builder(LossFunctions.LossFunction.MCXENT)
     .weightInit(WeightInit.XAVIER)
     .activation("softmax")
     .nIn(2).nOut(outputNum).build())
     .backprop(true).pretrain(false)
     .build
val network:MultiLayerNetwork = new
MultiLayerNetwork(multiLayerConfig)
network.init
network.setUpdater(null)
val sparkNetwork:SparkDl4jMultiLayer = new
SparkDl4jMultiLayer(sc,network)
val nEpochs:Int = 6
val listBuffer = new ListBuffer[Array[Float]]()
(0 until nEpochs).foreach{i =>
val net:MultiLayerNetwork =
sparkNetwork.fit("file:///<path>/
iris_shuffled_normalized_csv.txt",4,recordReader)
```

```
            listBuffer +=(net.params.data.asFloat().clone())
            }
            println("Parameters vs. iteration Output: ")
            (0 until listBuffer.size).foreach{i =>
            println(i+"\t"+listBuffer(i).mkString)}
        }
    }
```

As we can see, the output value predicted by our model is not accurate. This is because we have initialized the weights randomly and only forward propagated once. We need our neural network to optimize the weights on each of the links between the input layer to the hidden layer to the final output layer. This is achieved with a technique called backpropagation, which we will discuss in the next section.

Gradient descent and backpropagation

Let's consider the following linear regression example where we have a set of training data. Based on the training data, we use forward propagation to model a straight line prediction function, **h(x)**, as in the following diagram:

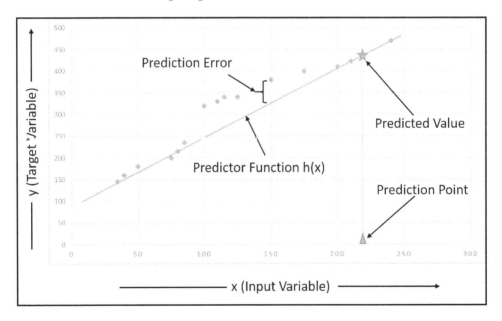

Figure 4.11: Forward propagation to model a straight line function

The difference between the actual and predicted value for an individual training sample contributes to the overall error for the prediction function. The goodness of fit for a neural network is defined with a cost function. It measures how well a neural network performed with respect to the training dataset when it modeled the training data.

As you can imagine, the cost function value in the case of the neural network is dependent on the weights on each neuron and the biases on each of the nodes. The cost function is a single value and it is representative of the overall neural network. The cost function takes the following form in a neural network:

$$C\ (W, X, Y)$$

- W represents weights for the neural network
- X^r represents the input values of a single training sample
- Y^r represents the output corresponding X^r

As we saw in `Chapter 3`, *Learning from Big Data*, the cost for all the training data points can be expressed as a sum of squared error. With this, we get our fifth equation for the neural network which represents the cost:

- $C\ (W, X^r, Y^r) = J = \sum 1/2\ (y - y^\wedge)^2$

Since the input training data is contextual and something that we cannot control, the goal of a neural network is to derive the weights and biases so as to minimize the value of the cost function. As we minimize the cost, our model is more accurate in predicting values for the unknown data input. There is a combination of weights, W, that gets us the minimum cost. Refer to figure 4.3, we have nine individual weights in our neural network. Essentially, there is a combination of these nine weights that gets us the minimum cost for our neural network. Let's further simplify our example and assume that we just have one weight that we want to optimize in order to minimize the cost of the neural network hypothesis. We can initialize the weight to a random value and test a high number of arbitrary values and plot the corresponding cost on a simple two-dimensional graph, as follows:

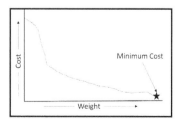

Figure 4.12: Weight-to-cost graph

It may be computationally easy and feasible to calculate the minimum cost for a large number of input weights selected at random. However, as the number of weights increases (nine in our case) along with the number of input dimensions (just two in our example), it becomes computationally impossible to get to the minimum cost in a reasonable amount of time. In real-world scenarios, we are going to have hundreds or thousands of dimensions and highly complex neural networks with a large number of hidden layers and hence a large number of independent weight values.

As we can see, the brute-force optimization method for optimizing the weights will not work for a large number of dimensions. Instead, we can use a simple and widely used **gradient descent** algorithm in order to significantly reduce the computational requirement in training the neural network. In order to understand gradient descent, let's combine our five equations into a single equation, as follows:

$$J = \Sigma \ 1/2 \ (y - f(\ f(X \ W^{(1)}) \ W^{(2)}) \ )^2$$

In this case, we are interested in finding the rate of change in J with respect to W, which can be represented as a partial derivative, as follows:

$$J = \frac{\partial J}{\partial W}$$

If the derivative equation evaluates to a positive value, we are going up the hill and not in the direction of minimum cost, and if the derivative equation evaluates to a negative value, we are descending in the right direction:

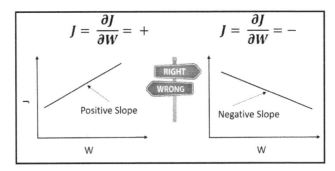

Figure 4.13: Positive slope versus Negative

Since we know the direction of negative slope, or the descent in the direction of reduced cost for the neural network, we can save the cost of computation while going in the wrong direction for the combinations of the weight values. We can iteratively go down the hill and stop at a point where the cost gets to a minimum and does not change significantly with a change in weight.

The neural network is trained when we get the combination of weights that results in the minimum value for the cost function. With the increase in the number of dimensions and the number of hidden layers, the optimization level due to the application of gradient descent increases and it is possible to train the neural network. However, the gradient descent works well only for a convex function relationship between weights and the cost. If the relationship is non-convex, the gradient descent algorithm my get stuck in a local minima instead of global minima. This is illustrated in the following diagram:

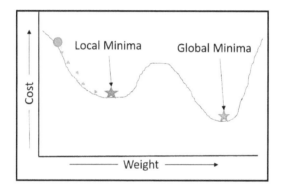

Figure 4.14: Graph of local minima and global minima

Depending on how we use our input data in conjunction with the weights matrix, it may not matter whether the cost function graph is non-convex in nature if we use the training examples and the corresponding weights one at a time in order to test multiple values in the direction of negative slope or gradient descent. This technique is called stochastic gradient descent. As the number of features increase, the gradient descent becomes computationally intensive and unreasonable for very complex problems and neural networks.

Stochastic gradient descent is an iterative technique that can distribute the work units and get us to the global minima in a computationally optimal way. In order to understand the difference between gradient descent and the stochastic gradient descent, let's look at the pseudocode for each:

Gradient Descent

```
for ( i in all_training_examples)
   gradient_descent_params = evaluate_gradient(loss_function, data, parameters)
   parameters = parameters – learning_rate * gradient_descent_params
```

Stochastic Gradient Descent

```
for (i in all training_examples)
   random_shuffle(training_data)
      for (single_example in training_data)
         gradient_descent_params = evaluate_gradient(loss_function, single_example, parameters)
         parameters = parameters – learning_rate * gradient_descent_parameters
```

Figure 4.15: Difference between gradient and stochastic descent

Gradient descent pseudocode

We proceed with the gradient descent pseudocode:

1. Let w be some initial value that can be chosen randomly.
2. Compute the $\partial J/\partial W$ gradient.
3. If $\partial J/\partial W < t$, where t is some predefined threshold value, *EXIT*. We found the weight vector that gets the minimum error for the predicted output.
4. Update W. $W = W - \varepsilon \ (\partial J/\partial W)$ [ε is called the learning rate. It needs to be chosen carefully, if it is too large, the gradient will overshoot and we will miss the minimum. If it is too large, it will take too many iterations to converge].

So far, we have traversed the ANN in one direction, which is termed as forward propagation. The ultimate goal in training the ANN is to derive the weights on each of the connections between the nodes so as to minimize the prediction error. One of the most popular technique is termed backpropagation. The fundamental idea is that once we know the difference between the actual value of the predictor variable based on the training example, the error is calculated.

The error in the final output layer is a function of the activation values of the nodes on the previous hidden layer. Each node in the hidden layer contributes with a different degree for the output error. The idea is to fine-tune the weights on the connectors so as to minimize the final output error. This will essentially help us to define how the hidden units should look based on the input and how the output is intended to look. This is an online algorithm that receives training input, one at a time. We feed forward to get predictions for a class by multiplying weights and the application of the activation function, get prediction errors based on the true label, and push the error back into the network in the reverse direction.

Backpropagation model

The backpropagation model can be conceptually represented as follows:

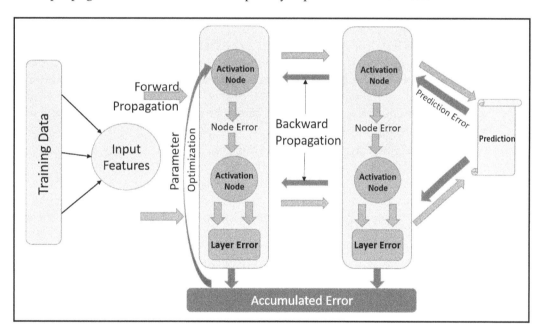

Figure 4.16: Backpropagation model

The backpropagation algorithm can easily be implemented in a staged manner. This is computationally less demanding compared to the gradient descent:

- **Initialize the model**: In this step, the model is randomly initialized to a point where the weights are selected with mathematical approximation and randomness. This is the first step in the feed-forward network.
- **Propagate forward**: In this step, all the input units, hidden units, and the output units are activated after adding the sum of the products of the neuron units and weights starting from the input units with the training dataset. The output is calculated by the application of the activation to the final output unit. Understandably, the output at this stage is going to be far from the ideal expected output.
- **Cost calculation**: At this point, we have the expected output (based on the training dataset) and the actual output from an untrained neural network. The cost function is typically a sum of squared errors for each of the training data points. This is a performance matrix of how well the neural network fits the training dataset as well as an indication of how well it is able to generalize the unknown input values that the model is expected to receive once trained. Once the loss function is established, the goal of the model training is to reduce the error in subsequent runs and for the majority of the possible input that the model will encounter in the real scenario.
- **Mathematical derivation of the loss function**: The loss function is optimized using the derivative of the error with respect to the weights on each of the connections within the neural network. For each of the connections in the neural network at this point, we calculate how much effect the change in value of a single weight (across the entire network) has on the loss function. Here are some of the possible scenarios when we calculate the cost derivative with respect to the weights:
    - At a particular weight value we have a loss of 0, the model accurately fits the input training dataset.
    - We can have a positive value for the loss function but the derivative is negative. In this situation, an increase in weight will decrease the loss function.
    - We can have a positive value for the loss function and the derivative is also positive. In this situation, a decrease in weight will decrease the loss function.

- **Backpropagation**: At this stage, the error in the output layer is back-propagated to the previous hidden layer and subsequently back to the input layer. On the way, we calculate the derivative and adjust the weights in a similar manner as in the previous step. The technique is called auto-differentiation in the reverse direction of the forward propagation. At each node, we calculate the derivative of the loss and adjust the weight on the previous connector.

- **Update the weights**: In the previous step, we calculated the derivatives on each of the nodes in all the layers by propagating the overall error backward. In a simplified manner, *New Weight = Old weight - (Derivative Rate * Learning Rate)*. The learning rate needs to be carefully selected with multiple experiments. If the value is too high, we may miss the minima and if the value is too low the model will converge extremely slowly. The weight on each connection is updated with following guidelines:

  - When the derivative of the error with respect to the weight is positive, the increase in weight will proportionally increase the error and the new weight should be smaller.

  - When the derivative of the error with respect to the weight is negative, the increase in weight will proportionally decrease the error and the new weight should be larger.

  - If the derivative of the error with respect to the weight is 0, no further updates to the weights are required and the neural network model has converged.

Overfitting

As we have seen in the previous sections, gradient descent and backpropagation are iterative algorithms. One forward and corresponding backward pass through all the training data is called an epoch. With each epoch, the model is trained and the weights are adjusted for minimizing error. In order to test the accuracy of the model, as a common practice, we split the training data into the training set and the validation set.

The training set is used for generating the model that represents a hypothesis based on the historical data that contains the target variable value with respect to the independent or input variables. The validation set is used to test the efficiency of the hypothesis function or the trained model for the new training samples.

Across multiple epochs we typically observe the following pattern:

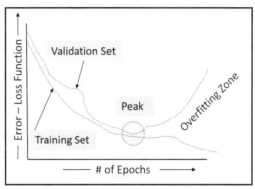

Figure 4.17: Graph of overfitting model

As we train our neural network through a number of epochs, the loss function error is optimized with every epoch and the cumulative model error tends to 0. At this point, the model has trained itself with respect to the training data. When we validate the hypothesis with the validation set, the loss function error reduces until a peak. After the peak, the error again starts to increase, as illustrated in the preceding figure.

At this point, the model has memorized the training data and it is unable to generalize itself for a new set of data. Each epoch after this point comes under an overfitting zone. The model has stopped learning after this point and it will produce incorrect results or outcomes. One of the easiest ways to prevent overfitting and create a model that generalizes well is to increase the amount of training data. With an increase in training data, the neural network is tuned for more and more real-world scenarios and hence generalizes well. However, with every increase in the training dataset, the computational cost of each epoch proportionately increases.

The machine has a finite capacity for modeling the data. The capacity of the ANN for modeling can be controlled by changing the number of hidden units, modifications, and optimizations of the number of training iterations, or changing the degree of nonlinearity for the activation functions. Overfitting can be controlled by reducing the number of features. Some features have insignificant contribution to the overall model behavior and hence the outcome. Such features need to be algorithmically identified with multiple experiments and iterations and eliminated from the final model generation. We can also use regularization techniques wherein all the features are used but with a varying degree of weightage based on the significance of the feature on the overall outcome.

Another popular regularization technique for preventing overfitting is dropout. With this technique, the nodes in the ANN are ignored (dropped) during the training phase. The neurons that are ignored are selected in a random manner.

Recurrent neural networks

So far, we have seen the ANNs where the input signals are propagated to the output layer in the forward pass and the weights are optimized in a recursive manner in order to train the model for generalizing the new input data based on the training set provided as input.

A special case real-life problem is optimizing the ANN for training sequences of data, for example, text, speech, or any other form of audio input. In simple terms, when the output of one forward propagation is fed as input for the next iteration of training, the network topology is called a **recurrent neural network** (**RNN**).

The need for RNNs

In the case of the feed-forward networks, we consider independent sets of inputs. In the case of image recognition problems, we have input images that are independent of each other in terms of the input dataset. In this case, we consider the pixel matrix for the input image. The input data for one image does not influence the input for the next image that the ANN is trying to recognize. However, if the image is part of a sequence or a frame within a video input, there is a correlation or dependence between one frame to the next frame.

This is also the case in audio or speech input to the ANN. Another limitation of the ANNs we have seen so far is that the length of the input layer needs to be constant. For example, a network that recognizes an image of 27 x 27 pixels as input will consistently be able to take input of the same size for training and generalization loops. An RNN can accommodate input of variable lengths and hence is more susceptible to the changes in input signals.

In summary, the RNNs are good at dependent input and input with variable lengths.

Structure of an RNN

A simple representation of an RNN is when we consider the output of one iteration as the input to the next forward propagation iteration. This can be illustrated as follows:

$$y^{(t)} = g_y\left(W_y h^{(t)}\right)$$

$$h(t) = g_h\left(W_I x^{(t)} + W_R h^{(t-1)}\right)$$

Figure 4.18: Output of one iteration as input to the next propagation iteration

A liner unit that receives input, x_I, applies a weight, W_I, and generates a hypothesis with an activation function metamorphosis into an RNN when we feed a weight matrix, W_R, back to the hypothesis function output in time with the introduction of a recurrent connection.

In the preceding example, t represents the activation in t time space. Now the activity of the network not only depends on the input signal, weights, and the activation function, but also on the activity of the previous timestamp. In the equation format, everything is the same except for the introduction of an additional parameter that represents output from the previous activation in time *(t-1)*.

Training an RNN

The RNN can be trained by unrolling the recurring unit in time into a series of feed-forward networks:

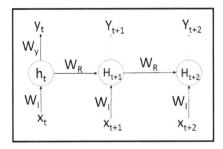

Figure 4.19: Unrolling the recurring unit into a series of feed-forward networks

The leftmost unit is the activity of the network in time, t, which is a typical feed-forward network with x_t as input at time, t. This is multiplied by the weight matrix, W_I. With the application of the activation function, we get the output, y_I, at time, t. This output is fed as input to the next unit along with the contextual and time input for the next unit in time, $t+1$. If you notice, there is a fundamental difference in the feed-forward network and the RNN.

The weights within various input, hidden, and output layers in a feed-forward network are different from each other and represent the significance of a dependent variable and the connections on the overall output. In the case of the RNN, the weights across the units (W_R) that are unrolled in time are the same. Since we are going to have an output at each of the units, we are going to have a cost associated with each of the units. Let's assume the cost of the first unit at timestamp t is C_t and subsequent units as C_{t+1} and C_{t+2}. The RNN training can be mathematically represented as:

$$\frac{\partial C}{\partial W_R} = \sum_t \frac{\partial C_t}{\partial W_R} \quad \Longrightarrow \quad \frac{\partial C_2}{\partial W_R} = \frac{\partial C_2}{\partial y_2} \frac{\partial y_2}{\partial h_2} \frac{\partial h_2}{\partial g} \frac{\partial g}{\partial a} \frac{\partial a}{\partial W_R}$$

Figure 4.20: RNN training mathematical expression

In this case, we are combining the gradients across units to calculate the overall cost of the network. Since the weights are shared across the units, the cost function is a derivative with respect to the weights and we can derive this with the same backpropagation and gradient descent methods.

Once the RNN is trained, it can be used primarily for the scenarios where the input are dependent on each other. In the case of language translation, we can use the connections between two keywords to predict the next word in the sequence in order to increase the accuracy of the language translation model.

Frequently asked questions

Q: Are ANNs exactly the same as the biological neurons in terms of information storage and processing?

A: Although it cannot be stated with 100% certainty that the ANNs are an exact replica in terms of memory and processing logic, there is evidence in medical science that the basic building block of a brain is a neuron, and neurons are interconnected. When the external stimulus is obtained or when is is generated by the involuntary processes, the neurons react by communicating with each other by the transmission of neurosignals. Although the functioning of the brain is very complex and far from fully understood, the theory of ANNs has been evolving and we are seeing a great deal of success in modeling some of the very complex problems that were not possible with traditional programming models. In order to make modern machines that possess the cognitive abilities of the human brain, there needs to be more research and a much better understanding of the biological neural networks.

Q: What are the basic building blocks of an ANN?

A: The ANN consists of various layers. The layer that receives input from the environment (independent variables) is consumed by the input layer. There is a final layer that emits output of the model based on the generalization of the training data. This layer is called the output layer. In between the input and output layers there can be one or many layers that process the signals. These layers are called hidden layers. The nodes within each of the layers are connected by synopse or connectors. Each of the connectors has an optimum weight so as to reduce the value of the cost function that represents the accuracy of the neural network.

Q: What is the need for nonlinearity within an ANN?

A: The neural networks are mathematical models where the input are multiplied by the synopse weights and the sum of all the node connection products constitutes the value on a node. However, if we do not include nonlinearity with an activation function, multi-layer neural networks will not exist. In that case, the model can be represented with a single hidden layer. We will be able to model very simple problems with linear modeling. In order to model more complex, real-world problems, we need multiple layers and hence nonlinearity within the activation functions.

Q: Which activation functions are most commonly used in building the ANNs?

A: Commonly used activation functions within the ANNs are:

- **Sigmoid function**: The output value is between *0* and *1*. This function takes a geometrical shape of *S* and hence the name sigmoid.
- **Tanh function**: The hyperbolic tangent function (`tanh`) is a slight variation of the sigmoid function that is 0-centered.
- **Rectified Linear Unit** (**ReLu**): This is the simplest, computationally optimized, and hence most popularly used activation function for the ANNs. The output value is *0* for all negative input and the same as the value of input for positive input.

Q: What is a feed-forward ANN and how are the initial values of weights selected?

A: A single pass through the network from the input layer to the output layer via the hidden layers is called a forward pass. During this, the nodes are activated as sum products of the node values and the connection weights. The initial values of the weights are selected randomly and as a result, the first pass output may deviate from the expected output based on the training data. This delta is called the network cost and is represented with a cost function. The intuition and goal for the ANN is to ultimately reduce the cost to a minimum. This is achieved with multiple forward and backward passes through the network. One round trip is called an epoch.

Q: What is the meaning of model overfitting?

A: Model overfitting occurs when the model is learning the input and cannot generalize on the new input data. Once this happens, the model is virtually not usable for real-world problems. The overfitting can be identified by the variation in model accuracy between the runs on training and validation datasets.

Q: What are RNNs and where are they used?

A: RNNs are the recurrent neural networks that utilize the output of one forward pass through the network as an input for the next iteration. RNNs are used when the input are not independent of each other. As an example, a language translation model needs to predict the next possible word based on the previous sequence of words. ANNs have great significance in the field of natural language processing and audio/video processing systems.

Summary

In this chapter, we introduced the most important concept in realizing intelligent machines, which is artificial neural networks. The ANNs are modeled against the biological brain. While the theory of ANN existed for decades, the advent of distributed computing power along with access to unprecedented volumes of data has enabled development in this exciting field of research.

In this chapter, we introduced the basic building blocks of the ANNs and simple techniques to train the models in order to generalize the model for producing outcomes for the new datasets.

This introduction is a building block for the next chapter, which will dive deeper into the implementation aspects of the neural networks.

5
Deep Big Data Analytics

In the previous chapter, we established the fundamental theory of **artificial neural networks** (**ANNs**) and how they emulate human brain structure for generating output based on a set of inputs with the help of interconnected nodes. The nodes are arranged in three types of layers: input, hidden, and output. We understood the basic and mathematical concepts of how the input signal is carried through to the output layer and the iterative approach that ANNs take for training weights on neuron connections. Simple neural networks with one or two hidden layers can solve very rudimentary problems. However, in order to meaningfully utilize ANNs for real-world problems, which involve hundreds or thousands of input variables, involve more complex models, and require the models to store more information, we need more complex structures that are realized with large numbers of hidden layers. These types of networks are called Deep Neural Networks and utilizing these Deep Neural Networks for modeling the real data is termed deep learning. With the addition of nodes and their interconnections, the Deep Neural Networks can model unstructured input, such as audio, video, and images.

In this chapter, we will explore how deep learning can be utilized for addressing some important problems in big data analytics, including extracting complex patterns from massive volumes of data, semantic indexing, data tagging, fast information retrieval, and simplifying discriminative tasks such as classification. We are going to cover:

- The building blocks of deep learning:
    - Gradient descent
    - Backpropagation
    - Non-linearities
    - Dropout
- Specialized neural net architectures for structured data
- Building data preparation pipelines
- Hyperparameter tuning
- Leveraging distributed computing for deep learning

The proposed examples will be implemented using the **Deeplearning4j** (**DL4J**) Java framework.

Deep learning basics and the building blocks

In the previous chapters, we established the fact that the machine learning algorithms generalize the input data into a hypothesis that fits the data so that the output, based on the new values, can be predicted accurately by the model. The accuracy of the model is a function of the amount of the input data along with variation in the values of the independent variables. The more data and variety, the more computation power we require to generate and execute the models. The distributed computing frameworks (Hadoop, Spark, and so on) work very well with the large volumes of data with variety. The same principles apply to ANNs.

The more input data we have along with variations, the more accurate the models can be generated, which requires more storage and computation power. Since the computation power and storage is available with the development of the big data analytics platforms (in-premise as well as on the cloud), it is possible to experiment with large neural networks with hundreds or thousands of nodes in the input layer, and hundreds or thousands of hidden layers. These types of ANNs are called Deep Neural Networks.

While these models are computationally heavy, they produce accurate results and get better with more data, unlike the traditional algorithms that plateau in terms of performance at some point. After the plateau point, even after adding more data, the model accuracy for traditional mathematical models does not increase by a great margin. The Deep Neural Networks perform better in terms of accuracy and reliability with increasing amount of data. The use of these multi-layered neural networks for hypothesis generation is generally termed deep learning. The difference between a **Simple Neural Network** and a **Deep Neural Network** can be depicted as follows:

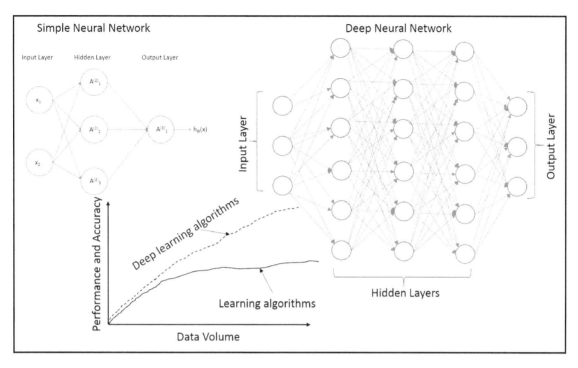

Simple ANN versus Deep Neural Network

For supervised learning problems, the Deep Neural Networks have proven to provide encouraging results, especially when it comes to mapping some of the functions with high complexity levels. With sufficiently large datasets with labeled training examples, the Deep Neural Networks are able to train the connection weights so that there is no loss of intelligence and the model accurately represents the historical facts based on data, and at the same time has a level of generalization that suits most of the mission critical applications. Remember, the generic and common objective of all the learning methods is to minimize the cost function. The cost function value is inversely proportional to the model's accuracy.

Let us mathematically define the cost function for a Deep Neural Network. This is also termed the mean squared error function. This function will always be positive since it takes the square of the difference:

$C(w,b) = 1/2n \sum_{x} \|y(x) - a\|^2$	w: collection of all the weights in the network b: all the biases n: training data size (number of samples) a: vector of outputs from the network corresponding to x as input value

Let's look at some of the methods of Deep Neural Networks learning.

Gradient-based learning

In the previous chapter, we primarily discussed the single hidden layer perceptron model or the simple neural networks, in that chapter we also introduced the concept of gradient descent. Gradient descent, as applicable to the Deep Neural Network, essentially means we define the weights and biases for the neuron connections so as to reduce the value of the cost function. The network is initialized to a random state (random weights and bias values) and the initial cost value is calculated. The weights are adjusted with the help of the **derivative** of cost with respect to weights on the Deep Neural Network.

 In mathematics, the derivative is a way to show the rate of change, that is, the amount by which a function is changing at one given point.

For functions that act on real numbers, it is the slope of the tangent line at a point on a graph:

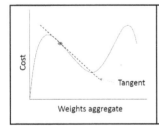

The dotted line is a tangent at a point on the cost function. The cost function represents the aggregate difference between the expected and the actual output from the deep neural network.

In a typical classification problem, where we are trying to predict the output classes based on the training data, we should be able to define the model's accuracy based on the number of correct predictions. In that case, it will not be possible to understand the effect of various weight values on the classification output. Instead, the Deep neural network is trained to produce a cost value that is a quadratic function of the input variables. With this, tuning various weight and bias values has a small gradient effect on the prediction confidence for a particular class.

The gradient-based learning can be visualized with an object that is rolling downhill in the direction of the lowest point in the valley. Gravity is the driving force that always moves the object in the direction of the lowest point. The gradient descent algorithm works in a similar manner. The slope is calculated at a random point initially; if the slope is negative, the weights and biases are modified in the same direction. Let's consider $\triangle(w_1, b_1)$ as a small movement for the cost value in the direction of (w_1, b_1) and $\triangle(w_2, b_2)$ as the small movement in the (w_2, b_2) direction. We can define the change in the value of cost function as:

$$\triangle C \approx \frac{\mathrm{d}C}{\mathrm{d}(w_1, b_1)} \triangle(w_1, b_1) + \frac{\mathrm{d}C}{\mathrm{d}(w_2, b_2)} \triangle(w_2, b_2)$$

The goal is to choose values of (w_i, b_i) so that $\triangle C$ is a negative value. In order to meet this goal, let's define $\triangle V$ as a vector of changes in (w_i, b_i):

$$\triangle V = (\triangle(w_1, b_1), \triangle(w_2, b_2)^T$$

Let's now define a gradient vector of the cost function as a vector of partial derivatives:

$$\nabla C = (\frac{\mathrm{d}C}{\mathrm{d}(w_1, b_1)}, \frac{\mathrm{d}C}{\mathrm{d}(w_2, b_2)})^T$$

We can now represent the change in the value of the cost function as:

$$\triangle C \approx \nabla C . \triangle V$$

The gradient vector, ∇C, establishes a relationship between changes in weight bias values (wi, bi) and the changes in the value of the cost function, C. This equation allows choice of all the weights and biases, $\triangle V$, so that we get a negative value for $\triangle C$. As a special case, if we choose $\triangle V = -\eta \nabla C$, where η is the learning rate (small value that defines the step size for the gradient descent). With this, the change in the value of the cost function becomes:

$$\triangle C \approx -\eta \nabla C . \nabla C = -\eta ||\nabla C||^2$$

Since the square value of ∇C is always going to be ≥ 0, $\triangle C$ will always be ≤ 0. That means cost, C, is always going to decrease, which is the intended behavior of the gradient descent. We change the value of weights and biases as $(w_i, b_i) = (w_i, b_i) - \eta \nabla C$. This rule is used in an iterative manner to reach the minimum cost value with the gradient descent algorithm. With gradient descent, we need to carefully choose the value of η so that the function is approximated properly. If the value is too great, the descent will miss the minima, and for too small a value, the steps will be small and the convergence will take a lot of time and computation. Applying the gradient descent to the deep neural network, we need to repeatedly apply the following updates and calculate the cost with each iteration leading to the minimum value for the cost function. The combinations of weights and biases at the minimum cost value is the optimization for the deep neural network and provides the required generalization:

$$wi = w'i = wi - \eta \frac{dC}{dw_i}$$

$$b_i = b'_i = b_i - \eta \frac{dC}{db_i}$$

While this iterative technique works mathematically, it becomes computationally demanding as the number of training inputs goes on increasing. As a result, the learning time increases. In most practical scenarios, the stochastic gradient descent is utilized. This is a variation of gradient descent in which we randomly pick up a small number of inputs. The gradient is averaged over these small numbers of input. This speeds up the gradient to the minimum cost.

Backpropagation

Backpropagation, or backprop, is used to efficiently calculate the gradient of the cost function, C. In simple terms, the goal of backprop is to compute the rate of change of the cost, C, with respect to the weights, $(\frac{dC}{dw})$, and the biases, $(\frac{dC}{db})$.

In order to clarify the intuition behind backprop, let's consider following deep neural network:

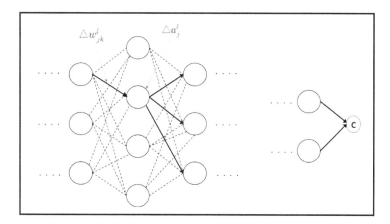

Imagine that we have made a small change, $\triangle w^l_{jk}$, in the weight value of some weight, w^l_{jk}, in the network. Due to this weight change, a corresponding change in the activation, $\triangle a^l_j$, for the connected neuron takes place. This change propagates to the output layer and ultimately affects the value of the cost function, as denoted by the solid lines in the earlier diagram. This change in cost, $\triangle C$, can be related to change in weight, $\triangle w^l_{jk}$, with the following equation:

$$\triangle C \approx \frac{dC}{dw^l_{jk}} \triangle w^l_{jk}$$

This equation allows us to establish the relationship between a small change, $\triangle w^l_{jk}$, and the overall cost, C, which also leads to computation of $\frac{dC}{dw^l_{jk}}$. The change in the value of the activation function for a connected neuron, $\triangle a^l_j$ ($j^{it}h$ neuron in l^{th} layer), is caused by the weight change. This change can be represented as follows:

$$\triangle a^l_j \approx \frac{da^l_j}{dw^l_{jk}} \triangle w^l_k$$

This change in activation changes the activation for all the neurons in the next and subsequently connected layers, shown by the solid arrows in the earlier formula. The change can be represented as follows:

$$\triangle a_q^{l+1} \approx \frac{da_q^{l+1}}{da_j^l} \triangle a_j^l$$

Based on the value of change in the activation value, $\triangle a_j^l$, we calculated earlier, the equation can be rewritten as follows:

$$\triangle a_q^{l+1} \approx \frac{da_q^{l+1}}{da_j^l} \frac{da_j^l}{dw_{jk}^l} \triangle w_k^l$$

The chain reaction based on the change in weight for one of the connections propagates to the end and affects the cost, C, which can be depicted as follows:

$$\frac{dC}{dw_{jk}^l} = \sum \frac{dC}{da_m^L} \frac{da_m^L}{da_n^{L-1}} \frac{da_m^{L-1}}{da_p^{L-2}} \cdots \frac{da_q^{l+1}}{da_j^l} \frac{da_j^l}{dw_{jk}^l}$$

This is the equation for backpropagation, which gives the change in rate for cost, C, with respect to the weights in the network.

Non-linearities

Let's consider two types of feature spaces, where $x1$ and $x2$ are independent variables and y is a dependent variable that takes a values based on $x1$ and $x2$:

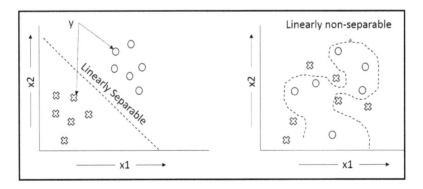

In the first instance, the input features are linearly separable with a straight line that represents the separation boundary. In other words, the space is linearly separable. However, in the second instance, the features space is inconsistent and cannot be separated with a line. We need some type of nonlinear or quadratic equation in order to derive the decision boundary. Most of the real-world scenarios are represented with the second type of feature space.

The deep neural networks receive data at the input layer, process the data, map it mathematically within the hidden layers, and generate output in the last layer. In order for the deep neural network to understand the feature space and model it accurately for predictions, we need some type of non-linear activation function. If the activation functions on all the neurons are linear, there is no significance for the deep neural networks. All the linear relationships across layers can be aggregated in single linear function that eliminates the need for multiple hidden units. In order to model the complex feature spaces, we require non-linearities within the nodes' activation functions. In the case of the more complex data input, such as images and audio signals, the deep neural networks model the feature space with weights and biases on the connectors.

The non-linear activations define whether a neuron fires or not based on the input signal and the applied activation function. This introduces enough non-linearity across the layers of a deep neural network in order to model hundreds and thousands of training data samples. The typical nonlinear functions that are deployed in the deep neural networks are:

- **Sigmoid function**: This is a mathematical function that takes the shape of *'S'* and ranges between *0* and *1*. This takes a mathematical form of $f(x) = \dfrac{1}{1 + e^{-x}}$.
- **Tanh function**: This is a variation of the sigmoid for which the values range from *-1* to *1*. This nonlinear function takes the mathematical form of $tanh(x) = \dfrac{e^x - e^{-x}}{e^x + e^{-x}}$.
- **Rectified linear unit (RELU)**: This function outputs *0* for any negative value of *x* and equals the value of *x* when it is positive: $f(x) = max(0, x)$.

Dropout

Dropout is a popular regularization technique used to prevent overfitting. When the deep neural network memorizes all the training data due to the limited size of the samples and a network of right depth is utilized for training, it does not generalize well enough to produce accurate results with the new test data. This is termed overfitting. Dropout is used primarily for preventing overfitting. This is a simple technique to implement. During the training phase, the algorithm selects the nodes from the deep neural network to be dropped (activation value set to *0*). With each epoch, a different set of nodes is selected based on a predefined probability. For example, if a dropout rate of *0.2* is selected, during each of the epochs, there is 20% chance that the node will not participate in the learning process. The network with dropout can be visualized as follows:

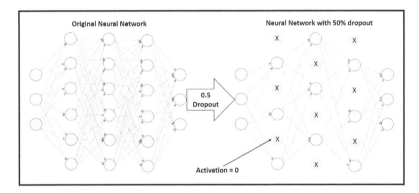

By dropping out the nodes, a penalty is added to the loss function. Due to this, the model is prevented from memorizing by learning interdependence between neurons in terms of activation values as well as corresponding connecting weights. As a result of the dropout where the activation on the dropped-out units is *0*, we are going to have a reduced value on the subsequent nodes in the network, we need to add a multiplication factor of *1 - drop_out_rate (1 - 0.5 in our case)* to the nodes that are participating in the training process. This process is called inverted dropout. With this, the activation on the participating node is $a = a/(1 - drop\_out\_percentage) = a/(1 - 0.5) = a/0.5 = a * 2$. In order to further optimize the dropout process, on the same training example, multiple iterations of the dropout with different nodes randomly eliminated can be applied. This technique also helps to eliminate the memorizing effect of the deep neural network and generalizes the training model further. Since the number of units in the neural network are reduced, each epoch through the network is optimized in terms of the time it takes through the iteration, including the backpropagation.

However, with the tests on multiple datasets and neural network sizes, it is observed that the number of iterations required for convergence are doubled with dropout (at a 50% dropout rate) and the overfitting zone is eliminated, as shown in the following diagram:

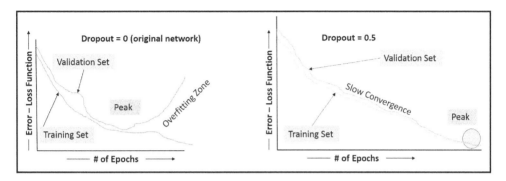

Building data preparation pipelines

The deep neural networks are best suited for supervised learning problems where we have access to historical datasets. These datasets are used for training the neural network. As seen in diagram 5.1, the more data we have at our disposal for training, the better the deep neural network gets in terms of accurately predicting the outcome for the new and unknown data values by generalizing the training datasets. In order for the deep neural networks to perform optimally, we need to carefully procure, transform, scale, normalize, join, and split the data. This is very similar to building a data pipeline in a data warehouse or a data lake with the help of the **ETL** (Extract Transform and Load with a traditional data warehouse) and **ELTTT** (**Extract Load and Transform** multiple times in modern data lakes) pipelines.

We are going to deal with data from a variety of sources in structured and unstructured formats. In order to use the data in deep neural networks, we need to convert it into a numerical representation and make it available in multi-dimensional arrays. DataVec is a popular Apache 2.0 library for generic machine-learning operations that we listed earlier. DataVec supports many data sources out-of-the-box. These data sources cover the majority of the types typically used within the data science community.

The data sources and types supported by DataVec are listed in the following table:

Data Type	Description
CSV	Comma separated files. The data fields (attributes are separated by COMMA ',' character)
Raw Test Data	Tweets, Text Documents and so on
Image Data	The images are stored as the two dimensional array of pixels. The pixels are represented as an integer value in various color scales. For example, the grey scale image contains 256 unique sheds represented by numbers between 0 and 255
LibSVM Data	LibSVM is an open machine library which specifies the data representation in a structured schema
Matlab (MAT) format	This is a binary file format which is internally used by MatLab. It includes arrays, variables, functions
JSON, XML, YAML	These are text formats which are defined by semantic rules and support hierarchical reprentation of the data

A generic machine learning pipeline consists of standard steps, such as data extraction from source, ingestion, preparation, model training and retraining, model deployment, and predictions (class prediction or regression value). The pipeline can be visualized as follows:

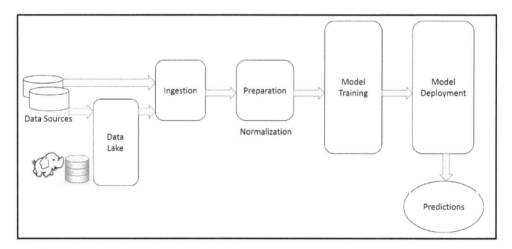

There are more and more devices and systems generating data in digital formats. These data assets are typically pushed into data lake structures that are based on distributed computing frameworks. Many organizations are also adopting a *cloud-first* strategy. The majority of the data loads are computation is moving to cloud infrastructure and platforms. For the machine learning, and specifically for the use cases based on deep neural networks, we need to carefully define the data ingestion and processing pipelines.

The DataVec API has libraries that make it easy to get the data in the format that the neural networks can understand. The primary component is the vectorization and hence the API is called DataVec. This is a process by which the data attributes are converted into numerical formats and regularized for the specific use case requirements. DataVec has a similarity in dealing with input and output data. The structures are defined to suit parallel processing and to work seamlessly with distributed file systems, such as HDFS.

 The **Hadoop Distributed File System** (**HDFS**) is a distributed file system designed to run on commodity hardware. It has many similarities with existing distributed file systems. However, the differences from other distributed file systems are significant. HDFS is highly fault-tolerant and is designed to be deployed on low-cost hardware. HDFS provides high throughput access to application data and is suitable for applications that have large datasets.

There are three primary entities in HDFS, as well as DataVec, for storing and loading the data for processing.

- **InputFormat**: This defines the structural semantic of the data. It confines to a predefined schema. The validators are implemented for validation based on the InputFormat. The input formats are defined in such a way that they can be easily split for distributed processing. The most commonly used input formats are:
  - **FileInputFormat**: This is a file-based format and treats a file as an independent and unique object. The format is tied with an input directory in which the data file is present. This format can also read and process all the files in a directory. Once all the files are loaded, the splits are created based on the underlying distributed file system rules.
  - **TextInputFormat**: The Hadoop MapReduce framework utilizes this as the default format. The best-suited and default format is a comma-separated data structure that typically contains a newline character as a record separator.
  - **SequenceFileInputFormat**: This format is used for reading the sequence files.
- **InputSplit**: This object is created from the InputFormat and represents the data logically. The splits are divided into records. The records can be independently processed in a distributed manner by Hadoop.
- **RecordReader**: This object reads the records defined by the InputSplit. It generates key-value pairs based on the indexing of the datasets. This makes it easy for the Mapper to read in sequences of available data chunks for processing.

These concepts are also implemented in the DataVec API for facilitating distributed parallel processing. DataVec also supports the OutputFormats that are largely interoperable. The vector formats most commonly generated with DataVec are ARFF and SVMLight. The framework also provides extensibility for incorporating custom input formats. Once the formats are defined with the DataVec interfaces, the framework handles those in the same way as the predefined formats. Vectorization of the datasets is the central focus for the DataVec library.

The numerical vectors are the only suitable input formats as well as the processing formats for the deep neural networks. The API also supports transformation libraries for massaging the data and filtering out the insignificant records and attributes. Once the data is ingested it is available for utilizing in training and testing the models. Normalization is one of the important preparation steps in order to optimize the learning process.

This step is important when the neural networks are deep within multiple hidden layers and the data input features vary in the scale. This variance results in slow convergence and takes a very long time for the deep neural network to learn. One of the most common normalization technique is 0-1 range normalization. In this, the input values are normalized between 0 and 1 without affecting the data quality or losing any data.

Let's demonstrate normalization using the Weka framework:

1. Open the Weka explorer and select the `iris.atff` file. This is a simple dataset with four features and a class output variable with three possible output values:

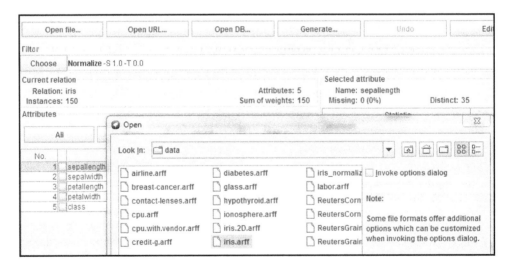

2. Review the attributes and their original value distribution:

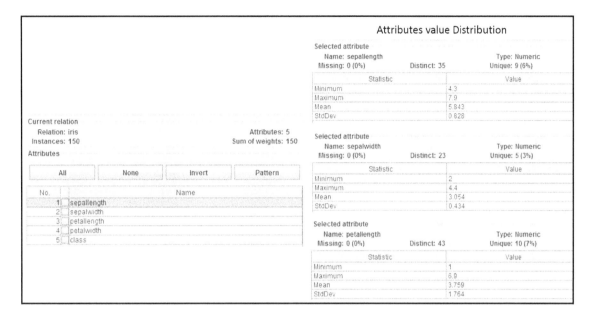

3. Apply the normalization filter. Choose the filter under **filters** | **unsupervised** | **attribute** | **Normalize** and apply the filter to the selected dataset:

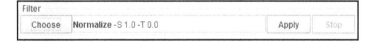

4. Check the attribute values after normalization. The values are all in the range between **0** and **1**:

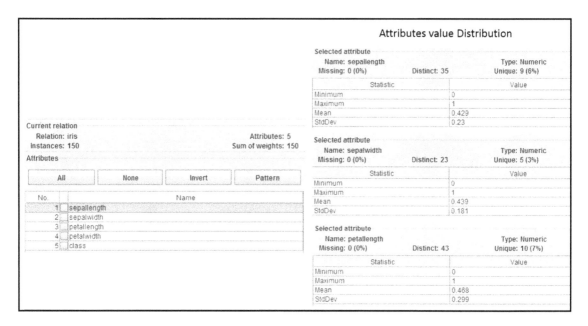

These normalized values in the range of **0** and **1** produce the same training model and hence the output. However, with normalization, we optimize the learning performance for the deep neural network. Here is the Java code for applying normalization in the data preparation pipeline using the `deeplearning4j` library:

```
package com.aibd.dnn;

import org.datavec.api.records.reader.RecordReader;
import org.datavec.api.records.reader.impl.csv.CSVRecordReader;
import org.datavec.api.split.FileSplit;
import org.datavec.api.util.ClassPathResource;
import org.deeplearning4j.datasets.datavec.RecordReaderDataSetIterator;
import org.nd4j.linalg.dataset.DataSet;
import org.nd4j.linalg.dataset.api.iterator.DataSetIterator;
import org.nd4j.linalg.dataset.api.preprocessor.NormalizerMinMaxScaler;

public class Normalizer {

    public static void main(String[] args) throws  Exception {
        int numLinesToSkip = 0;
        char delimiter = ',';
```

```
        System.out.println("Starting the normalization process");
        RecordReader recordReader = new
CSVRecordReader(numLinesToSkip,delimiter);

        recordReader.initialize(new FileSplit(new
ClassPathResource("iris.txt").getFile()));
        int labelIndex = 4;
        int numClasses = 3;

        DataSetIterator fulliterator = new
RecordReaderDataSetIterator(recordReader,150,labelIndex,numClasses);

        DataSet dataset = fulliterator.next();

        // Original dataset
        System.out.println("\n{}\n" + dataset.getRange(0,9));

        NormalizerMinMaxScaler preProcessor = new NormalizerMinMaxScaler();
        System.out.println("Fitting with a dataset...............");
        preProcessor.fit(dataset);
        System.out.println("Calculated metrics");
        System.out.println("Min: {} - "   + preProcessor.getMin());
        System.out.println("Max: {} - " + preProcessor.getMax());

        preProcessor.transform(dataset);
        // Normalized dataset
        System.out.println("\n{}\n" + dataset.getRange(0,9));
    }
}
```

Here is the output from the program:

```
==========Original Values =======
[[5.10, 3.50, 1.40, 0.20],
 [4.90, 3.00, 1.40, 0.20],
 [4.70, 3.20, 1.30, 0.20],
 [4.60, 3.10, 1.50, 0.20],
 [5.00, 3.60, 1.40, 0.20],
 [5.40, 3.90, 1.70, 0.40],
 [4.60, 3.40, 1.40, 0.30],
 [5.00, 3.40, 1.50, 0.20],
 [4.40, 2.90, 1.40, 0.20]]

==========Normalized Values =======
[[0.22, 0.62, 0.07, 0.04],
 [0.17, 0.42, 0.07, 0.04],
 [0.11, 0.50, 0.05, 0.04],
 [0.08, 0.46, 0.08, 0.04],
```

```
[0.19, 0.67, 0.07, 0.04],
[0.31, 0.79, 0.12, 0.12],
[0.08, 0.58, 0.07, 0.08],
[0.19, 0.58, 0.08, 0.04],
[0.03, 0.38, 0.07, 0.04]]
```

Practical approach to implementing neural net architectures

While the deep neural networks are good at generalizing the training data with multi-layered iteratively-generated models, the practical application of these algorithms and theory requires careful consideration of various approaches. This section introduces general guiding principles for using the deep neural networks in practical scenarios. At a high level, we can follow a cyclic process for deployment and the use of deep neural networks, as depicted in this diagram:

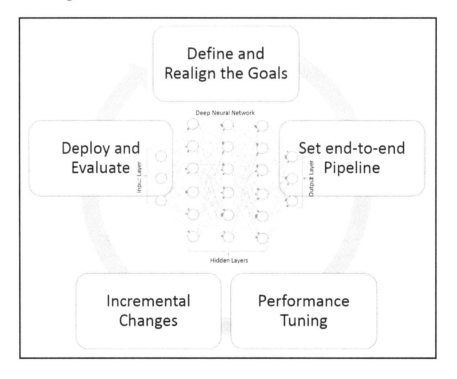

We explain the preceding diagram as follows:

- **Define and realign the goals**: This is applicable not only to the deep neural networks but in general use of the machine learning algorithms. The use-case-specific goals related to the choice error metric and threshold target value for the metric need to be set as the first step. The goal around the error metric defines the actions in the subsequent stages of architectural design and various design choices. It is unrealistic to set the goal of zero error for most of the practical use cases. This is due to the stochastic nature of most of the real scenarios where the training data is often insufficient and cannot model the environment with certainty.

- **Set the end-to-end pipeline**: Once the goals are determined and the expected threshold metrics are set up, the next step is to set up the end-to-end pipeline. While the pipeline is going to be different based on the use case and available data assets, in this section we will learn the generic guidelines. When the use case is to implement supervised learning with fixed and small numbers of input parameters in vector form (for example, defining the housing price based on various factors, such as the square foot area, number of rooms, location, start with a feed-forward network). Initialize this network with fully connected nodes. In case of a matrix structure data such as image pixels, use a convolutional neural network architecture. When the input is a sequence of data that depends on the previous value chain, use a recurrent network topology. Early stopping and dropout can be used as the strategies when the training set contains a large number of examples and input features.

- **Performance tuning**: Once we have the basic pipeline setup completed, we need to evaluate the performance of the model. There is a decision point between trying out a set of new models or model parameters, or adding more data to the training set. As a general guiding principle, the initial model should be tested through multiple iterations by adding more data and evaluating its impact on the model performance. Measure the model performance on the training set. If the model is not performing well on the training set, the first step is to increase the number of hidden units in the network. With this, the model is able to identify minor and deeper insights in the training data. The performance needs to be evaluated based on multiple tests by setting different values for the learning rate. Despite this, if the model's performance on the training data does not improve, there may be an issue with the quality of the training data. The datasets need to be carefully evaluated and cleansed before running further optimizations.

Once the model is performing well on the training data, we need to test the performance with the test data. If the model is performing well within the set threshold in the first step, the model is well generalized and good to be utilized with real data. If the model does not perform well on the test data, we need to gather more data and train the model again for better generalization. As a rule of thumb, the marginal addition of data does not improve the performance by a great deal. We need to consider adding data in multiples of the original dataset in order to achieve significant performance gain and reduce generalization error.

- **Incremental changes**: The summary-level goal for deploying the deep neural networks is to minimize the error in the real data when the model is deployed. In order to achieve that, we need to make incremental changes to the configuration parameters. This is termed hyperparameter tuning. Some of the hyperparameters which typically result in quick gains are number of hidden units, learning rate, convolution kernel width, implicit zero padding, weight decay coefficient and dropout rate. Apart from these, different volumes of the training data are randomly tested for incrementally optimizing the model performance. We will cover this topic in detail in the next section.

- **Deploy and evaluate**: Once the threshold goals for the model's performance are achieved, the model can be deployed in the real environment. Due to the stochastic nature of most of the environments, the model performance needs to be constantly evaluated, especially for mission-critical applications. At this stage, we also need to consider strategies for automated hyperparameter-tuning based on the historical trends with the model's deployment in production. With increasing degrees of historical data on the model's performance with different values of manually-, as well as automatically-selected hyperparameter values, it is also possible to treat the hyperparameter values, the volume of the training data as an input set of the dependent variables, and the model's performance as the dependent variable. A simplified technique, such as Bayesian regression, can be used for further optimization at runtime in an automated manner.

In the next section, we will take a look at some of the guiding principles for tuning the runtime parameters for the deep neural networks.

Hyperparameter tuning

Imagine a sound system that has a high quality speaker and mixer system. You must have seen a series of buttons on the console that independently control a specific parameter of sound quality. The bass, treble, and loudness are some of the controls that need to be properly set for a great experience. Similarly, a deep neural network is only as good as the setting of various controlling parameters. These parameters are called hyperparameters, and the process of controlling various parameters at a value that gets the best performance in terms of training/execution time as well as accuracy and generalization of the model. Similar to the sound equalizer example, multiple hyperparameters need to be tuned together for optimum performance. There are two strategies typically used when choosing a combination of hyperparameters:

- **Grid search**: The hyperparameters are plotted on a matrix and the combination that gets the best performance is selected for the model that is deployed in the real scenario. With grid search, the number of iterations to the yield ratio is poor.
- **Random search**: In the case of random search, the hyperparameter values are selected at random. In this case, with the same number of iterations as the grid search, there is a better chance of reaching the optimum values for the hyperparameters. The difference between grid search and random search can be depicted with the diagram as follows:

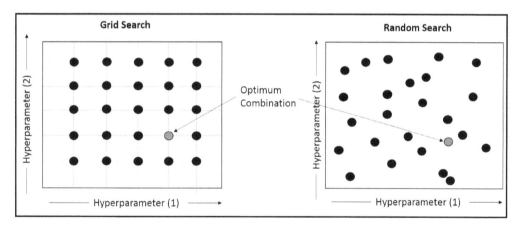

A variation of the random search technique can be deployed in order to reduce the number of iterations through the search space. The technique is broadly categorized as **Coarse to Fine** search. In this case, the random search is run for a few iterations and once a region with higher optimization combination is identified, the search space is limited to a smaller zone of hyperparameter values. With this technique, the search is confined to a region and hence optimized. The coarse-to-fine technique can be visualized as follows:

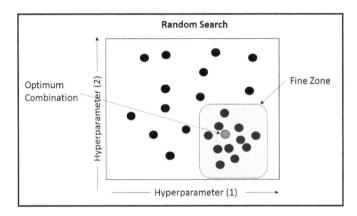

During initial search iterations, the entire space is searched. As the optimum hyperparameter values are found, the search space is restricted to a fine zone. With this, the hyperparameters are finely tuned with a relatively smaller number of iterations. With these techniques for searching for the right set of hyperparameters, let's now look at some of the most commonly used hyperparameters with deep neural networks.

Learning rate

In the *Gradient-based learning* section of this chapter, we established the equations for weight and bias updates for the deep neural network as follows:

$$wi = w'i = wi - \eta \frac{\mathrm{d}C}{\mathrm{d}w_i}$$

$$b_i = b'_i = b_i - \eta \frac{\mathrm{d}C}{\mathrm{d}b_i}$$

In these equations, the learning rate is denoted by η. The learning rate for the gradient descent algorithm defines the size of the step that algorithm takes with each training set instance. If the learning rate is too high, the average loss across the gradient descent steps will be high. In this case, the algorithm may miss the global minima. An extremely low learning rate will result in slow convergence, as depicted in this diagram:

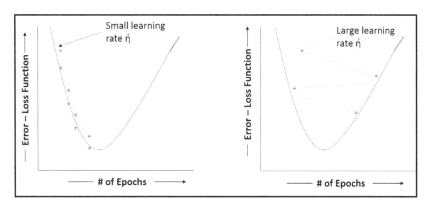

If there is an opportunity to tune only one hyperparameter, this parameter needs to be tuned. As a standard, the value of the learning rate needs to be less than 1 and greater than 10^{-6}. Another widely used strategy with the learning rate is to adapt to a decreasing learning rate with time (training iterations). During the initial iterations, the learning rate is kept constant and once the model is close to convergence (when the change in the value of loss function degrades to a minimum), the learning rate is modified with a small fraction of the original learning rate. Typically, a 0.001 fraction of the initial learning rate is recommended for optimum convergence to global minima. Another strategy for quicker convergence using parallel processing and train with mini batches. These batches independently tune the learning rate hyperparameter with small batches defined by a factor between 1 and 100. When the mini batch factor is 1, the algorithm behaves as the gradient descent algorithm. As an example, when the factor value is 20, the training data samples are at 5% and are distributed for independent tuning of the learning rate, η.

Number of training iterations

This hyperparameter is useful for avoiding overfitting. As the model converges (the loss function value plateaus at a point and does not change with epochs), it tends to overfit the training data and moves towards a non-generalized zone in which the test samples do not perform as well as the training data. Setting the number of training iterations carefully around the plateau region ensures early stopping and hence a robust model that generalizes well.

While the hyperparameters are tuned and their effect on the overall cost function is evaluated, the early stopping can be disabled. However, once all the other hyperparameters are fully tuned, we can dynamically set the number of training iterations based on the plateau region for the loss function.

 Stopping immediately after convergence is not a good strategy. It is recommended to continue the iterations for about 10% of the total epochs that resulted in near convergence. Controlling the number of training iterations is a good strategy to reduce the computation requirement for the model.

Number of hidden units

The performance of the deep neural network can be tweaked by selecting and changing the number of hidden units, n_h, in each of the layers. As a general guideline, it is recommended to select a larger-than-required n_h value initially. This ensures enough generalization for the network. However, the higher the value of n_h, the greater the computational requirement for training the deep neural network. This hyperparameter can also be tuned at the level of a layer. Each individual layer can have a different and optimal value for n_h based on the results from multiple iterations on the test data. In such cases, the first layer that is connected to the input layer is recommended to be overcomplete (having more nodes than the optimum value). This strategy helps to generalize the data better than having a lean first layer and more populated layers toward the output layer.

Number of epochs

One iteration through the entire dataset forward and backward in the deep neural network is called as an **epoch**. With each epoch, the network typically uses a backpropagation algorithm to adjust weights and biases. It is important to choose the right number of epochs. If the number of epochs is too high, the network will potentially overfit the data and not generalize on the new set of input.

If the number of epochs is too low, the network will underfit the data and will not perform well, even on the training data. There is no rule of thumb for selecting the number of epochs for a deep neural network. The number depends on the diversity of the dataset and the volume of the data. A recommended strategy is to start with a high number of epochs, and once the loss function does not vary significantly between multiple epochs, the training can be stopped.

Experimenting with hyperparameters with Deeplearning4j

Let's build a simple neural network to demonstrate the effects of various hyperparameters on model performance. We will create a simple neural network that can add two numbers based on the randomly generated training data. The training data has two independent variables, *x1* and *x2*, and an output variable, *y1* = *x1* + *x2*. Here is a pictorial view of the network we will generate with the deeplearning4j library:

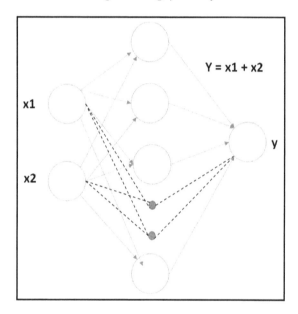

Here is the utility code for generating the sample data: *x1* and *x2* as the input independent variables, and *y* as the output (dependent) variable:

```
// Method to generate the training data based on batch size passed as
parameter
private static DataSetIterator generateTrainingData(int batchSize, Random
rand){

    // container for the sum (output variable)
    double [] sum = new double[nSamples];
    // container for the first input variable x1
    double [] input1 = new double[nSamples];
    //container for the second input variable x2
    double [] input2 = new double[nSamples];
```

```
    // for set size of the sample in configuration, generate random
    // numbers and fill the containers
    for (int i= 0; i< nSamples; i++) {
        input1[i] = MIN_RANGE + (MAX_RANGE - MIN_RANGE) *
rand.nextDouble();
        input2[i] =  MIN_RANGE + (MAX_RANGE - MIN_RANGE) *
rand.nextDouble();
        // fill the dependent variable y
        sum[i] = input1[i] + input2[i];
    }
    // Format in the deeplearning4j data structure
    INDArray inputNDArray1 = Nd4j.create(input1, new int[]{nSamples,1});
    INDArray inputNDArray2 = Nd4j.create(input2, new int[]{nSamples,1});
    INDArray inputNDArray = Nd4j.hstack(inputNDArray1,inputNDArray2);
    INDArray outPut = Nd4j.create(sum, new int[]{nSamples, 1});
    DataSet dataSet = new DataSet(inputNDArray, outPut);
    List<DataSet> listDs = dataSet.asList();
    Collections.shuffle(listDs,rand);
    return new ListDataSetIterator(listDs,batchSize);
}
```

Here is the code for the method that generates the multi-layer neural network with configurable hyperparameters:

```
/** Method for generating a multi-layer network
 * @param numHidden - the int value denoting number of nodes in the hidden
unit
 * @param iterations - number of iterations per mini-batch
 * @param learningRate - The step size of the gradient descent algorithm
 * @param numEpochs - number of full passes through the data
 * @param trainingDataIterator - the iterator through the randomly
generated training data
 * @return the model object (MultiLayerNetwork)
 * */
private static MultiLayerNetwork generateModel(int numHidden, int
iterations, double learningRate, int numEpochs, DataSetIterator
trainingDataIterator ) {

    int numInput = 2;   // using two nodes in the input layer
    int numOutput = 1;  // using one node in the output layer
    MultiLayerNetwork net = new MultiLayerNetwork(new
NeuralNetConfiguration.Builder()
        .seed(SEED)
        .iterations(iterations)
.optimizationAlgo(OptimizationAlgorithm.STOCHASTIC_GRADIENT_DESCENT)
        .learningRate(learningRate)
        .weightInit(WeightInit.XAVIER)
        .updater(Updater.NESTEROVS)
```

```
            .list()
            .layer(0, new DenseLayer.Builder().nIn(numInput).nOut(numHidden)
                .activation(Activation.TANH)
                .build())
            .layer(1, new OutputLayer.Builder(LossFunctions.LossFunction.MSE)
                .activation(Activation.IDENTITY)
                .nIn(numHidden).nOut(numOutput).build())
            .pretrain(false).backprop(true).build()
    );
    net.init();
    net.setListeners(new ScoreIterationListener(1));

    //Train the network on the full dataset, and evaluate in periodically
    double startTime = System.currentTimeMillis();
    for( int i=0; i<nEpochs; i++ ){
        trainingDataIterator.reset();
        net.fit(trainingDataIterator);
    }
    double endTime = System.currentTimeMillis();
    System.out.println("Model Training Time = " + (endTime - startTime));
    return net;
}
```

This model can be tested by passing different values of the hyperparameters, as follows:

```
public static void main(String[] args){

    //Generate the training data
    DataSetIterator iterator =
generateTrainingData(batchSize,randomNumberGenerator);

        // Test 1: -----------------------------------------------------
        //Set the values of hyperparameters
        int nHidden = 10;
        int iterations = 1;
        double learningRate = 0.01;
        int nEpochs = 200;
        double startTime = System.currentTimeMillis();
        MultiLayerNetwork net =
generateModel(nHidden,iterations,learningRate,nEpochs,iterator);

        double endTime = System.currentTimeMillis();
        double trainingTime = (endTime - startTime);

        // Test the addition of 2 numbers
        INDArray input = Nd4j.create(new double[] { 0.6754345,
0.3333333333333 }, new int[] { 1, 2 });
        INDArray out = net.output(input, false);
```

```
            double actualSum = 0.6754345 + 0.3333333333333;
            double error = actualSum - out.getDouble(0);
            System.out.println("Hidden Layer Count, Iterations, Learning Rate,
Epoch Count, Time Taken, Error");
            System.out.println(""+nHidden + "," + iterations + "," +
learningRate + "," + nEpochs + "," + trainingTime + "," + error );
            // -------------------------------------------------------------
```

With this code, the output will be printed on the console as follows:

```
Hidden Layer Count, Iterations, Learning Rate, Epoch Count, Time Taken,
Error
--------------------------------------------------------------------------
10,1,0.01,200,11252.0,-3.5079920391032235
10,1,0.02,200,1,3781.0,-2.8320863346049325
10,1,0.04,200,1,3152.0,-9.223153362650587
10,1,0.08,200,1,3520.0,NaN
5,1,0.01,200,2960.0,-0.725370417017652
```

Alternatively, the deeplearning4j library provides a visualization interface with the UI library. The UI library can be included as Maven dependency, as follows:

```
<dependency>
    <groupId>org.deeplearning4j</groupId>
    <artifactId>deeplearning4j-ui_2.10</artifactId>
    <version>${dl4j.version}</version>
</dependency>
```

The user interface can be quickly enabled by adding the following lines of code:

```
//Initialize the user interface backend
static UIServer uiServer = UIServer.getInstance();

//Configure where the network information (gradients, score vs. time) is to
be stored.
static StatsStorage statsStorage = new InMemoryStatsStorage();

// Once the MultiLayerNetwork object is initialized, register the
StateStorage instance as a //listener.

net.setListeners(new StatsListener(statsStorage));
```

With this simple code snippet, the framework enables a UI on port `9000` on the `localhost`:

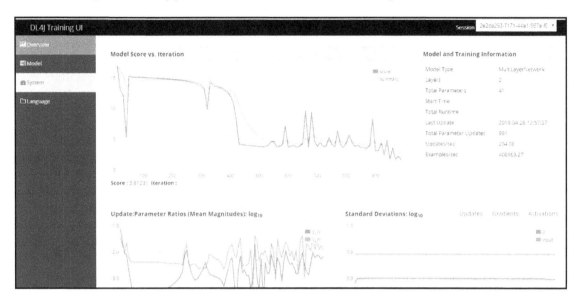

The network structure can be visualized with the **Model** view user interface:

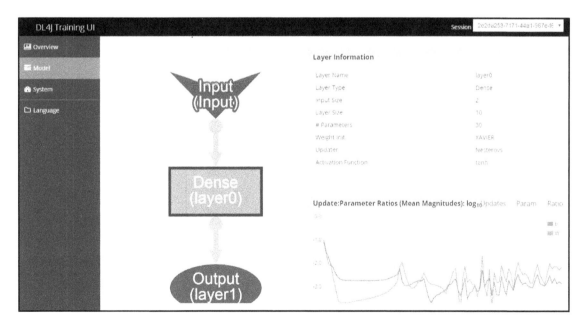

Distributed computing

As we have seen in *figure 5.1*, the performance of the neural network improves with an increasing volume of training data. With more and more devices generating data that can potentially be used for training and model generation, the models are getting better at generalizing the stochastic environment and handling complex tasks. However, with more data and more complex structures for the deep neural networks, the computational requirements increase.

Even though we have started leveraging GPUs for deep neural network training, the vertical scaling of the compute infrastructure has its own limitations and cost implications. Leaving the cost implications aside, the time it takes to train a significantly large deep neural network on a large set of training data is not reasonable. However, due to the nature and network topology of the neural networks, it is possible to distribute the computation on multiple machines at the same time and merge the results back with a centralized process. This is very similar to Hadoop, as a distributed computing batch processing engine, and Spark, as an in-memory distributed computing framework. With deep neural networks, there are two approaches for leveraging distributed computing:

- **Model Distribution**: In this approach, the deep neural network is broken into logical fragments that are treated as independent models from a computational perspective. The results from these models are combined by a central process, as depicted in this diagram:

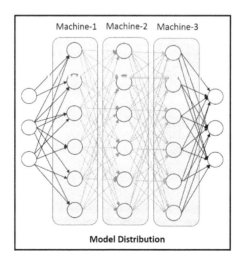

Model Distribution

- **Data Distribution**: In this approach, the entire model is copied to all the nodes participating in the cluster and the data is distributed in chunks for processing. The master process collects the output from the individual nodes and produces the final outcome, shown as follows:

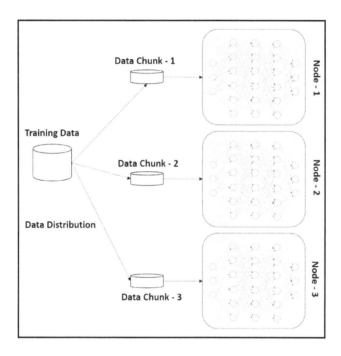

The data distribution approach is very similar to Hadoop's MapReduce framework. The MapReduce job creates the input splits based on predefined and run-time configuration parameters. These chunks are sent to the independent nodes for processing by the map tasks in a parallel manner.

The output from the map tasks is shuffled for relevance (simple sort) and is given as input to the reduce tasks for generating intermediate results. The individual MapReduce chunks are combined to produce the final result. The data distribution approach is more naturally suitable for Hadoop and Spark frameworks and it is a more widely researched approach at this time. The deep neural networks that leverage data distribution primarily deploy a parameter-averaging strategy for training the model.

This is a simple but efficient approach for training a deep neural network with data distribution:

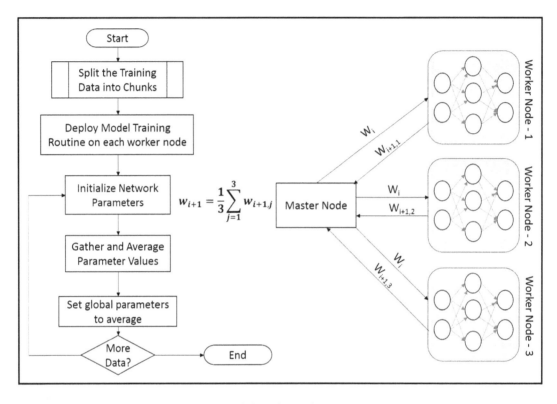

Based on these fundamental concepts of distributed processing, let's review some of the popular libraries and frameworks that enable parallelized deep neural networks.

Distributed deep learning

With an ever-increasing number of data sources and data volumes, it is imperative that the deep learning application and research leverages the power of distributed computing frameworks. In this section, we will review some of the libraries and frameworks that effectively leverage distributed computing. These are popular frameworks based on their capabilities, adoption level, and active community support.

DL4J and Spark

We have coded the examples in this chapter with deeplearning4j library. The core framework of DL4J is designed to work seamlessly with Hadoop (HDFS and MapReduce) as well as Spark-based processing. It is easy to integrate DL4J with Spark. DL4J with Spark leverages data parallelism by sharding large datasets into manageable chunks and training the deep neural networks on each individual node in parallel. Once the models produce parameter values (weights and biases), those are iteratively averaged for producing the final outcome.

API overview

In order to train the deep neural networks on Spark using DL4J, two primary wrapper classes need to be used:

- `SparkDl4jMultiLayer`: A wrapper around DL4J's MultiLayerNetwork
- `SparkComputationGraph`: A wrapper around DL4J's ComputationGraph

The network configuration process for the standard, as well as the distributed, mode remains same. That means, we configure the network properties by creating a `MultiLayerConfiguration` instance. The workflow for deep learning on Spark with DL4J can be depicted as follows:

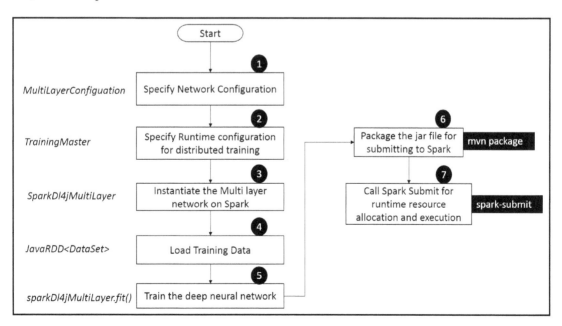

Here are the sample code snippets for the workflow steps:

1. Multilayer network configuration:

```
MultiLayerConfiguration conf = new NeuralNetConfiguration.Builder()
.optimizationAlgo(OptimizationAlgorithm.STOCHASTIC_GRADIENT_DESCENT
).iterations(1)
    .learningRate(0.1)
    .updater(Updater.RMSPROP)    //To configure: .updater(new
RmsProp(0.95))
    .seed(12345)
    .regularization(true).l2(0.001)
    .weightInit(WeightInit.XAVIER)
    .list()
    .layer(0, new
GravesLSTM.Builder().nIn(nIn).nOut(lstmLayerSize).activation(Activa
tion.TANH).build())
    .layer(1, new
GravesLSTM.Builder().nIn(lstmLayerSize).nOut(lstmLayerSize).activat
ion(Activation.TANH).build())
    .layer(2, new
RnnOutputLayer.Builder(LossFunctions.LossFunction.MCXENT).activatio
n(Activation.SOFTMAX)        //MCXENT + softmax for classification
        .nIn(lstmLayerSize).nOut(nOut).build())
.backpropType(BackpropType.TruncatedBPTT).tBPTTForwardLength(tbpttL
ength).tBPTTBackwardLength(tbpttLength)
    .pretrain(false).backprop(true)
    .build();
```

2. Set up the runtime configuration for the distributed training:

```
ParameterAveragingTrainingMaster tm = new
ParameterAveragingTrainingMaster.Builder(examplesPerDataSetObject)
        .workerPrefetchNumBatches(2) //Async prefetch 2 batches
for each worker
        .averagingFrequency(averagingFrequency)
        .batchSizePerWorker(examplesPerWorker)
        .build();
```

3. Instantiate the Multilayer network on Spark with `TrainingMaster`:

```
SparkDl4jMultiLayer sparkNetwork = new SparkDl4jMultiLayer(sc,
config, tm);
```

4. Load the shardable training data:

```
public static JavaRDD<DataSet> getTrainingData(JavaSparkContext
sc) throws IOException {
    List<String> list = getTrainingDatAsList(); // arbitrary sample
method
    JavaRDD<String> rawStrings = sc.parallelize(list);
    Broadcast<Map<Character, Integer>> bcCharToInt =
sc.broadcast(CHAR_TO_INT);
    return rawStrings.map(new StringToDataSetFn(bcCharToInt));
}
```

5. Train the deep neural network:

```
sparkNetwork.fit(trainingData);
```

6. Package the Spark application as a `.jar` file:

```
mvn package
```

7. Submit the application to Spark runtime:

```
spark-submit --class <<fully qualified class name>> --num-executors
3 ./<<jar_name>>-1.0-SNAPSHOT.jar
```

 The DeepLearning4j official website provides extensive documentation for running the deep neural networks on Spark: `https://deeplearning4j.org/spark`.

TensorFlow

TensorFlow is the most popular library created and open sourced by Google. It uses data-flow graphs for numerical computations and deals with Tensor as the basic building block. A Tensor can simply be considered as an *n*-dimensional matrix. TensorFlow applications can be seamlessly deployed across platforms and it can run on GPUs and CPUs, along with mobile and embedded devices. TensorFlow is designed as a large-scale distributed training that supports new machine learning models, research, and granular-level optimizations.

TensorFlow is quick to install and start experimenting with. The latest version of TensorFlow can be downloaded from `https://www.tensorflow.org/`. The site also contains extensive documentation and tutorials.

Keras

Keras is a high-level neural network API, written in Python and capable of running on top of TensorFlow. For more information, refer to `https://keras.io/`.

TensorFlow and Keras hold the top two spots in terms of adoption and mention by researchers in scientific papers. The stack ranking of the frameworks and libraries as per `arxiv.org` is as follows:

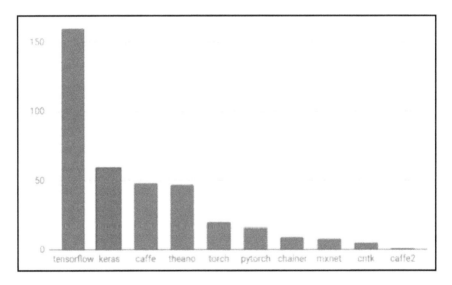

Source: arXiv (Oct 2017)

Frequently asked questions

Q: What is the difference between machine learning and deep learning?

A: Deep learning is a specialized implementation of machine learning as an abstract concept. Machine learning algorithms are primarily the functions that draw lines through the data points in the case of supervised learning algorithms. The feature space is mapped as a multi-dimensional representation. This representation generalizes the datasets and can predict the value or the state of the actor for new environment states. Deep learning algorithms also model the real-world data within the context. However, they take a layered approach in creating the models. Each layer in the network specializes in a specific part of the input signal, starting from the high-level, more generic features in the initial layers, to the deeper and granular features in the subsequent layers toward the output layer. These networks are capable of training themselves based on some of the popular algorithms, such as backpropagation. Another difference between deep learning and machine learning is the performance with respect to the addition of data. As seen in *figure 5.1*, the machine learning algorithms plateau at a certain data volume threshold. However, the deep learning algorithms keep improving with the addition of training data. Typically, deep learning algorithms need more time and computation power to train compared to the traditional machine learning models.

Q: What is the difference between epoch, batch size, and iterations for a deep neural network?

A: We come across these terminologies when the data size is high. An epoch is one forward and backward pass through the entire training dataset. In most of the real-world scenarios, the training dataset is so high that it is computationally very difficult to pass the entire data through one epoch. In order to make the training through the deep neural network computationally feasible, the entire dataset is divided into training batches. The number of training examples in one batch is called the **batch size**. The number of batches to complete one epoch is called an **iteration**. For example, if the training data size is 10,000 and the batch size is 2,000, one epoch will be completed in five iterations.

Q: Why do we need non-linear activation functions in deep neural networks?

A: Within the real-world, stochastic environments, and feature spaces, nonlinearities are more common than linear relationships. The neural networks learn by learning about the features with a layered structure where each layer stores a specific feature set from the training data. With a linear activation function applied at all the nodes within different layers, the linearity can be aggregated in one layer and there is no point in having a multi-layered network. Without a multilayered network, it is not possible to model the stochastic input and generalize the model.

Q: How do we measure the performance of a deep neural network?

A: As a general principle, the performance of the deep neural network is a factor of how well it is able to generalize the real-world data once the network is deployed in production use. There are times when the model performs very well on the training data but does not perform well on the test data due to overfitting. While there are many parameters on which the deep neural network needs to be evaluated, three primary metrics help us in understanding the model performance at a broad level:

- **Receiver operating curve** (**ROC**): Based on the predicted data points, this is a plot between the false positive rate on the x axis and the true positive rate on the y axis. Typically, the ROC curve takes the following shape when plotted with a test with perfect discrimination. The closer the curve stays to the upper-left corner, the greater the accuracy and hence the performance of the network:

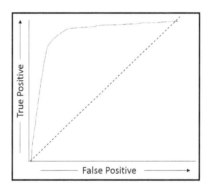

- **Precision and recall**: Precision defines the ratio of the number of correct classifications to the total number of training input. This is a general indication of how often the model is correct. Recall measures the utility of the model within the search space in terms of finding the correct output. These scores are always seen in combination and they constitute the F1 score for the model. If one of these parameters is low, the overall F1 score is also low.

Q: What are some of the implementation areas of deep neural networks?

A: Deep learning can be applied in variety of fields, such as automatic speech recognition, image recognition, natural language processing, medical image processing, recommendation systems, and bioinformatics.

Summary

In this chapter, we took our understanding of the ANNs further, to the deep neural networks that contain more than one, and up to hundreds and thousands of, hidden layers. The learning based on these deep neural networks is called deep learning. Deep learning is evolving as one of the most popular algorithms for solving some of the extremely complex problems within a stochastic environment. We have established the fundamental theory behind the working of deep neural networks and looked at the building blocks of gradient based-learning, backpropagation, nonlinearities, and the regularization technique- dropout. We have also reviewed some of the specialized neural network architecture's CNNs and RNNs.

We have also studied practical approaches for building data preparation pipelines and looked at the examples of applying regularization using the Weka library along with the DataVec library. We have studied some practical approaches for implementing neural network architectures. We have also reviewed a set of hyperparameters that affect the performance of the deep neural networks, and defined best practices for tuning those hyperparameters.

We experimented with the deeplearning4j library to demonstrate hyperparameter tuning and how to visualize the neural network with the deeplearning4j UI library. The deep neural networks are computationally heavy and hence need more processing power as we we add more data, and consequently more hidden layers and nodes within each hidden unit. It is imperative that we leverage the distributed computing frameworks for deep learning. We reviewed some of the basics of distributed computing and how to integrate deeplearning4j with Spark.

In the next chapter, we are going to transform from the area of artificial intelligence to Machine Learning. We will understand the basics of NLP, along with the mathematical intuition and practical guidelines with the implementation of NLP-based systems.

6
Natural Language Processing

Machine learning, or artificial intelligence, is based on data that can be structured or unstructured. **Natural language processing** (**NLP**) is an area of algorithms that is focused on processing unstructured data. This chapter is focused on unstructured data with a natural language text format. Organizations always have large corpuses of unstructured text data, either in the form of word documents, PDFs, email body, or web documents. With advances in technology, organizations have started relying on large volumes of text information. For example, a legal firm has lots of information in the form of bond papers, legal agreements, court orders, law documents, and so on. Such information assets are made up of textual information that is domain-specific (legal in this case). It is imperative that in order to utilize these valuable textual assets, and convert the information into knowledge, we require intelligent machines to be able to understand the text as-is, without any human intervention. NLP for big data uses tons of text data from various sources to determine relationships and patterns across contents received from those sources. It helps in identifying trends which will be utilized in use cases like recommendation engines. This chapter introduces the basic concepts behind NLP with practical examples.

We can divide NLP into two types of approaches, supervised NLP and unsupervised NLP. The supervised learning NLP approach involves using supervised learning algorithms such as Naive Bayes and Random Forests. In these algorithms, models are created based on the predicted output given to them for training an input set. That means supervised learning approaches are not self-learning but they train and fine-tune models based on the target output provided to them. Unsupervised learning algorithms do not rely on the fact that the target output is provided to them for model training. They draw deductions from input records given to them as a result of multiple iterations over data learning from the output of previous iterations, and tuning weights and parameters to optimize results. **Recurrent neural nets** (**RNN**) is one of the common unsupervised learning algorithms used in natural language processing. We will explore all these techniques in this chapter.

Overall, we will cover the following topics:

- Natural language processing basics
- Text preprocessing
- Feature extraction
- Applying NLP techniques
- Implementing sentiment analysis

Natural language processing basics

Before we state some of the high-level steps involved in NLP, it is important to establish a definition of NLP. In simple terms, NLP is a collection of processes, algorithms, and tools used by intelligent systems to interpret text data written in human language for actionable insights. The mention of text data makes one fact about NLP very evident. NLP is all about interpreting unstructured data. NLP organizes unstructured text data and uses sophisticated methods to solve a plethora of problems, such as sentiment analysis, document classification, and text summarization. In this section, we will talk about some of the basic steps involved in NLP.

In the subsequent sections, we will take a deep dive into those steps. The following diagram represents some of the basics hierarchical steps involved in NLP:

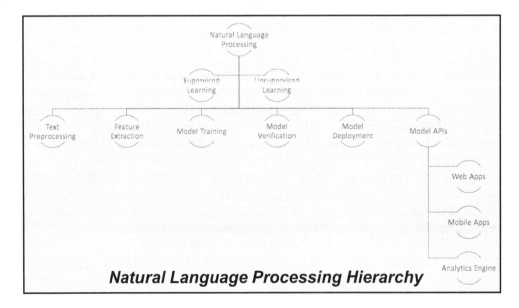

Natural Language Processing Hierarchy

Let us look at each of these steps briefly:

- **Type of machine learning**: NLP can be performed either using supervised learning algorithms or as unsupervised learning algorithms. Supervised learning algorithms include Naive Bayes, SVM, and Random Forest. Unsupervised learning algorithms include **Feed Forward Neural Networks** (**Multi Layer Perceptron**) and **Recurrent Neural Network** (**RNN**). One important thing to note here is that the preprocessing and feature-extraction steps are same for both classes of algorithms. What differs is how you train your model. Supervised learning requires labeled output as their input, and unsupervised learning would predict the outcome without any labeled output.

- **Tex preprocessing**: This step is required because raw natural text cannot be used in NLP systems. This will result in bad or not-very-accurate output. Some of the common text preprocessing steps are removing stop words, replacing capital letter words, and removing special characters. Another common step in text preprocessing is part of-speech tagging, which is also called annotation. Text normalization in the form of stemming and lemmatization is also applied.

- **Feature extraction**: For any ML algorithm to work on text, these texts have to be converted into some form of numerical input. Feature extraction employs common techniques of converting input text to numerical input in the form of vectors.

- **Model training**: Model training is process of establishing or finding a mathematical function that can be used to predict the outcome based on the given input. The process of finding a function involves multiple iterations and parameter tuning.

- **Model verification**: This step is the process of verifying models resulting from the model training process. Generally, you divide your training dataset into an 80:20 ratio. 80% of data is used for model training and 20% of the data is used for validating the correctness of the model. In the case of discrepancies, you fine-tune your model creation steps and re-run the validations.

- **Model deployment and APIs**: After the models have been verified, you deploy your models so that they can be used to predict the outcomes in the context of enterprise applications. You can save these models on a storage location where they can be read in-memory and can be applied to a dataset to predict its outcome. In distributed processing, they are generally saved in a Hadoop-distributed file system so that Hadoop batch processes can read and apply those models. In the case of web applications, they are stored in the form of Python pickle files, and these pickle files are read and processed upon each prediction request. Although, for applications to use this, you would require API layers to be exposed on top of it. These API layers can be restful APIs or come in the form of packaged jars deployed to the location where applications are hosted. Once the APIs are exposed, they can be used by a variety of web applications, mobile applications, or analytics or BI engines.

Text preprocessing

Preprocessing the data is the process of cleaning and preparing the text for classification and derivation of meaning. Since our data may have a lot of noise, uninformative parts, such as HTML tags, need to be eliminated or re-aligned. At the word level, there might be many words that do not make much impact on the overall semantic of the textual context. Text preprocessing involves a few steps, such as extraction, tokenization, stop words removal, text enrichment, and normalization with stemming and lemmatization. In addition to these, some of the basic and generic techniques that improve accuracy involve converting the text to lower case, removing numbers (based on the context), removing punctuation, stripping white spaces (sometimes these add to noise in the input signal), and eliminating the sparse terms that are infrequent terms in the document. In the subsequent sections, we'll analyze some of these techniques in detail.

Removing stop words

Stop words are words that occur more frequently in the sentence and make the text heavier and less important for the analysis, they should be excluded from the input. Having stop words in your text confuses your algorithm as these stop words do not have contextual meaning and increase dimensional features of your term vectors. Therefore, it is imperative that these stop words be removed for better model accuracy. Examples of stop words are `I`, `am`, `is`, and `the`. One of the ways to remove the stop words is to have a precompiled list of the stop words and then remove those stop words from the document (text used to train the model).

With Spark, we can use the `StopWordsRemover` library, which has its own list of default stop words for many natural languages. We can also provide a list of stop words with the `stopWords` parameter. Another way to remove the less significant words from the document is based on their frequency of occurrence; if the word's frequency is low, we can remove those words, this is also known as **pruning**.

Here is a sample code for using the Spark library. With this library, the process of stop words removal is parallelized and we can quickly perform a stop words removal on a large volume of data in a distributed manner:

```
import java.util.Arrays;
import java.util.List;

import org.apache.spark.ml.feature.StopWordsRemover;
import org.apache.spark.sql.Dataset;
import org.apache.spark.sql.Row;
import org.apache.spark.sql.RowFactory;
import org.apache.spark.sql.types.DataTypes;
import org.apache.spark.sql.types.Metadata;
import org.apache.spark.sql.types.StructField;
import org.apache.spark.sql.types.StructType;

StopWordsRemover remover = new StopWordsRemover()
  .setInputCol("raw")
  .setOutputCol("filtered");

List<Row> data = Arrays.asList(
  RowFactory.create(Arrays.asList("I", "am", "removing", "the", "stop",
"words")),
  RowFactory.create(Arrays.asList("from", "a", "large", "volume",
"of","data"))
);

StructType schema = new StructType(new StructField[]{
  new StructField(
    "raw", DataTypes.createArrayType(DataTypes.StringType), false,
Metadata.empty())
});

Dataset<Row> dataset = spark.createDataFrame(data, schema);
remover.transform(dataset).show(false);
```

Stemming

Different forms of a word often communicate essentially the same meaning. Consider an example of a search engine when a user searches `shoe` or when they search for `shoes`. The intent of the user is the same and the search result is still going to be shoes from different brands. But the presence of both words can confuse models. So for better accuracy, we need to convert these different forms of the word in its row format. **Stemming** is converting a word in a text into its raw format. For example, introduction, introduced, and introducing all turn into introduce after stemming. The purpose of this method is to remove various suffixes, to reduce the number of words. Also, this helps the model to avoid confusion while getting trained. Many stemming algorithms are available, such as porter stemming, snowball stemming, and Lancaster stemming. Most of the stemming algorithms in the following sections are available in multiple natural languages.

Porter stemming

Porter stemming is one form of the stemming algorithm that removes suffixes from base words or terms in the English dictionary. The whole purpose of Porter Stemmer is to improve the performance of the NLP model training exercise. It does so by removing suffixes from a word and bringing it to its base form. This way, the number of terms is reduced and the memory footprint and complexity of your term space is also minimized. Porter is not dictionary-based. It does not use any stem dictionary to identify suffixes that need to be removed. It is based on a set of generic rules. Some people see this as a drawback as its working is pretty straightforward and does not take care of the lower-level contextual nitty-gritty of English words. Porter stemming is used for its simplicity and speed. Porter stemming has five steps that are applied on the word until one of them satisfies. For example, consider step 1 in porter stemming, which is as explained in the following blocks:

SSESS -> SS   - This rule converts SSESS suffix of the word into SS.
For example, prepossess - > preposs

IES -> I   - This rule converts IES suffix of the word into I.
For example, ties -> ti

SS -> SS   - If the word has SS as suffix this won't change.
For example, Success -> Success

S -> - If the word has S as suffix this would remove the suffix.
For example, Pens -> Pen

Please refer to `http://www.cs.toronto.edu/~frank/csc2501/Readings/R2_Porter/Porter-1980.pdf` for a detailed explanation of the porter stemming algorithm.

Snowball stemming

This is also known as **Porter2**. The Porter2 algorithm is implemented as the English Stemmer (based on Snowball). This algorithm was developed as a framework to use for languages other than English. This is better in accuracy than porter algorithms. The snowball rule example is given as follows:

```
ied or ies ->  replace by i if preceded by more than one letter, otherwise
by ie.
ties -> tie,
cries -> cri
So as we can see with porter ties we stemmed into ti whereas with snowball
it becomes tie.
```

For more details, refer to `http://snowballstem.org/algorithms/english/stemmer.html`.

Lancaster stemming

A very aggressive stemming algorithm, sometimes to a fault. With porter and snowball, the stemmed representations are usually fairly intuitive to a reader, not so with Lancaster, as many shorter words will become totally obfuscated. The fastest algorithm here, it will greatly reduce your working set of words, but if you want more distinction, this is not the tool to use. The Lancaster rule example is given in the following block:

```
ies -> y - This rule converts ies suffix of the word into y.
cries -> cry
So with Lancaster stemming as we see cries stemmed into cry which more
better stemmed.
```

Lovins stemming

In 1968, Lovins JB published this stemming algorithm. The approach taken by Lovins is bit different, but it does start with removing suffixes from the word. It comes to the conclusion in a two-step process. It first removes the longest possible suffix from a word. It is a single-pass algorithm that removes the single largest suffix from a word. Secondly, it applies set of rules on the resulting longest suffix to transform it into a word. This algorithm is rules- and dictionary-based. It is faster and usually is less memory intensive. It is able to convert words such as getting into get or words such as mice to mouse. Sometimes this algorithm can be inaccurate due to many suffixes not available in its dictionary. Moreover, it frequently fails to form a word from a stemmed word or even if a word is formed, it may not have the same meaning as the original word.

Dawson stemming

This stemmer extends the same approach as the Lovins stemmer with a list of more than a thousand suffixes in the English language. Here is the generic algorithm for the Dawson stemmer:

```
1. Get the input word
2. Get the matching suffix
     2a. The suffix pool is reverse indexed by length
     2b. The suffix pool is reverse indexed by the last character
3. Remove longest suffix from the word with exact match.
4. Recode the word using a mapping table
5. Convert stem into a valid word.
```

The advantages of the Dawson stemmer are as follows:

- It covers a wider range of suffixes and hence produces a more accurate stemming output
- It is a single-pass algorithm, which makes it efficient

Lemmatization

Lemmatization is a bit different from stemming. Stemming generally removes end characters from a word with the expectation that they will get the correct base word. However, sometimes it results in removing suffixes that add meaning to a word. Lemmatization tries to overcome this limitation of stemming. It tries to find out the base form of the word, called the lemma, based on a vocabulary of words that it has and a morphological analysis on words. It uses the `WordNet` lexical knowledge dictionary to get the correct base form of a word. However, this has its limitation as well, for example, it requires part-of-speech tagging otherwise it will treat everything as a noun.

N-grams

N-gram is a continuous sequence of N-words or tokens in a given sentence or continuous sequence of text. **N** is defined as an integer value starting from 1. So, N-Gram could be Uni-Gram(N=1), Bi-Gram(N=3) or Tri-Gram(N=3). N-gram algorithms or programs identify all continuous adjacent sequences of words in a given sentence tokens. It is a Windows-based functionality starting from the left-most word position and then moving windows by one step. Let's see it with an example sentence, **This is Big Data AI Book**. See the following example of Uni-Gram, Bi-Gram, and Tri-Gram examples:

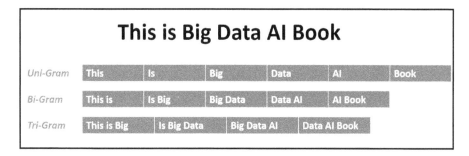

N-grams is used for developing efficient features that are passed to supervised machine learning models, such as SVMs and Naive Bayes, for training and prediction. The idea is to use tokens, such as Bi-Grams, instead of just Uni-Grams so that these machine learning models can learn efficiently.

Using N-grams tends to capture the context in which words are used together in a given document. As shown in the previous example, Tri-Grams can give your machine learning algorithm more context so that the next set of words can be predicted better. However, what should be the optimal value of N, is something that needs to be determined based on your dataset and after doing sufficient data exploration and analysis. A larger value of N does not always mean a better result. You should make very informed decisions about the value of *N*.

Feature extraction

As mentioned earlier in this chapter, the NLP system does not understand string values. They need numerical input to build models, sometimes they are also called numerical features. Feature extraction in NLP is converting a set of text information into a set of numerical features. Any machine learning algorithm that you are going to train would need features in numerical vector forms as it does not understand the string. There are many ways text can be represented as numerical vectors. Some such ways are One hot encoding, TF-IDF, Word2Vec, and CountVectorizer.

One hot encoding

One hot encoding is the binary sparse vector representation of text. In this encoding, the resulting binary vector is all zero-value except at the position or index of the token where it is one. Let's look at it with an example. Suppose there are two sentences: This is Big Data AI Book. This is book explains AI algorithms on Big Data. Unique tokens (nouns) for earlier sentences would be {data, AI, book, algorithms}. The one hot encoding representation for these tokens would be like the following:

	data	*AI*	*book*	*Algorithms*
data	1	0	0	0
AI	0	1	0	0
book	0	0	1	0
Algorithms	0	0	0	1

The Encoded Sparse Vector Representation would look like the following:

$$
\begin{aligned}
data &= [1,0,0,0] \\
AI &= [0,1,0,0] \\
book &= [0,0,1,0] \\
Algorithms &= [0,0,0,1]
\end{aligned}
$$

TF-IDF

The TF-IDF method of feature extraction uses a scalar product of **term frequency** (**TF**) and **inverse document frequency** (**IDF**) to calculate the numerical vector of a token or term. TF-IDF not only calculates the importance of a word in a specific document but also measures its importance in other documents of a corpus. Moreover, it tries to normalize any word that is overly frequent in the entire corpus.

TF, or Term Frequency, is a term's occurrence in a document. We can use the `HashingTF` library in Spark to compute the term's frequency. `HashingTF` creates the sparse vector corresponding to each document representing index and frequency. For example, if we consider the `extraction of the feature using HashingTF extraction method` text string, then the TF of every word in the earlier document using `HashingTF` would be the following:

```
1  import org.apache.spark.ml.feature.{HashingTF, IDF, Tokenizer}
2
3  val exampleData = spark.createDataFrame(Seq(
4    (0.0, "extraction of the feature using HashingTF extraction method")
5  )).toDF("label", "sentence")
6
7  val tokenizer = new Tokenizer().setInputCol("sentence").setOutputCol("words")
8  val tokensData = tokenizer.transform(exampleData)
9
10 val hashingTF = new HashingTF()
11   .setInputCol("words").setOutputCol("rawFeatures").setNumFeatures(10)
12 val features = hashingTF.transform(tokensData)
13 features.select("rawFeatures")show(truncate=false)
```

TF Using HashingTF

The output of `HashingTF`:

```
+-----------------------------------------------+
|rawFeatures                                    |
+-----------------------------------------------+
|(10,[0,3,4,5,6,8],[1.0,1.0,2.0,1.0,1.0,2.0])|
+-----------------------------------------------+
```

In the preceding screenshot, we can see the first array is the extracted features from the document, and the second array is the `Array[SparseVector]`, which represents the index and frequency. For an instance, the `extraction` word occurs twice in the document so we can see the frequency of the word is 2. With `HashingTF`, tokenized word array may not be in the same sequence as the vector array.

TF measures the importance of a word in a particular document only and not with respect to the entire corpus of documents. Moreover, overly frequent words in a large document may not be that important with respect to the entire corpus. This can hamper the prediction output as words that appear less frequently may be of higher importance with respect to the entire corpus. This is where IDF comes into the picture; it represents the inverse of the share of the documents in which the regarded term can be found. The lower the number of containing documents relative to the size of the corpus, the higher the factor. The reason why this ratio is not used directly but instead its logarithm, is because otherwise the effective scoring penalty of showing up in two documents would be too extreme. The following is the sample example on how to calculate TF-IDF together:

```scala
1   import org.apache.spark.ml.feature.{HashingTF, IDF, Tokenizer}
2
3   val exampleData = spark.createDataFrame(Seq(
4     (0.0, "extraction of the feature using HashingTF extraction method")
5   )).toDF("label", "sentence")
6
7   val tokenizer = new Tokenizer().setInputCol("sentence").setOutputCol("words")
8   val tokensData = tokenizer.transform(exampleData)
9
10  val hashingTF = new HashingTF()
11    .setInputCol("words").setOutputCol("TF").setNumFeatures(10)
12  val features = hashingTF.transform(tokensData)
13  val idf = new IDF().setInputCol("TF").setOutputCol("IDF")
14  val idfModel = idf.fit(features)
15  val rescaledData = idfModel.transform(features)
16  rescaledData.select("label", "TF","IDF").show(truncate=false)
```

Code to calculate IDF

The IDF code output is as follows:

```
+------+--------------------------------------------+------------------------------------------------+
|label|TF                                           |IDF                                             |
+------+--------------------------------------------+------------------------------------------------+
|0.0  |(10,[0,3,4,5,6,8],[1.0,1.0,2.0,1.0,1.0,2.0])|(10,[0,3,4,5,6,8],[0.0,0.0,0.0,0.0,0.0,0.0])|
+------+--------------------------------------------+------------------------------------------------+
```

The goal of TF-IDF is to find words of higher relevance. The algorithm keeps track of the local relevance of a word in a document using TF calculations and the global relevance of a word in the entire training corpus using IDF calculations. Finally, both the calculations are multiplied to get the final weights of a word. However, we encourage you to get a feel for how this can be applied to your NLP system as TF-IDF ranking behavior may not give relevant results in your use case. You can apply multiple adjustments to the corpus to get the desired behavior. The following is the mathematical formula for TF-IDF:

The formula to calculate **Term Frequency (TF)**

$$tf_{t,d} = n_{t,d} / \sum_{i=0}^{i=N} n_{i,d}$$

Where t is the term or word in a document, d. $n_{t,d}$ is the count of term, t, in a document, d. $\sum_{i=0}^{i=N} n_{i,d}$ is the count of all terms in a document.

The formula to calculate **Inverse Document Frequency (IDF)**:

$$idf_t = \log_{10}(N/df_t)$$

Where df_t is term frequency in a document and N is the total number of documents in a corpus.

The TF-IDF weight formula is:

$$w_{t,d} = (1 + (1 + tf_{t,d})).idf_t$$

CountVectorizer

CountVectorizer and **CountVectorizerModel** works on count of words(tokens). It uses words in text documents to build vectors containing count of tokens. It has provisions of using dictionary of words to identify tokens that can be taken as input to algorithms. If dictionary is not available CountVectorizer uses its own estimator to build the vocabulary. Based on that vocabulary it generates CountVectorizerModel, a sparse representations of training documents. This model acts as input to NLP algorithms like LDA.

CountVectorizer counts the word frequencies for the document, whereas TF-IDF gives us the importance of the word with regards to the whole corpus. CountVectorizer is one of the tools used to convert the text to a vector that can passed as a feature to the machine learning model. Similar to TF-IDF, this model also produces sparse representations for the documents over the vocabulary. For example, if we consider the `extraction of the feature using countvectorizer extraction method` text string, then the output would look something like this:

```
1  import org.apache.spark.ml.feature.{CountVectorizer, CountVectorizerModel,Tokenizer}
2
3
4  val exampleData = spark.createDataFrame(Seq(
5    (0.0, "extraction of the feature using countvectorizer extraction method")
6  )).toDF("label", "sentence")
7
8  val tokenizer = new Tokenizer().setInputCol("sentence").setOutputCol("words")
9  val tokensData = tokenizer.transform(exampleData)
10
11 val cvModel: CountVectorizerModel = new CountVectorizer()
12   .setInputCol("words")
13   .setOutputCol("features")
14   .setVocabSize(3)
15   .setMinDF(1)
16   .fit(tokensData)
17
18 cvModel.transform(tokensData).select("words","features").show(false)
```

Code to calculate CountVectors

The output of the CountVector code:

```
+----------------------------------------------------------------------------+------------------------+
|words                                                                       |features                |
+----------------------------------------------------------------------------+------------------------+
|[extraction, of, the, feature, using, countvectorizer, extraction, method]  |(3,[0,1,2],[2.0,1.0,1.0])|
+----------------------------------------------------------------------------+------------------------+
```

We can see in the earlier example that the first words array is the extracted features from the document, similar to TF-IDF, but the second features array is the `Array[SparseVector]`, which represents the index and word frequency that is ordered from highest to lowest. Also, here 3 is the vocabulary size, which means CountVectorizer picks and is equal to the distinct words in the document, which is 3 in our case. You can customize this in Spark.

Word2Vec

In a typical feature extraction from text, numerical vectors are created based on unique labels given to them. However, these uniquely-labeled sparse vectors do not represent the context in which each word has appeared. In other words, it does not specifically state or represent the relationship a given word exhibits with other words in a corpus. That means unsupervised learning algorithms that learn from data processing cannot be leveraged much. These algorithms cannot leverage relationships or contextual information about the word. Therefore, a new class of algorithms for feature extraction is developed that preserves the context or relationship information among words. This new class of algorithms is called Word-Embedding feature-extraction algorithms. These classes of algorithms represent sparse vectors into continuous **vector space models** (**VSM**).

In VSM, similar words are mapped to nearby points so that they form a cluster of similar words. Word2Vec is a predictive method based on word-embedding algorithms that can be implemented in two ways, the **continuous bag of words** model (**CBOW**) and the **Skip-Gram** model.

CBOW

Most of the prediction models are based on the words or contexts that have appeared in past words. Based on their learning from past words, they predict the next word. CBOW, in contrast to this, uses N words before and after the word in question to predict the outcome. It uses a continuous representation of a bag of words to predict the outcome. However, order is of no significance here. CBOW takes context in the form of a window of words and predicts the word.

The following figure represents how CBOW works:

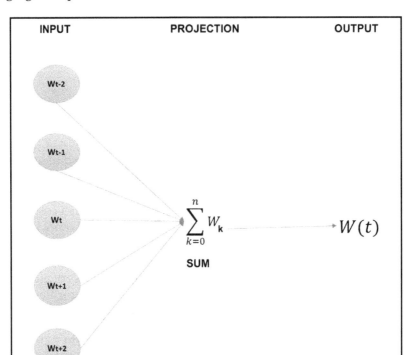

Word2Vec: CBOW

Based on the previous diagram, CBOW can be formalized as:

$$J_\varnothing = \frac{1}{T} \sum_{t=1}^{T} \log_p (W_t | W_{t-n}, \ldots, W_{t-1}, \ldots, W_{t+1}, \ldots W_{t+n})$$

The previous formula is based on a window of n words around a target word. t represents the time step. The word window spans across the previous words and the next words.

Skip-Gram model

The Skip-Gram model works opposite of the CBOW model. It predicts the context based on the current word. In other words, it uses a central world to predict words appearing before and after the main word. The following figure represents the Skip-Gram model:

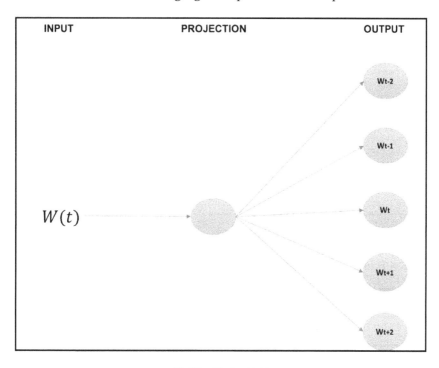

Word2Vec: Skip-Gram Model

Based on the previous diagram, Skip-Gram can be formalized as:

$$J_\emptyset = \frac{1}{T} \sum_{t=1}^{T} \sum_{-n \le j \le n} \log_p \left(W_{t+j} | W_t \right)$$

The skip-gram model calculates and sums up the logarithmic probabilities of the previous and next, n, words surrounding the target word, W_t.

The following is code to calculate Word2Vec using the Skip-Gram model in Spark:

```
1   import org.apache.spark.ml.feature.{Word2Vec,Tokenizer}
2   import org.apache.spark.ml.linalg.Vector
3   import org.apache.spark.sql.Row
4
5   val exampleData = spark.createDataFrame(Seq(
6     (0.0, "extraction of the feature using word2Vec extraction method")
7   )).toDF("label", "sentence")
8
9   val tokenizer = new Tokenizer().setInputCol("sentence").setOutputCol("words")
10  val tokensData = tokenizer.transform(exampleData)
11
12  val word2Vec = new Word2Vec()
13    .setInputCol("words")
14    .setOutputCol("features")
15    .setVectorSize(3)
16    .setMinCount(0)
17  val model = word2Vec.fit(tokensData)
18  val result = model.transform(tokensData)
19  result.select("words","features").show(false)
```

Word2Vec: Skip-Gram code in Spark

The Word2Vec Skip-Gram Spark code output is as follows:

```
+--------------------------------------------------------------+------------------------------------------------------------------------------+
|words                                                         |features                                                                      |
+--------------------------------------------------------------+------------------------------------------------------------------------------+
|[extraction, of, the, feature, using, word2vec, extraction, method]|[-0.036735267378389835,-0.017351628514006734,0.014259896153816953]|
+--------------------------------------------------------------+------------------------------------------------------------------------------+
```

Applying NLP techniques

Generally, for any class of NLP problems, you first apply text preprocessing and feature extraction techniques. Once you have reduced the noise in the text and are able to extract features out of text, you perform various machine learning algorithms to solve different NLP classes of NLP problems. In this section, we will cover one such problem, called **text classification**.

Text classification

Text classification is one of the very common use cases of NLP. Text classification can be used for use cases such as email SPAM detection, identifying retail product hierarchy, and sentiment analysis. This process is typically a classification problem wherein we are trying to identify a specific topic from a natural language source of a large volume of data. Within each of the data groups, we may have multiple topics discussed and hence it is important to classify the article or the textual information into logical groups. Text classification techniques help us to do that.

These techniques require a good deal of computing power if the data volume is huge and it is recommended to use a distributed computing framework for text classification. As an example, if we want to classify the legal documents that exist in a knowledge repository on the internet, we can use text classification techniques for the logical separation of various types of documents. The following illustration represents a typical text classification process that is done in two phases:

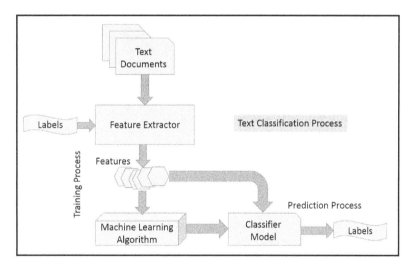

Let's now look at how text classification can be performed using Spark. We will divide our code into four parts: text preprocessing, feature extraction, model training/verification, and prediction. We will use the Naive Bayes' algorithm for model training and prediction. But before we deep dive into the code, let's walk you through how NB works. We will also give you a brief overview of another algorithm, Random Forest, which can be used in text classification.

Introduction to Naive Bayes' algorithm

The **Naive Bayes** (**NB**) classifier is a very powerful algorithm for the classification task. NB is very good in cases where we use natural language processing for text analytics. As with the name, Naive means independent or no relation, and the NB algorithm assumes that there is no relation between features. As its name suggests, it works on Bayes' theorem.

So what is Bayes' theorem? Bayes' theorem finds out the probability of an event in the future based on events that have already occurred. This type of probability is also called **conditional probability**. This probability is context-based and context is determined by a knowledge of events that have already occurred.

The following is mathematical expression of Bayes' theorem:

$$P(A/B) = \frac{P(B/A)P(A)}{P(B)}$$

For any given two events, *A* and *B*, Bayes' theorem calculates *P(A|B)* (the probability of event *A* occurring when event *B* has happened) from *P(B|A)* (the probability of event *B* occurring, given that event *A* has already occurred).

Naive Bayes tries to classify data points into classes. It calculates the probability of each data point belonging to a class. Then each of the probabilities are compared to get the highest probability, and the second highest probability is determined.

The highest probability class is considered the primary class, and the second highest probability is considered the secondary class. When you have multiple classes - for example, suppose we are classifying fruits as either apple, banana, orange, or mango, then we have more than two classes where we are classifying a fruit - it is known as MultiNomial Naive Bayes, and if we would have only two classes - for example, email as either spam or non-spam - it would be Binomial MultiNomial Naive Bayes. The NB algorithm would be clearer with the following example:

A pathology lab is performing a test of a disease, D, with two results, Positive or Negative. They guarantee that their test result is 99% accurate: if you have the disease, you will test positive 99% of the time. If you don't have the disease, you will test negative 99% of the time. If 3% of all the people have this disease and test gives the positive result, what is the probability that you have the disease?

For solving the preceding problem, we will have to use conditional probability. The following mathematical calculation shows how the NB conditional probability would be applied mathematically:

```
Probability of people suffering from Disease D, P(D) = 0.03 = 3%
Probability that test gives "positive" result and patient have the disease,
P(Pos | D) = 0.99 =99%
Probability of people not suffering from Disease D, P(~D) = 0.97 = 97%
Probability that test gives "positive" result and patient does have the
disease, P(Pos | ~D) = 0.01 =1%
For calculating the probability that the patient actually have the disease
i.e, P( D | Pos) we will use Bayes theorem:
P( D | Pos) = (P(Pos | D) * P(D)) / P(Pos)
We have all the values of numerator but we need to calculate P(Pos):
P(Pos) = P(D, pos) + P( ~D, pos)
                   = P(pos|D)*P(D) + P(pos|~D)*P(~D)
                   = 0.99 * 0.03 + 0.01 * 0.97
                   = 0.0297 + 0.0097
                   = 0.0394
Let's calculate, P( D | Pos) = (P(Pos | D) * P(D)) / P(Pos)
                   = (0.99 * 0.03) / 0.0394
                   = 0.753807107
```

The preceding example shows that there is approximately a 75% chance of a patient having the disease.

Random Forest

Random Forest is the class of algorithms that comes under the supervised learning algorithm category. It is based on forests of trees, which is similar to decision trees in certain contexts. Random Forest algorithms can be used for both classification and regression problems. A decision tree gives the set of rules that are used in building models, which can be executed against a test dataset for the prediction. In decision trees, we first calculate the root node. To calculate the root node, we use information gain. For example, if you want to predict whether your friend will accept a job offer or not. You need to feed the training dataset of the offers they have accepted to the decision tree. Based on this, the decision tree will come up with a set of rules that you will be using in the prediction. So let's say a rule can be if salary > 50K, then your friend will accept the offer. A decision tree algorithm can overfit as it is very flexible. To avoid this model overfitting in a decision tree, we can perform the pruning. The following is the pseudocode for the Random Forest algorithm:

1. Randomly select k features from total m features. Where $k \ll m$.
2. Among the k features, calculate the node, d, using the best split point.

3. Split the node into daughter nodes using the best split.
4. Repeat steps 1 to 3 until *l* number of nodes has been reached.
5. Build the forest by repeating steps 1 to 4 for *n* number times to create *n* number of trees.

Once we have trained the model using the previous steps, for prediction we need to pass the test features through all rules created by the different trees in the forest. If we want to understand by example, suppose you want to purchase a mobile phone and you have decided to ask your friends which phone is best for you. In this case, your friends might ask you some random question about the features you like and suggest a suitable phone. Here, each friend is the tree, and with the combination of all the friends, we form the forest.

Once you collect the suggestions from your friends (trees, in terms of the Random Forest algorithm), you will count which type of phone has the most votes, and you will might purchase that one. Similarly, in Random Forest, each tree will predict a different target variable that we will sum with respect to that key. The key with the highest count, predicted by the maximum number of trees, is the final target variable.

Naive Bayes' text classification code example

The following code represents how to perform text classification using the NB algorithm:

```
import org.apache.spark.ml.{Pipeline, PipelineModel}
import org.apache.spark.ml.classification.{NaiveBayes, NaiveBayesModel}
import org.apache.spark.ml.feature.{StringIndexer, StopWordsRemover,
HashingTF, Tokenizer, IDF, NGram}
import org.apache.spark.ml.linalg.Vector
import org.apache.spark.sql.Row

//Sample Data
val exampleDF = spark.createDataFrame(Seq(
(1,"Samsung 80 cm 32 inches FH4003 HD Ready LED TV"),
(2,"Polaroid LEDP040A Full HD 99 cm LED TV Black"),
(3,"Samsung UA24K4100ARLXL 59 cm 24 inches HD Ready LED TV Black")
)).toDF("id","description")

exampleDF.show(false)

//Add labels to dataset
val indexer = new StringIndexer()
  .setInputCol("description")
  .setOutputCol("label")

val tokenizer = new Tokenizer()
```

```
    .setInputCol("description")
    .setOutputCol("words")

val remover = new StopWordsRemover()
    .setCaseSensitive(false)
    .setInputCol(tokenizer.getOutputCol)
    .setOutputCol("filtered")

val bigram = new
NGram().setN(2).setInputCol(remover.getOutputCol).setOutputCol("ngrams")


val hashingTF = new HashingTF()
    .setNumFeatures(1000)
    .setInputCol(bigram.getOutputCol)
    .setOutputCol("features")

val idf = new IDF().setInputCol(hashingTF.getOutputCol).setOutputCol("IDF")

val nb = new NaiveBayes().setModelType("multinomial")
val pipeline = new
Pipeline().setStages(Array(indexer,tokenizer,remover,bigram,
hashingTF,idf,nb))
val nbmodel = pipeline.fit(exampleDF)
nbmodel.write.overwrite().save("/tmp/spark-logistic-regression-model")

val evaluationDF = spark.createDataFrame(Seq(
(1,"Samsung 80 cm 32 inches FH4003 HD Ready LED TV")
)).toDF("id","description")

val results = nbmodel.transform(evaluationDF)
results.show(false)
```

The following screenshot represents the results output:

Implementing sentiment analysis

In the following code snippet, we have implemented sentiment analysis based on the NLP theory we discussed in this chapter. It uses SPARK libraries on Tweeter JSON records to train models for identifying sentiments like `happy` or `unhappy`. It looks for keywords like `happy` in the twitter messages and then flags it with value 1 indicating that this message represents a happy sentiment. Other messages are flagged with value 0 which represents unhappy sentiment. Finally TF-IDF algorithm is applied to train models:

```
import org.apache.spark.ml.feature.{HashingTF, RegexTokenizer,
StopWordsRemover, IDF}
import org.apache.spark.sql.functions._
import org.apache.spark.ml.classification.LogisticRegression
import org.apache.spark.ml.Pipeline
import org.apache.spark.ml.classification.MultilayerPerceptronClassifier
import org.apache.spark.ml.evaluation.MulticlassClassificationEvaluator
import scala.util.{Success, Try}
import sqlContext.implicits._

val sqlContext = new org.apache.spark.sql.SQLContext(sc)

var tweetDF = sqlContext.read.json("hdfs:///tmp/sa/*")
tweetDF.show()


var messages = tweetDF.select("msg")
println("Total messages: " + messages.count())

var happyMessages =
messages.filter(messages("msg").contains("happy")).withColumn("label",lit("
1"))
val countHappy = happyMessages.count()
println("Number of happy messages: " + countHappy)

var unhappyMessages = messages.filter(messages("msg").contains("
sad")).withColumn("label",lit("0"))
val countUnhappy = unhappyMessages.count()
println("Unhappy Messages: " + countUnhappy)

var allTweets = happyMessages.unionAll(unhappyMessages)
val messagesRDD = allTweets.rdd

val goodBadRecords = messagesRDD.map(
  row =>{
      val msg = row(0).toString.toLowerCase()
      var isHappy:Int = 0
```

```
      if(msg.contains(" sad")){
        isHappy = 0
      }else if(msg.contains("happy")){
        isHappy = 1
      }
      var msgSanitized = msg.replaceAll("happy", "")
      msgSanitized = msgSanitized.replaceAll("sad","")
      //Return a tuple
      (isHappy, msgSanitized.split(" ").toSeq)
  }
)

val tweets = spark.createDataFrame(goodBadRecords).toDF("label","message")

// Split the data into training and validation sets (30% held out for
validation testing)
val splits = tweets.randomSplit(Array(0.7, 0.3))
val (trainingData, validationData) = (splits(0), splits(1))

val tokenizer = new
RegexTokenizer().setGaps(false).setPattern("\\p{L}+").setInputCol("msg").se
tOutputCol("words")

val hashingTF = new
HashingTF().setNumFeatures(1000).setInputCol("message").setOutputCol("featu
res")

val idf = new IDF().setInputCol(hashingTF.getOutputCol).setOutputCol("IDF")

val layers = Array[Int](1000, 5, 4, 3)
val trainer = new MultilayerPerceptronClassifier().setLayers(layers)

val pipeline = new Pipeline().setStages(Array(hashingTF,idf,trainer))
val model = pipeline.fit(trainingData)

val result = model.transform(validationData)
val predictionAndLabels = result.select("message","label","prediction")
predictionAndLabels.where("label==0").show(5,false)
predictionAndLabels.where("label==1").show(5,false)
```

The output is as follows:

```
scala> predictionAndLabels.where("label==1").show(5,false)
+------------------------------------------------------------------------------------+-----+----------+
|message                                                                             |label|prediction|
+------------------------------------------------------------------------------------+-----+----------+
|[, birthday, michael, scott]                                                        |1    |1.0       |
|[, birthday, サプライズ西野カナのコンサートグッズを買いに来たフリしてーいいなと思ったら rthttps//tco/mdjncxctnn]|1    |1.0       |
|[, birthday, ☐, x, chloelittlexo]                                                   |1    |1.0       |
|[, if, she, does, need, help, or, my, 2, cents, ill, be, , to, apply]               |1    |1.0       |
|[_drxo, , birthday, mamas♥, enjoy, your, day]                                       |1    |1.0       |
+------------------------------------------------------------------------------------+-----+----------+
only showing top 5 rows

scala> predictionAndLabels.where("label==0").show(5,false)
+----------------------------------------------------------------------------------------------------------+-----+----------+
|message                                                                                                   |label|prediction|
+----------------------------------------------------------------------------------------------------------+-----+----------+
|[rt, fran_cec, i, feel, un, i, feel, so, , ive, lost, the, bestfriend, that, i, ever, had]                |0    |0.0       |
|[rt, christa_marie79, stefanimichele9, im, , but, , , that, you, are, growing, up, but, , that, you, are, a, wonderful, mommy, and, a, be]|0    |0.0       |
|[rt, regalbasil, ciara, amp, keke, palmer, keep, yall, mad, as, they, live, the, , part, is, i, see, bw, doing, most, of, the, damage, cant, be, , or, caref…]|0    |0.0       |
|[rt, trash_mobb, not, , not, , kinda, just, floating]                                                     |0    |0.0       |
|[rt, fursonajail, im, just, so, , now, all, the, fucking, time, because, i, know, what, its, like, to, be, , thankyoudan, for, making, me, h…]|0    |1.0       |
+----------------------------------------------------------------------------------------------------------+-----+----------+
only showing top 5 rows
```

The result after implementing sentiment analysis

The previous implementation is very basic form of NLP based sentimental analysis and should be seen as a just simple example to understand sentimental analysis. There are more advanced techniques that can be applied on this example to make it more adaptable towards enterprise grade applications.

Frequently asked questions

Q: What are some of the common use cases of natural language processing?

A: Natural Language processing is branch of Machine learning algorithms that process text data to produce meaningful insights. A few of the common use cases of NLP are answering questions asked by the user, sentimental analysis, language translation to a foreign language, search engines, and document classifications. The key point to understand here is that if you want to perform analytics/machine learning on data represented by text/sentences/word format, NLP is the way to go.

Q: How is feature extraction relevant to NLP?

A: Machine learning algorithms work on mathematical forms. Any other forms, such as Text, need to be converted into mathematical forms to apply machine learning algorithms. Feature extraction is converting forms, such as texts/images, into numerical features, such as Vectors. These numerical features act as an input to Machine learning algorithms. Techniques such as TF-IDF and Word2Vec are used to convert text into numerical features. In a nutshell, feature extraction is a mandatory step to perform NLP on text data.

Summary

In this chapter, we reviewed one of the most important techniques for the evolution of intelligent machines to understand and interpret human language in its natural form. We covered some of the generic concepts within NLP with sample code and examples. It is imperative that the NLP technique and our understanding of the text gets better with more and more data assets used for training.

Combining NLP with an ontological worldview, intelligent machines can derive meaning from the text based assets at the internet scale and evolve to a know-everything system that can complement the human ability to comprehend vast amounts of knowledge, and use it at the right time with the best possible actions based on the context.

In the next chapter, we are going to look at fuzzy systems and how those systems combined with NLP techniques can take us closer to creating systems that are very close to the human ability to derive meaning from vague input, rather than exact input as required by computers.

7
Fuzzy Systems

In the previous chapter, we saw an overview of the theory and techniques for building intelligent systems that are capable of processing natural language input. It is certain that there will be a growing demand for machines that can interact with human beings via natural language. In order for the systems to interpret the natural language input and react in the most reasonable and reliable way, the systems need a great degree of fuzziness. The biological brain can very easily deal with approximations in the input compared to the traditional logic we have built with computers. As an example, when we see a person, we can infer the quotient of *oldness* without explicitly knowing the age of the person. For example, if we see a a two-year-old baby, on the oldness quotient, we interpret the baby as *not old* and hence *young*. We can easily deal with the ambiguity in the input. In this case, we do not need to know the exact age of the baby for a fundamental and very basic interpretation of the input.

This level of fuzziness is essential if we want to build intelligent machines. In real-world scenarios, we cannot depend on the exact mathematical and quantitative input for our systems to work with, although our models (deep neural networks, for example) require actual input. The uncertainties are more frequent and the nature of real-world scenarios are amplified by the incompleteness of contextual information, characteristic randomness, and ignorance of the data. The human reasoning levels are capable enough to deal with these attributes in the real world. A similar level of fuzziness is essential for building intelligent machines that can complement human capabilities, in real sense of the term.

In this chapter, we are going to understand the fundamentals of the fuzzy logic theory and how it can be implemented for building the following:

- Adaptive network-based fuzzy inference systems
- Classifiers with fuzzy c-means
- Neuro-fuzzy-classifiers

We will be covering the following topics in the chapter:

- Fuzzy logic fundamentals
- ANFIS network
- Fuzzy C-means clustering
- NEFCLASS

Fuzzy logic fundamentals

Let's quickly understand how human interactions are seamless, even with a degree of vagueness within our statements. A statement such as *John is tall* does not have any indication of John's exact height in inches or centimeters. However, within the context of the conversation, two people communicating with each other can understand and infer from it. Now, consider that this conversation is taking place between two teachers in a school about a second grade student, John. Within this context, the statement *John is tall* means a certain height and we are really good at understanding and inferring contextual meaning from this vague information. The fundamental concept of fuzzy logic originates from the fact that with an increase in the complexity of the environmental context, our ability to make precise and exact statements about the state diminishes, yet in spite of that, the human brain is capable of drawing precise inferences. Fuzzy logic represents a degree of truth instead of the absolute (mathematical at times) truth. Let's represent the difference between traditional logic and fuzzy logic with a simple diagram:

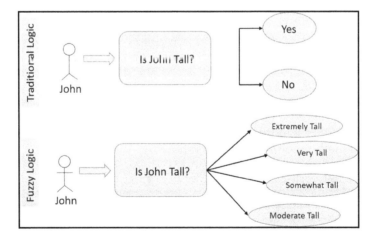

While the traditional computing frameworks are better suited for traditional logic, the intelligent systems we intend to build need to adapt to fuzzy input based on context. The computing frameworks need to transition from absolute truth, *yes/no*, to partial truth, *extremely tall*, *very tall*, and so on. This is very similar to the human reasoning paradigm in which the truth is partial and falseness is a diminishing degree of truth.

Fuzzy sets and membership functions

In our example, all the possible answers to the question of the height of a person constitute a set. Since there is enough uncertainty within each of the values, it is termed a **fuzzy set**. In this case, the fuzzy set is =k, {"Very tall", "Somewhat tall", "Moderately tall"}. Each member of the set has a mathematical value that represents the level or degree of membership. In our example, the set can be represented, along with the degree of membership, as {"Extremely tall":1.0, "Very tall":0.8, "Somewhat tall":0.6, "Moderately tall":0.2}. The input can be plotted on a curve that represents the values in the fuzzy set along with the degrees of membership:

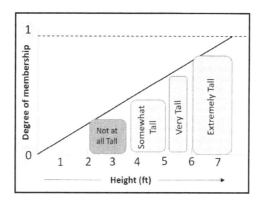

Let's define some standard terminology around fuzzy sets. A fuzzy set is typically marked with character 'A', which represents the data space parameter X (measure of tallness, in this case). The fuzzy set, A, is defined using a membership function, $\mu_A(X)$, which associates each value within A with a real number between 0 and 1, denoting the grade of membership within A.

The membership space is also termed the **universe of discourse**, which simply refers to all the possible values within set *A*. Within the value space, the membership function needs to satisfy only one condition: that the degree of membership for all the fuzzy set members should be between 0 and 1. Within this constraint, the membership functions can take any form (Triangular, Sigmoid, Step, Gaussian, and so on) depending on the dataset and the predicament context. Here is a representation of the member functions for our dataset that denotes tallness for a person:

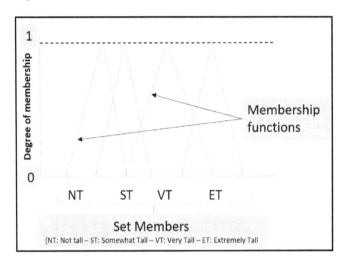

The linguistic variables (**NT/ST/VT/ET**) can be related to the numerical variables (actual height of a person in inches) with a level of approximation or fuzziness.

Attributes and notations of crisp sets

A **crisp set** is a collection of entities that can be clearly separated as members versus non-members, for example, a set of living objects versus non-living objects. In this case, the container fully includes or fully excludes the elements. There are several ways in which crisp sets can be defined:

- A set of even numbers greater than 0 and less than 10
  - $A = \{2,4,6,8\}$
- A set of elements that belong to another set, *P* and *Q*
  - *A = {x | x is an element belonging to P and Q}*

- $\mu_A(X) = 1$ if $(x \in A)$, 0 if $(x \notin A)$
- Φ: Represents a null or empty set
- Power set $P(A) = \{X \mid x \subseteq A\}$: This is a set containing all the possible subsets of A
- For the crisp sets A and B containing a super-set of elements within X:
    - $x \subset A \Longrightarrow x$ belongs to A
    - $x \notin A \Longrightarrow x$ does not belong to A
    - $x \subset X \Longrightarrow x$ belongs to the entire universe X
- Consider crisp sets A and B on X space
    - $A \subset B \Longrightarrow A$ is completely part of B *(if $x \in A$ then $x \in B$)* - implicit reasoning
    - $A \subseteq B \Longrightarrow A$ is contained in or equivalent to B
    - $A = B \Longrightarrow A \subset B$ or $B \subset A$

Operations on crisp sets

Similar to the mathematical numerals, we can perform certain operations on crisp sets:

- **Union**: $A \cup B = \{x \mid x \in A \ OR \ x \in B\}$
- **Intersection**: $A \cap B = \{x \mid x \in A \ AND \ x \in B\}$
- **Complement**: $\bar{A} = \{x \mid x \notin A, x \in X\}$
- **Difference**: $A - B = A \mid B = \{x \mid x \notin A \ and \ x \notin B\} \Longrightarrow A - (A \cap B)$

This is how we we represent these operations:

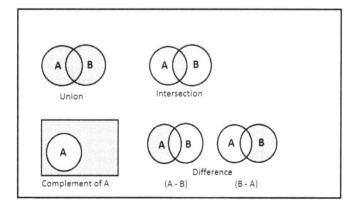

Properties of crisp sets

Crisp sets demonstrate certain properties, as follows:

- **Commutivity**:
  - $A \cup B = B \cup A$
  - $A \cap B = B \cap A$

- **Associativity**:
  - $A \cup (B \cup C) = (A \cup B) \cup C$
  - $A \cap (B \cap C) = (A \cap B) \cap C$

- **Distributivity**:
  - $A \cup (B \cap C) = (A \cup B) \cap (A \cup C)$
  - $A \cap (A \cup C) = (A \cap B) \cup (A \cap C)$

- **Idempotency**:
  - $A \cup A = A$
  - $A \cap A = A$

- **Transitivity**:
  - If $A \subseteq B \subseteq C$ then $A \subseteq C$

Fuzzification

Digital computers are designed and programmed to primarily work with crisp sets. This means they are able to apply logical operations and computational reasoning based on the classical sets. In order to make intelligent machines, we require a process called **fuzzification**. With this process, the digital inputs are translated into fuzzy sets.

Membership of the fuzzy sets corresponds to a certain degree of certainty for the fuzzy set. Fuzzification is a process by which we move gradually from precise symbols to vagueness for the element representations, which translates measured numerical values into fuzzy linguistic values. Consider a set of numbers that are close to integer value 5:

$A_{classic} = \{3,4,5,6,7\}$

$A_{fuzzy} = \{0.6/2, 0.8/3, 1.0/4, 1.0/5, 1.0/6, 0.8/7, 0.6/8\}$

Fuzzification is a process for defining the membership degree of the set members. In the case of the classic set, the membership degree is 1 or 0. Whereas in the fuzzy set, the membership degree varies between 0 and 1. The following diagram illustrates a dataset representation for **Poorness of Grades**. Assume that a student gets grades from 0 to 100 on the exam. 0 is the minimum and hence the poorest grade, and 100 is the maximum and hence *not a poor* grade at all:

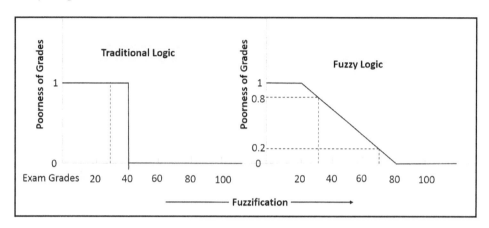

If a student scores 30 in the exam, with traditional logic, they have received poor grades, since the poorness of grades is a step function that treats all the grades below 40 as poor and higher than 40 as not-poor. In the case of fuzzy logic, if a student gets 30, they have a 0.8 degree of a poor grade and if the student scores 70, they have a 0.2 degree of a poor grade. The fuzzy sets do not need to be distinct and they can union, intersect, complement, and differentiate with each other:

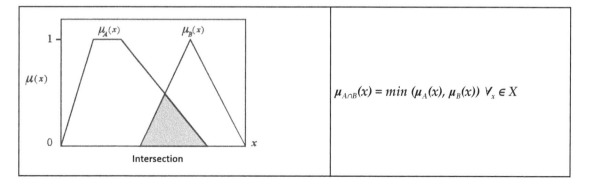

$$\mu_{A \cap B}(x) = min\ (\mu_A(x),\ \mu_B(x))\ \forall_x \in X$$

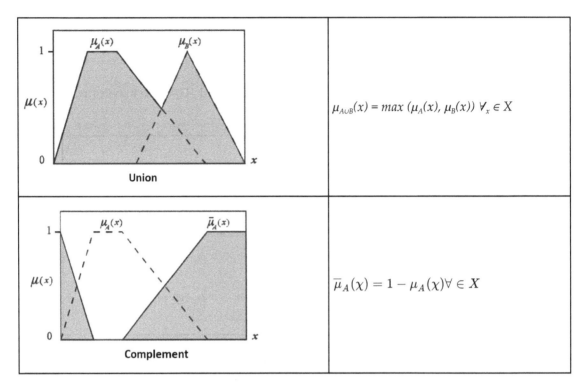

Union	$\mu_{A\cup B}(x) = max \; (\mu_A(x), \; \mu_B(x)) \; \forall_x \in X$
Complement	$\bar{\mu}_A(\chi) = 1 - \mu_A(\chi) \forall \in X$

The fuzzy function can take any complex form based on the contextual data-based reasoning. Membership for elements in a fuzzy set that follows the fuzzy function can be ensured in multiple ways, depending on the context:

- Membership as similarity
- Membership as probability
- Membership as intensity
- Membership as approximation
- Membership as compatibility
- Membership as possibility

Membership functions can be generated in two ways:

- **Subjective**: Intuition/expertise/knowledge
- **Automatic**: Clustering/neural nets/genetic algorithms

Defuzzification

Defuzzification is a process by which the actionable outcomes are generated as quantifiable values. Since computers can only understand the crisp sets, it can also be seen as a process of converting fuzzy set values based on the context into a crisp output. Defuzzification interprets the membership value based on the shape of the membership function into a real value. The defuzzified value represents the action to be taken by the intelligent machine based on the contextual inputs. There are multiple defuzzification techniques available; the one that is used for a given problem depends on the context.

Defuzzification methods

We have the following defuzzication methods:

- Center of sums method
- **Center of gravity (COG)/ centriod of area (COA)** method
- Center of area / **bisector of area (BOA)** method
- Weighted average method
- Maxima methods:
    - **First of maxima method (FOM)**
    - **Last of maxima method (LOM)**
    - **Mean of maxima method (MOM)**

Fuzzy inference

Fuzzy inference is the actual process that brings everything together to formulate the actions for the intelligent machines. The process can be depicted as follows:

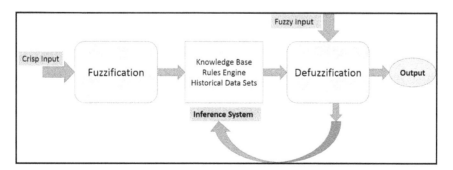

In traditional systems, the inputs are received as crisp sets. The crisp input are fuzzified as membership functions and the input fuzzy sets are aggregated with union/complement/differentiation techniques. Once the aggregated membership function is obtained, we apply the knowledge base, rules, and utilize historical datasets before defuzzifying the input set into an actionable output value.

Modern intelligent systems need to work with fuzzy input directly; the fuzzification process is part of the environmental context. The machines need to interpret natural language input to create a seamless experience for end users. A fuzzification unit needs to support the application of various fuzzification methods to convert the crisp input into fuzzy sets.

ANFIS network

In earlier chapters, we saw the theory and practical applications of ANNs. When we combine the general theory of ANNs with fuzzy logic, we are able to get a neuro-fuzzy system that is a very efficient and powerful mechanism for modeling the real world input into intelligent machines, and producing output that are based on the adaptive judgement of a machine. This brings the computational frameworks very close to how a human brain would interpret the information and is able to take action within split seconds. Fuzzy logic itself has the ability to interpenetrate between human and machine interpretations of the data, information, and knowledge. However, it does not have an inherent capability to translate and model the process of transformation of human thought processes into rule based, self-learning, **fuzzy inference systems** (**FIS**).

ANNs can be utilized for automatically adjusting the membership functions based on the environmental context and training the network interactively in order to reduce the error rate. This forms the basis of **Artificial Neuro-Fuzzy Inference Systems** (**ANFIS**). ANFIS can be considered as a class or type of adaptive networks that are equivalent to fuzzy inference systems that use the hybrid learning algorithm.

Adaptive network

This is a type of feed-forward neural network with multiple layers that often uses a supervised learning algorithm. This type of network contains a number of adaptive nodes that are interconnected, without any weight value between them. Each node in this network has different functions and tasks. A learning rule that is used affects parameters in the node and reduces error levels at the output layer.

This neural network is usually trained with backpropagation or gradient descent. Due to the slowness in convergence, a hybrid approach can also be used, which accelerates the convergence and potentially avoids local minima.

ANFIS architecture and hybrid learning algorithm

At the core of the ANFIS architecture is the adaptive network that uses the supervised learning algorithm. Let's understand this with a simple example. Consider that there are two inputs, x and y, and an output, z. We can consider the use of two simple rules in the method of *if-then* as follows:

Rule 1: If x is A_1 and y is B_1 then $z_1 = p_1 x + q_1 x + r_1$

Rule 2: If x is A_2 and y is B_2 then $z_2 = p_2 y + q_2 y + r_2$

 A1, A2 and *B1, B2* are the membership functions of each input x and y. *p1, q1, r1* and *p2, q2, r2* are linear parameters of the fuzzy inference model.

Let's illustrate this with a diagram:

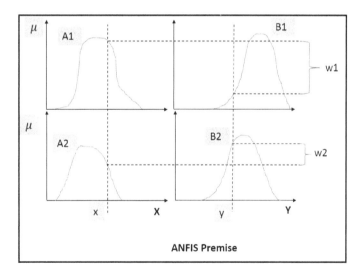

The ANFIS architecture in this case can be considered a five-layer neural network. The first and fourth layers contain an adaptive node and the other layers contain fixed nodes, as we have already seen in the previous chapters on ANNs. The network is illustrated in the following diagram:

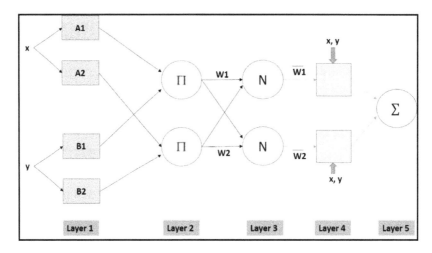

- **Layer 1**: This layer consists of two adaptive nodes that adapt to a function parameter based on the input values (x and y). The output from each of these nodes denotes the degree of membership corresponding to the input value (refer the ANFIS premise in the previous diagram). The membership function, as we have seen in the previous sections, can take any form (Gaussian, bell function, and so on). The parameters in this layer are termed premise parameters:
    - $z1 = p1x + q1y + r1$
    - $z2 = p2x + q2y + r2$

- **Layer 2**: The nodes in this layer are fixed nodes that are non-adaptive in nature and resemble a hidden layer node in a neural network. The output from these nodes is obtained by multiplying the signal coming from the adaptive nodes and delivered to the next layer nodes. The nodes in this layer represent the firing strength of each of the rules that are inherited by the adaptive nodes in the previous layer.

- **Layer 3**: The nodes in this layer are also fixed nodes. Each node is a calculated value of the ratio between the nth rule's firing strength and the sum of all the rules' firing strength. The overall result represents the normalized firing strength.
- **Layer 4**: The nodes in this layer are the adaptive nodes. In this layer, the normalized firing strength from the previous layer nodes is multiplied with the output from the rule functions ($p_1x + q_1x + r_1$ and $p_2y + q_2y + r_2$). The output parameters from this layer are called consequent parameters.
- **Layer 5**: This is the output layer and has one fixed output node resembling the ANN. This node performs the summation on the signals from the previous layer. This is the overall output of the ANFIS network. This represents the quantitative actionable outcome from the fuzzy system. This output can be utilized in the control loop and back-propagated for training and optimization, eventually minimizing the error.

With this network topology in place, we can apply a hybrid learning algorithm in order to optimize the output and reduce the error. The hybrid algorithm also ensures that we are able to converge quicker and avoid local minima. The hybrid algorithm is a two-step process that essentially tweaks the parameters for the first and fourth adaptive layers based on the rule set.

During the forward pass, the parameters for the first layer (premise parameters) are kept constant and the parameters for the fourth layer (consequent parameters) are adjusted based on the **recursive least square estimator** (**RLSE**) method.

 Note that the consequent layer parameters are linear and we can accelerate the convergence rate in the learning process. Once the consequent parameters values are obtained, the data is passed through the input space and the aggregated membership functions, and the output is generated. The output is then compared with the actual output.

When the backward pass is executed, the consequent parameters obtained from the first step are kept constant and the premise parameters are tweaked with the learning method of gradient descent or backward propagation. The output is once again generated with the changed values for the premise parameters and compared with actual output for further tuning and optimization. Use of this hybrid algorithm, which combines RLSE and gradient descent, ensures faster convergence.

Fuzzy C-means clustering

In Chapter 3, *Learning from Big Data*, we saw the k-means clustering algorithm, which is an iterative unsupervised algorithm that creates k clusters for a dataset based on the distance from a random centroid in the first iteration step. The centriods are calculated in each iteration to accommodate new data points. This process is repeated until the centriods do not change significantly after a point. As a result of the k-means clustering algorithm, we get discrete clusters with data points. Each data point either belongs to a cluster or it does not. There are only two states for a data point in terms of cluster membership. However, in real-world scenarios, we have data points that may belong to multiple clusters with different degrees of membership. The algorithms that create fuzzy membership instead of crisp membership for the data points within a cluster are termed soft-clustering algorithms. C-means clustering is one of the most popular algorithms, which is iterative in nature and very similar to the k-means clustering algorithm.

Let's consider a dataset S that contains N data points. The goal is to cluster these N data points into C clusters:

$S = \{x_1, x_2, x_3, ..., x_N\}$

We are going to have C cluster membership functions (indicated by μ):

$\mu_1 = [\mu_1(x_1), \mu_1(x_2), \mu_1(x_3), ...\mu_1(x_n)]$

$\mu_2 = [\mu_2(x_1), \mu_2(x_2), \mu_2(x_3), ...\mu_2(x_n)]$

.

.

$\mu_c = [\mu_c(x_1), \mu_c(x_2), \mu_c(x_3), ...\mu_c(x_n)]$

For each of the clusters that are represented by the membership functions, we are going to have a centroid data point, denoted by V_i, corresponding to a fuzzy cluster $Cl_i (i = 1,2,3, ... C)$. With this background information and these notations, the optimization objective for the C-means clustering algorithm is defined as:

$$J_m = \sum_{i=1}^{c} \sum_{k=1}^{N_s} [u_i(k)]^m d^2(x_k, V_i)$$

N_s is the total number of input vectors; m represents the fuzziness index for the ith cluster (the higher the value of m, the higher the fuzziness). The fuzzy C-means algorithm minimizes J_m by selecting V_i and μ_i where $i = 1,2,3,...C$ by an iterative process. With these notations and the algorithm objective, here is the flowchart that represents the fuzzy C-means algorithm:

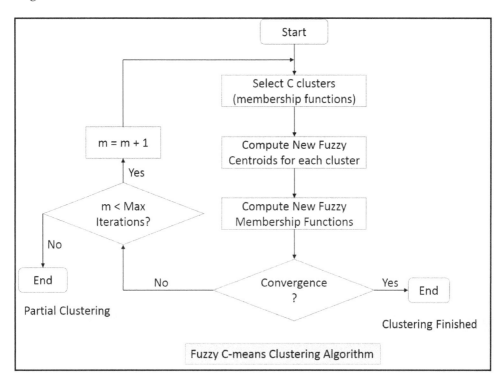

The flowchart is explained as follows:

- Initialization (Select the membership functions such that):

$$0 < \mu_i(x_k) < 1 \qquad for \ \ i = 1, 2, 3, ...C$$

$$\sum_{i=1}^{C} \mu_i(x_k) = 1$$

for k = 1,2,3, ...N_s

$$0 < \sum_{k=1}^{N_s} \mu_i(x_k) < N_s$$

for i = 1,2,3, ...C

- Compute fuzzy centroids for *i = 1,2,3, ...C* and *k = 1,2,3, ... N_s*:

$$V_i = \frac{\sum_{k=1}^{N_s} [\mu_i(x_k)]^m x_k}{\sum_{k=1}^{N_s} [\mu_i(x_k)]^m}$$

- Compute new fuzzy membership functions:

$$\mu_i(x_k) = \frac{\left(\frac{1}{d^2(x_k,V_i)}\right)^{\frac{1}{(m-1)}}}{\sum_{j=1}^{C} \left(\frac{1}{d^2(x_k,V_j)}\right)^{\frac{1}{(m-1)}}}$$

- Check for convergence:

    - If the membership functions do not change over iterations, the iterations can stop and the algorithm has converged
    - Once the algorithm converges, μ_i represents the fuzzy clusters
    - If the algorithm does not converge and the number of iterations is equal to the maximum iterations set as the parameter, we exit the loop without finding the optimum fuzzy clusters

The membership values for the data points obtained by the algorithm are not unique since there is a dependency on the initial random conditions. There is a possibility of this algorithm converging to a local minimum. If we set the threshold for the membership values, it is possible to produce hard clusters (same as the k-means clustering algorithm). For example, we can set the threshold value to *0.8*. If the cluster membership value is greater than *0.8*, we can consider it as a crisp membership value of *1* and less than *0.8* as *0*.

Let's implement this algorithm with Spark:

```
import org.apache.spark.mllib.linalg.Vectors
import scala.util.Random
import org.apache.spark.mllib.clustering._
import org.apache.spark.ml.clustering._
import org.apache.spark.mllib.clustering.KMeans
import org.apache.spark.mllib.clustering.FuzzyCMeans
import org.apache.spark.mllib.clustering.FuzzyCMeans._
import org.apache.spark.mllib.clustering.FuzzyCMeansModel

val points = Seq(
    Vectors.dense(0.0, 0.0),
    Vectors.dense(0.0, 0.1),
    Vectors.dense(0.1, 0.0),
    Vectors.dense(9.0, 0.0),
    Vectors.dense(9.0, 0.2),
    Vectors.dense(9.2, 0.0)
  )
  val rdd = sc.parallelize(points, 3).cache()

  for (initMode <- Seq(KMeans.RANDOM, KMeans.K_MEANS_PARALLEL)) {

    (1 to 10).map(_ * 2) foreach { fuzzifier =>

      val model = FuzzyCMeans.train(rdd, k = 2, maxIterations = 10, runs
= 10, initMode, seed = 26031979L, m = fuzzifier)

      val fuzzyPredicts = model.fuzzyPredict(rdd).collect()
      rdd.collect() zip fuzzyPredicts foreach { fuzzyPredict =>
        println(s" Point ${fuzzyPredict._1}")
        fuzzyPredict._2 foreach{clusterAndProbability =&gt;
          println(s"Probability to belong to cluster
${clusterAndProbability._1} " +
            s"is ${"%.6f".format(clusterAndProbability._2)}")
        }
      }
    }
  }
```

The program will output this fuzzy clustering:

Iteration - 1	Iteration - 10
| ```
Point [200.0]
Probability to belong to cluster 0 is 0.000219
Probability to belong to cluster 1 is 0.999781
Point [204.0]
Probability to belong to cluster 0 is 0.006037
Probability to belong to cluster 1 is 0.993963
Point [5.0]
Probability to belong to cluster 0 is 0.998991
Probability to belong to cluster 1 is 0.001009
Point [198.0]
Probability to belong to cluster 0 is 0.001727
Probability to belong to cluster 1 is 0.998273
Point [198.0]
Probability to belong to cluster 0 is 0.001727
Probability to belong to cluster 1 is 0.998273
Point [4.0]
Probability to belong to cluster 0 is 0.999958
Probability to belong to cluster 1 is 0.000042
Point [4.0]
Probability to belong to cluster 0 is 0.999958
Probability to belong to cluster 1 is 0.000042
Point [203.0]
Probability to belong to cluster 0 is 0.004299
Probability to belong to cluster 1 is 0.995701
Point [2.0]
Probability to belong to cluster 0 is 0.997964
Probability to belong to cluster 1 is 0.002036
Point [195.0]
Probability to belong to cluster 0 is 0.006995
Probability to belong to cluster 1 is 0.993005
Point [3.0]
Probability to belong to cluster 0 is 0.999244
Probability to belong to cluster 1 is 0.000756
Point [201.0]
Probability to belong to cluster 0 is 0.001302
Probability to belong to cluster 1 is 0.998697
``` | ```
Point [200.0]
Probability to belong to cluster 0 is 0.497199
Probability to belong to cluster 1 is 0.502801
Point [204.0]
Probability to belong to cluster 0 is 0.497317
Probability to belong to cluster 1 is 0.502683
Point [5.0]
Probability to belong to cluster 0 is 0.502447
Probability to belong to cluster 1 is 0.497553
Point [198.0]
Probability to belong to cluster 0 is 0.497136
Probability to belong to cluster 1 is 0.502864
Point [198.0]
Probability to belong to cluster 0 is 0.497136
Probability to belong to cluster 1 is 0.502864
Point [4.0]
Probability to belong to cluster 0 is 0.502424
Probability to belong to cluster 1 is 0.497576
Point [4.0]
Probability to belong to cluster 0 is 0.502424
Probability to belong to cluster 1 is 0.497576
Point [203.0]
Probability to belong to cluster 0 is 0.497288
Probability to belong to cluster 1 is 0.502712
Point [2.0]
Probability to belong to cluster 0 is 0.502379
Probability to belong to cluster 1 is 0.497621
Point [195.0]
Probability to belong to cluster 0 is 0.497036
Probability to belong to cluster 1 is 0.502964
Point [3.0]
Probability to belong to cluster 0 is 0.502401
Probability to belong to cluster 1 is 0.497599
Point [201.0]
Probability to belong to cluster 0 is 0.497229
Probability to belong to cluster 1 is 0.502771
``` |

NEFCLASS

In the previous chapters, we learned the general theory of neural networks, which resemble the human brain in terms of a network of computation units that are interconnected. The neural networks are trained by adjusting the weights on the synapses (connectors). As we have seen, the neural network can be trained to solve classification problems such as image recognition. The neural networks accept crisp input and adjust weights to produce output values (classification into a class). However, as we have seen in this chapter, the real-world input have a degree of fuzziness in the input as well as a degree of vagueness for the output.

The membership of the input and output variables in a specific cluster or a type is represented with a degree instead of a crisp set. We can combine the two approaches to formulate a **neuro-fuzzy-classifier** (**NEFCLASS**), which is based on fuzzy input and utilizes the elegance of a multi-layer neural network in order to solve the classification problem. In this section, we will understand the algorithm and intuition behind it.

At a high level, NEFCLASS consists of input, rule, and output layers. The neurons in these layers are hence called input neurons, rule neurons, and output neurons. Here is the generic structural representation of the NEFCLASS network:

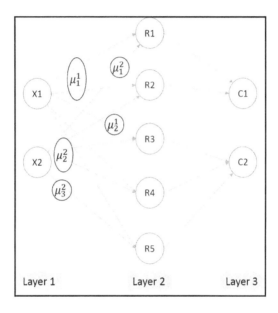

Layer 1 processes input data. The activation function in this layer is typically an identity function. The neurons in the hidden Layer 2 represent fuzzy rules that contain fuzzy sets in premise and conclusion sides (input and output, for simplicity).

In mathematics, an identity function, also called an identity relation, identity map, or identity transformation, is a function that always returns the same value that was used as its argument. In equations, the function is given by $f(x) = x$.

Typically, the fuzzy sets with triangular membership functions are used and a fuzzy set with a singleton membership function is used in the conclusion part. The premises of fuzzy rules become weights for the rule neurons in Layer 2. Finally, the conclusion of a rule is the connection from the rule neuron to the output layer. When we calculate the activation from the rule neurons in Layer 2, we use T-norm as the minimization function:

$a_R{}^P = \min\limits_{x \in U_1} \{W(x, R)(a_x{}^P)\}$	**W(x,R) represents the weight of connection between input neuron, x, and the rule neuron, R**

The weights for the rule neurons, given by the earlier formula, are shared for each fuzzy input value and one fuzzy set is used. From the rule neuron layer (Layer 2) to the classification layer (Layer 3), only one connection is attached. This represents the connection between the rule and the class.

The final layer is the output layer, which calculates the activation value for the given class on the basis of the activation of rules that indicate a given class as output. In this case, we use the maximum function indicated in the following:

$$a_c{}^P = \max\limits_{R \in U_2} \{a_R{}^P\}$$

After calculation of the activation in output neurons, the neuron with highest activation is chosen as a result of classification.

Frequently asked questions

Q: Why do we need fuzzy systems?

A: In our quest to build intelligent machines, we cannot continue to model the world with crisp or quantitative and definite inputs. We need to model systems like the human brain, which can easily understand and process input, even if they are not mathematical and contain a degree of vagueness. We need fuzzy systems in order to interpret real-world input and produce prescribed actions based on the context. Fuzzy systems can fuzzify and defuzzify the input and facilitate inseparability between natural events and computers.

Q: What are crisp sets and fuzzy sets? How are they different from one another?

A: Crisp sets have two possibilities for members. A particular element/data point/event is a member or a non-member of the crisp set. For example, days in a week from Monday to Sunday are members of the *days of the week* crisp set. Anything else apart from the seven days is not a member of the set. Members of fuzzy sets, on the other hand, belong to the fuzzy set with a degree of membership. This is how our natural language conversations happen. When we say a person is tall, we do not mention the exact height of the person. At that point, if tallness is considered as a membership function, a person with a certain height belongs to the fuzzy set with a degree.

Q: Do fuzzy sets support all the operations that are supported by crisp sets?

A: Yes, the fuzzy sets support all the operations supported by crisp sets, such as union, intersection, complement, and differentiation.

Summary

In this chapter, we understood the fundamental theory of fuzzy logic. It is imperative that as we build intelligent machines with ever-growing volumes of data that is available from discrete sources in structured, unstructured, and semi-structured forms, machines need the ability to interface with the real world in the same way as human beings do. We do not need explicit mathematical input to make our decisions. In the same way, if we are able to interpret natural language and apply fuzzy techniques to computation, we will be able to create smart machines that really complement humans.

The mathematical theory of fuzzy systems is decades old. However, with the advent of massive data storage and processing frameworks, practical implementations are possible especially with the convergence of fuzzy logic and deep neural networks, and a truly intelligent, self-learning system will be a reality very soon. This chapter has created the foundation for modeling and bringing our systems even closer to the human brain.

In the next chapter, we are going to visit genetic algorithms, where the AI systems derive inspiration from the natural process of evolution in cases where the brute-force approach is not computationally viable.

Genetic Programming

8

Big Data mining tools need to be empowered by computationally efficient techniques to increase their degree of efficiency. Using genetic algorithms over data mining creates great robust, computationally efficient, and adaptive systems. In fact, with an exponential explosion of data, data analytics techniques go on taking more time and inversely affect the throughput. Also, due to their static nature, complex hidden patterns are often left out. In this chapter, we want to show how to use genes to mine data with great efficiency. To achieve this objective, we are going to explore some of the basics of genetic programming and the fundamental algorithms. We are going to begin with some of the very basic principles of natural (biological) genetics and draw some parallels when it comes to applying the general theory to computer algorithms. We will cover the following:

- Genetic algorithm structure
- KEEL framework
- Encog machine learning framework
- Weka framework
- Attribute search with genetic algorithms in Weka

The genetic algorithms derive a lot of inspiration from nature and the following quotation is appropriate as we research nature for the evolution of intelligent machines:

"Nature has all the answers within itself. We need a state of mind that is tuned in harmony with Nature to find answers to all the questions that bother humanity."

—Gurunath Patwardhan (Vishnudas)

Life on our planet has evolved over a period of millions of years in a peculiar way by keeping some of the basic fundamentals constant. At the core of the process of evolution of various creatures, natural phenomena, and everything that we can tangibly perceive, there is a universal consciousness that operates within the framework of certain laws. Our quest to develop intelligent systems that match human intelligence cannot be complete if we do not derive meaning from universal consciousness and try to mimic some of the complex algorithms that nature is leveraging for boundless time. One such phenomenon is gene theory, which is one of the basic principles of biology. The core principle of this theory is that traits are passed from parents to offspring through gene transmission. Genes are located on chromosomes and consist of DNA. While the natural laws of biological evolution are very interesting to study, they are out of the scope of this book. We will be looking at generic principles of genetic evolution and how we can apply those to mimick a computer algorithm that helps us in reasonably mining huge volumes of data and derive actionable insights for intelligent machines.

The core principles that define genetic theory and sustain natural evolution generation after generations are:

- **Heredity**: This is a process by which offspring in the next generation receive selected characteristics from both parents. For example, there is a chance that the next generation of tall parents will be tall.
- **Variation**: In order to sustain evolution, there has to be a level of characteristic variation between reproducing partners. A new set of combinations and traits will not evolve if there is a lack of variation.
- **Selection**: This is a mechanism by which members of the population that demonstrate prominently better characteristics are selected as the ones that participate in the matching process and give birth to the next generation. Nature's selection criteria is subjective and context dependent and differs from species to species.
- **Reproduction**: In this process, the characteristics from the parents are carried forward into the next generation by a process of cross-selection and matching. In simple terms, some characteristics from each of the two parents are selected and prominently transferred while the same attribute is dormant for the other parent. While nature's algorithm for the selection of characteristic is not entirely random, it is far from being fully understood. This is nature's way of creating further variation with every generation.

- **Mutation**: This is an optional but essential step in natural evolution. In certain minimum cases, nature makes a modification in the chromosomal structure (at times due to some external stimulus and most of the time without a known or obvious trigger) to modify the characteristic behavior of the offspring entirely. This is another way by which nature introduces an even larger degree of variation and diversity since the natural selection process can only have so much variation.

Let's define the premise of the genetic algorithms that draw motivation from the natural process of evolution. We need intelligent computer programs that evolve within the search space of possible solutions in an optimal and self-evolving manner. As is typically the case, the search space is huge and it is computationally impossible to apply brute force in order to fetch the solution in a reasonable time. The genetic algorithms provide a quick breakthrough within the search space with a process very similar to the natural evolution process. In the next section, we will define the structure of a generic genetic algorithm and how it simplifies and optimizes solution discovery within the search space. Before we get there, here is some of the terminology that we are going to use:

- **Generation**: A generation is an iteration of the genetic algorithm. Initial random generation is called **generation zero**.
- **Genotype**: It defines the structure of a solution produced by the genetic algorithm. For example, *#ff0000* is the hexadecimal representation of the *red* color, which is the genotype for the color red.
- **Phenotype**: This represents the physical/tangible/perceived characteristic corresponding to the genotype. In the previous example, the color red is the manifestation or phenotype for genotype *#ff0000*.
- **Decoding**: This is a process that translates the solution from genotype to phenotype space.
- **Encoding**: This is a process that translates the solution from phenotype to genotype space.
- **Population**: This represents a subset of all possible solutions to the given problem.
- **Diversity**: It defines the relative uniqueness of each element of the selected population. A higher level of diversity is considered to be good for the convergence of the genetic algorithm.

Genetic algorithms structure

In this section, let's understand the structure of a genetic algorithm that finds the optimum solution for a problem where the search space is so huge that brute force cannot solve it. The core algorithm was proposed by John Holland in 1975. In general, Genetic Algorithm provides an ability to provide a good enough solution fast enough to be reasonable. The generic flow of a Genetic Algorithm is depicted in the diagram:

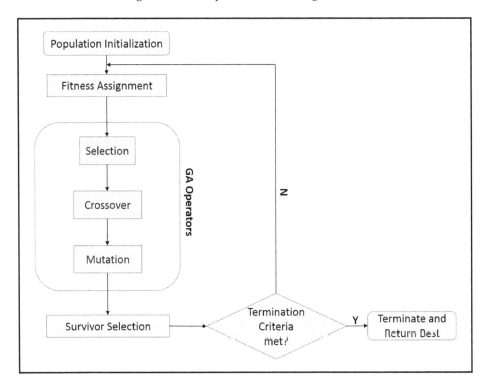

Let's try to illustrate Genetic Algorithm with a simple example. Consider that you have to find out a number (integer) in millions of values (the solution space). We can follow the steps in the algorithm and reach the target solution much quicker than application of a brute force method. Here is the implementation of the algorithm in Java:

1. Define the GA class with a simple constructor to initialize the population:

```
public GA(int solutionSpace, int populationSize,int targetValue,
int maxGenerations, int mutationPercent) {
    this.solutionSpace = solutionSpace; // Entire solution space in
which the algorithm needs to search
    this.populationSize = populationSize; // Size of the random
```

```
sample from the solution space
    this.targetValue = targetValue; // Value of the target solution
    this.maxGenerations = maxGenerations; // Maximum number of
generations (iterations) of the GA
    this.mutationPercent = mutationPercent; // This field defines
the percentage of new generation members to be mutated
    population = new int[this.populationSize]; // Initialize the
first generation
    for(int i=0; i< this.populationSize; i++) {
      population[i] = new Random().nextInt(this.solutionSpace);
    }
  }
```

2. Create a `fitness` function that defines the level of fitness for a particular solution in terms of its closeness to the actual solution. The higher the fitness value of a solution, the greater the chance of it getting retained in subsequent generations of the GA. In this case, we are making the fitness inversely proportional to the distance from the target value:

```
private int getFitness(int chromosome) {
  int distance = Math.abs(targetValue - chromosome);
  double fitness = solutionSpace / new Double(distance);
  return (int)fitness;
}
```

3. Select the next generation from the pool based on the `fitness` value. The higher the `fitness`, the more changes there are to make it to the next generation:

```
private ArrayList <Integer> getSelectionPool() {
  ArrayList <Integer> selectionPool = new ArrayList <Integer>();
  for(int i=0; i<this.populationSize; i++ ) {
    int memberFitnessScore = getFitness(this.population[i]);
    //System.out.println("Member fitness score = " +
memberFitnessScore);
    Integer value = new Integer(this.population[i]);
    for(int j=0; j<memberFitnessScore; j++) {
      selectionPool.add(value);
    }
  }
  return selectionPool;
}
```

4. In each generation, apply a minor mutation that changes the child element by a small margin. This includes variation and increases the chances of successfully finding the solution in a short amount of time:

```
for (int g=0; g<algorithm.maxGenerations; g++) {
System.out.println("********** Generation " + g + "
************");
  ArrayList <Integer> pool = algorithm.getSelectionPool();
  Random randomGenerator = new Random();
  int[] nextGeneration = new int[algorithm.populationSize];
  for(int i=0; i<algorithm.populationSize; i++) {
    if(pool.size() == 0)
      break;
    int parent1RandomIndex =
randomGenerator.nextInt(pool.size());
    int parent2RandomIndex =
randomGenerator.nextInt(pool.size());
    int parent1 = pool.get(parent1RandomIndex).intValue();
    int parent2 = pool.get(parent2RandomIndex).intValue();
    if(parent1 == algorithm.targetValue || parent2 ==
algorithm.targetValue) {
        System.out.println("Found a match !!! ");
        System.exit(1);
    }
    int child1 = (parent1 + parent2) > algorithm.solutionSpace ?
algorithm.solutionSpace - (parent1 + parent2) : (parent1 +
parent2);
    int child2 = Math.abs(parent1 - parent2);
    if (child1 == algorithm.targetValue || child2 ==
algorithm.targetValue) {
        System.out.println("Found a match !!! ");
        System.exit(1);
    }
    double mutatioRate = 0.001;
    float randomizer = new Random().nextFloat();
    if(randomizer < mutatioRate) {
      System.out.println("Mutating....");
      child1 += new Random().nextInt(1);
      child2 -= new Random().nextInt(1);
    }
    if(algorithm.getFitness(child1) >
algorithm.getFitness(child2))
        nextGeneration[i] = child1;
    else
      nextGeneration[i] = child2;
  }
  algorithm.population = nextGeneration;
```

Here are the program outputs in multiple runs. As we can see, we need to tune various parameters for the optimum performance of the algorithm:

Solution Space	Population Sample Size	Target Value	Mutation %	# of Generations to find the match
5000	1000	1234	1%	2
50000	1000	1234	1%	3
500000	1000	1234	1%	6
500000	2000	1234	1%	2
500000	2000	1234	10%	2
500000	10000	1234	1%	2

As we can see, implementing the Genetic Algorithm is simple and the core principles can be applied to more complex problems such as human gene profiling, signal processing, image processing, and so on. Based on the basic concepts we have covered so far in this chapter, there are lots of frameworks and models developed in order to leverage the **evolutionary algorithms** (EAs) for various data mining and related problems. In the next sections, we are going to review some of these frameworks at a high level.

KEEL framework

KEEL (**K**nowledge **E**xtraction based on **E**volutionary **L**earning) is a framework that can be used for various tasks, which translates data into information into knowledge assets. KEEL specifically assesses evolutionary algorithms for data mining based on regression, classification, unsupervised learning, and so on. The ultimate feat of machine intelligence will be when the computer programs are able to read the text and interpret and understand it the way human beings do. With this capability, combined with exponentially growing brute force computing power, we will be able to create a knowledge system that will possess supernatural powers when it comes to applying that knowledge to various problems like Genome decoding, studies of antibodies and so on that have plagued humanity for centuries.

The KEEL framework and similar frameworks are taking us a step closer to that goal with the fundamental idea of automatically discovering knowledge from datasets using evolutionary algorithms. Although EAs are powerful for solving a wide range of scientific problems, they can only be used with extensive programming expertise, and carefully tuning the parameters and experimenting with outcomes over a long stretch of time. KEEL empowers the user to use EAs quite easily without the need for extensive programming, allowing them to focus on the core data mining and extraction problems while providing a toolkit for ease of use. KEEL provides an extensive library of EAs along with easy-to-use software that comes in handy for considerably reducing the level of experience and knowledge required by researchers in evolutionary computing.

KEEL is a Java-based desktop application that facilitates the analysis of the behavior of evolutionary learning in different areas of learning and preprocessing tasks, making the management of these tasks easy for the user. The latest available version (3.0) of KEEL consists of the following modules:

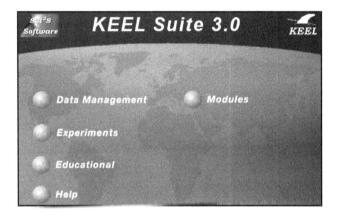

- **Data Management**: This is the core component for making the data available for analysis and running experiments using various algorithms and visualization techniques. It allows data imports from various sources, exporting the data to outbound systems and storage, visualizing the data and making edits (transformations based on use cases), and most importantly, making partitions if the data volume is large so that it can be distributed to various nodes if a compute and storage cluster is utilized (for example, the Hadoop framework). The application includes pre-loaded datasets for quick experimentation. Here is the view into data management within KEEL:

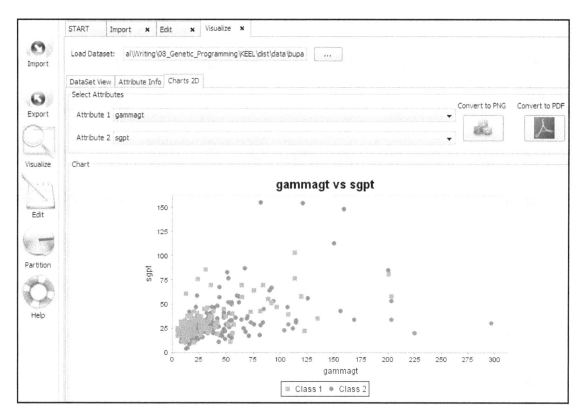

- **Experiments**: This section allows users to create experiments based on the imported datasets. There are some predefined experiments that the user can start with and they can build their own experiments based on the use cases and the available algorithms within KEEL. The framework provides various easy-to-use options such as type of validation, type of learning (**Classification/Regression/Unsupervised Learning**), and so on:

The experiments can be configured with an intuitive user interface that allows users to select the datasets along with the algorithm used during data preprocessing, processing, and post processing. Multiple pathways can be configured within the same experiment, leveraging various algorithms for comparison. The algorithms can be tuned by setting the relevant parameters, as seen in the following screenshot:

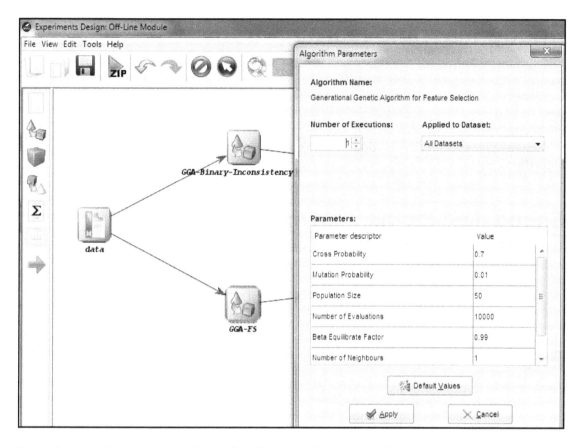

Once the experiments are configured and executed, the KEEL framework generates a directory structure and the files required for running them on the local machine, as well as a distributed computing environment. For example, the Java class can be embedded to run as a **user defined function** (**UDF**) within any of the Hadoop ecosystem components in order to leverage a parallel processing paradigm. The KEEL framework also allows extending the core libraries and algorithm coverage by providing APIs for extension.

The KEEL philosophy tries to include the fewest possible constraints for the developer, in order to simplify the inclusion of new algorithms within this tool. In fact, each algorithm has its source code in a single folder and does not depend on a specific structure of classes, making the integration of new methods straightforward.

Encog machine learning framework

Encog is an advanced ML framework that supports a variety of algorithms including Neural Networks and Genetic algorithms. It supports Java and .NET APIs along with a workbench that has an easy to use user interface for running various tests and experiments with the datasets. The training algorithm implementations are multi-threaded and support multi-core hardware. In this section, we are going to see general use of the Encog framework and specifically its support for **genetic programming** (**GP**) to implement **genetic algorithms** (**GAs**).

Encog development environment setup

The core libraries for the Encog framework can be acquired from the Git repository and built as a Maven project within your development environment as follows:

```
https://github.com/encog/encog-java-core
mvn package
```

Encog API structure

The core API is a simple object-oriented paradigm with three core functional blocks:

- **Machine learning methods**: Each model type in Encog is represented as a machine learning method. These machine learning methods implement the org.encog.ml.MLMethod interface as a marker interface. This super-class does not contain any method or define any behavior for the inheriting interfaces and only tags them as a machine learning method. A MLMethod is an algorithm that accepts data and provides some sort of insight into it. This could be a neural network, support vector machine, clustering algorithm, or something else entirely:
  - **MLRegression**: Used to define regression models, the ones that produce numerical output
  - **MLClassification**: Used to define classification models, the ones that classify the input variables into one of the output classes
  - **MLClustering**: Used to define clustering algorithms that take input data and place them into several clusters:

Here is the class diagram of the interfaces which are the fundamental building blocks of Encog framework:

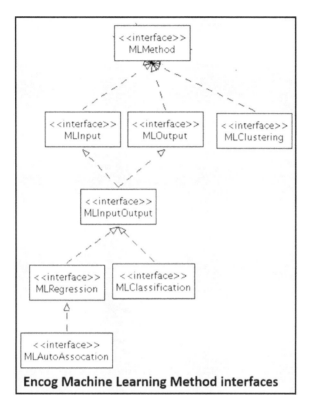

Encog Machine Learning Method interfaces

- **Encog Datasets**: Encog needs data to fit various machine learning methods. The data is accessed using a variety of dataset classes. The Encog data handling objects work with the following interfaces:
    - **MLData**: Used to hold a vector that will be input or output either to or from a model.
    - **MLDataPair**: Used as input **MLData** vectors for supervised learning. A training set is built with this data type.
    - **MLDataSet**: Provides a list of **MLDataPair** objects to trainer functions.

We can create new versions of any of these three interfaces. Encog also provides basic implementations of these classes such as **BasicMLData**, **BasicMLDataPair**, and **BasicMLDataSet**.

Encog supports an extensive implementation of evolutionary algorithms that support genetic programming. Here is a snapshot of various available classes:

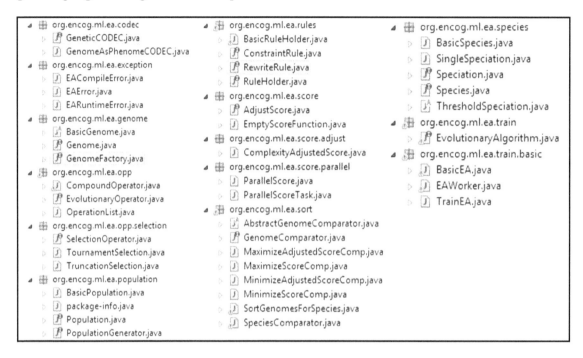

With these APIs, implementation of genetic algorithms is extremely easy with Encog using a level of abstraction. Here is some pseudocode for the implementation of genetic algorithms with Encog:

```
    Population pop = initPopulation();          // Initialize the initial
population (generation 0)
    CalculateScore score = new ScorerClass(pop.solutionSpace); // This is
the implementation of
// the scorer class

    genetic = new TrainEA(pop,score);                          // Train
the model with
    genetic.addOperation(0.9,new SpliceNoRepeat(POPULATION_SIZE)); // apply
crossover operation
    genetic.addOperation(0.1,new MutateShuffle());             // apply
mutation
    while (solutionCount < MAX_SAME_SOLUTION) {                 //
iterate over generations
        genetic.iteration();                                   // next
generation
```

```
        double thisSolution = genetic.getError();                    //
solution from next generation
    }
```

The Encog framework also provides an analyst workbench that is a handy user interface for running quick experiments with various datasets. The workbench uses the Encog core libraries and visualizes the output from various algorithms and test cycles. Here is a quick snapshot of the Encog workbench:

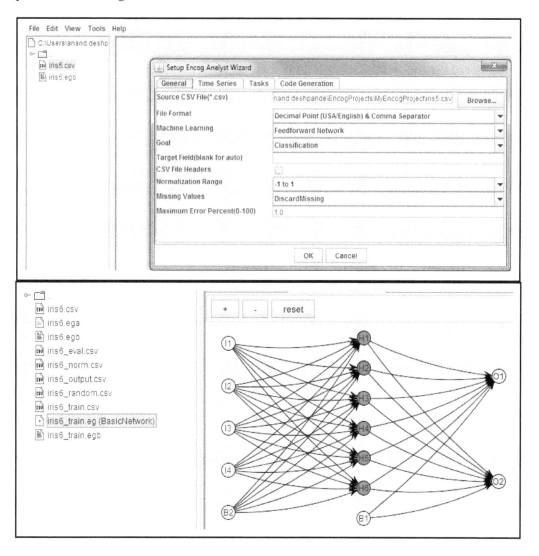

Introduction to the Weka framework

One of the handy tools in evaluating various data science algorithms is **Weka** (**Waikato Environment for Knowledge Analysis**). This is a suite of machine learning software written in the Java programming language. Weka is very popular since it can be extended to leverage additional algorithms and data mining techniques. In this section, we will be introduced to the generic concepts of Weka and specifically look at using it for the implementation of genetic algorithms.

Weka provides a great and intuitive visual user interface for data mining, analysis, and predictive modeling. Some of the features that make Weka a popular choice for the community are the following:

- Weka is available as a free tool to use under the GNU General Public license
- Weka is written in the Java programming language and compiles to byte code, which is easily portable across platforms
- Weka contains a rich library of machine learning algorithms and it can further be extended within the framework by creating hooks using the simple-to-use APIs
- The simple-to-use GUI makes it easy to train and compare various classifiers, clusters, and regression outputs

Here is a conceptual view of the Weka framework:

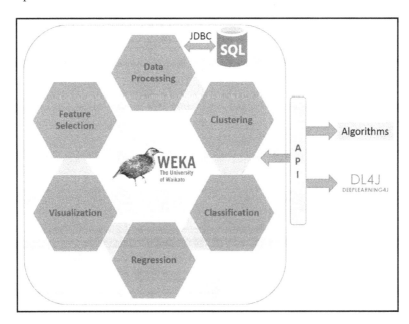

Weka supports ARFF (Attribute-Relation File *Format*), CSV (Comma Separated Values), and data formats for the datasets.

 An **ARFF** (**A**ttribute-**R**elation **F**ile **F**ormat) file is an ASCII text file that describes a list of instances sharing a set of attributes. ARFF files were developed by the Machine Learning Project at the Department of Computer Science of The University of Waikato for use with the Weka machine learning software.

ARFF files have two distinct sections. The first section is the header information, which is followed by the data information. The header of the ARFF file contains the name of the relation, a list of the attributes (the columns in the data), and their types.

An example header on the standard and typically used IRIS dataset looks as follows:

```
% 1. Title: Iris Plants Database
   %
% 2. Sources:
   %       (a) Creator: R.A. Fisher
   %       (b) Donor: Michael Marshall (MARSHALL%PLU@io.arc.nasa.gov)
   %       (c) Date: July, 1988
   %
   @RELATION iris

   @ATTRIBUTE sepallength   NUMERIC
   @ATTRIBUTE sepalwidth    NUMERIC
   @ATTRIBUTE petallength   NUMERIC
   @ATTRIBUTE petalwidth    NUMERIC
   @ATTRIBUTE class         {Iris-setosa,Iris-versicolor,Iris-virginica}
```

The data of the ARFF file looks as follows:

```
@DATA
   5.1,3.5,1.4,0.2,Iris-setosa
   4.9,3.0,1.4,0.2,Iris-setosa
   4.7,3.2,1.3,0.2,Iris-setosa
   4.6,3.1,1.5,0.2,Iris-setosa
   5.0,3.6,1.4,0.2,Iris-setosa
   5.4,3.9,1.7,0.4,Iris-setosa
   4.6,3.4,1.4,0.3,Iris-setosa
```

Lines that begin with % are comments.

The @RELATION, @ATTRIBUTE, and @DATA declarations are case insensitive.

Two of the advantages of Weka is that it includes a rich library of various algorithms for regression and classification, and there is an easy way to compare the algorithms based on the available dataset(s).

The latest version of Weka (3.8) can be downloaded from https://www.cs.waikato.ac.nz/ml/weka/downloading.html.

When we launch Weka, there are five possible applications to choose from:

- **Explorer**: This application provides an environment for exploring datasets with Weka.
- **Experimenter**: An environment for performing experiments and conducting statistical tests between learning schemas.
- **Knowledge Flow**: This environment supports the same features as explorer, but with a drag-and-drop interface. It supports incremental learning.
- **Workbench**: This is an all-in-one application that combines all the others within the perspectives that the user can select.
- **Simple CLI**: Provides a simple command-line interface that allows direct execution of Weka commands for operating systems that do not provide their own command line interface.

Here is a consolidated view of the initial launch screen in Weka:

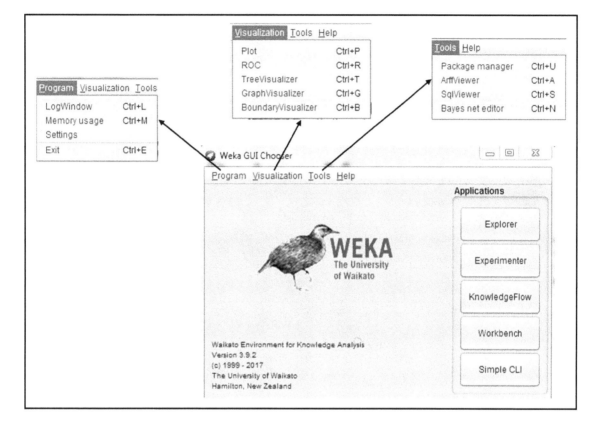

The visualizations allow us to explore the datasets visually with some basic options provided in the launch **Visualization** menu. In the **Tools** section, **Package manager** provides a graphical interface to Weka's package management system. This is one of the key benefits of Weka, that it can be very easily extended to include additional packages seamlessly.

Another handy tool provided by Weka is ARFF-Viewer. With this, we can quickly view the structure and contents of a data file in .arff format. Weka provides some of the pre-loaded datasets in its installation. Let's review one of the datasets that we will be using as an example to show some of the explorer features of Weka. Weka contains a **diabetes** dataset that has a set of independent variables and one dependent variable that defines whether a person is diabetic or not. Here is a snapshot of the .arff file viewer:

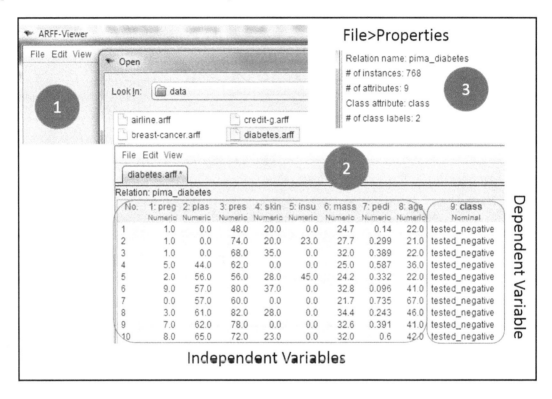

1. From the file selection menu, **Select** the .artf data file from available data files
2. Show all the fields (independent variable) in the dataset along with their data types and the output class (dependent variable)
3. Show the header properties of the file # of records, number of attributes, and the number of output classes

Weka Explorer features

While an introduction to the entire tool is out of scope for this book, we will review the Explorer section of the Weka toolkit.

Preprocess

This section allows us to choose and modify the data being acted upon. Weka allows users to select a data file in a large set of supported formats. The following is a screenshot of Weka Explorer:

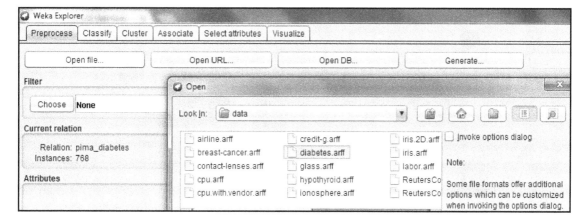

As you can see in the preceding screenshot, there are multiple choices for selecting the dataset from:

- **Open file...**: This option displays a file selection box to select the data file from the local disk or the network location.
- **Open URL**: This option displays a URL input box that accepts the HTTP URL endpoint for the dataset.
- **Open DB**: This option allows users to connect to a database and fetch the dataset. The database can be accessed via JDBC protocol provided that the network location for the database is accessible to the machine on which Weka is running.
- **Generate**: Allows the user to generate artificial data from various data generators.

Let's open the `dibetes.arff` file from the available datasets. It opens the following user interface:

1. **Filter**: The preprocesses section allows filters to be defined so that they transform the data in various ways. The filter box is used to set up the filters that are required. Weka provides a consistent user interface for the selection of filters and any other object types that are applied on the data. Once the filter is selected, the **Apply** button filters on the data based on the criteria specified in the filter.

2. **Current relation**: Once the data is loaded, the preprocesses panel shows a variety of information about the dataset:
   - **Relation**: The name of the relation as given in the file it was loaded from (@Relation in the ARFF file)
   - **Instances**: The number of records in the data
   - **Attributes**: The number of attributes (features) in the data

3. **Attributes**: This section shows all the attributes in the same sequence as they are present in the data file.

4. **Selected Attribute**: This section displays details about the selected attribute such as name, type, the % missing values, % unique values, along with minimum/maximum/mean and standard deviation for the attribute.

5. **Visualization:** This section shows the output class as a function of the selected attribute. The **Visualize All** button shows histograms for all the attributes in the data in a separate window, as follows:

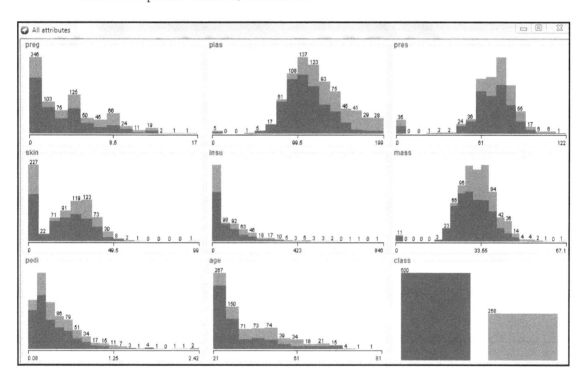

6. **Status bar**: This is a placeholder for the information and log entry based on the latest activity within the explorer

Classify

This section allows us to train different algorithms for the classification of the data into an output class. Weka provides a way to perform quick comparisons between various classification techniques. This facilitates the selection of the right algorithm, along with optimal parameters to be applied to the actual problem space. The following is a screenshot of the **Classify** section in Weka:

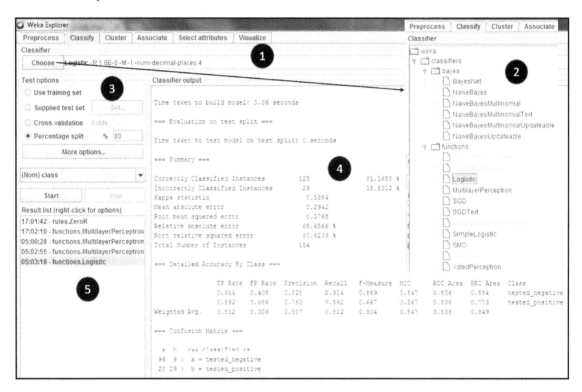

The following are the classifiers in the **Classify** section:

1. **Selecting a classifier**: This section has a text field that displays the name of the currently selected classifier.

2. **List of classifiers**: Clicking on the **Choose** button opens a list of available classifiers to select from. Weka provides a wide range of classifiers that can be seamlessly used. This can be extended very easily with the extension APIs and libraries provided by the Weka framework.

3. **Test options**: The results of applying a chosen classifier will be tested according to the options provided for testing. There are four primary test modes:

   • **Use Training Set**: The classifier is evaluated on how well it predicts the class of the instances it was trained on.

   • **Supplied Test Set**: The classifier is evaluated on how well it predicts the class of a set of instances loaded from a file.

   • **Cross Validation**: The classifier is evaluated by cross-validation, using a number of folds that are entered in the **Folds** text field.

   • **Percentage Split**: The classifier is evaluated on how well it predicts a certain percentage of the data that is held out for testing. The amount of data held out depends on the value entered in the % field.

4. **Classifier Output**: Depending on the classifier used, the output displays a variety of information:

   • **Run Information**: A list of information giving the learning scheme options, relation name, instances, attributes, and test mode that were involved in the process.

   • **Classifier Model**: A textual representation of the classification model that was produced on the full training data.

   • **Summary**: A list of statistics summarizing how accurately the classifier was able to predict the true class of instances under the chosen test mode.

   • **Detailed Accuracy by Class**: A more detailed pre-class break down of classifier's prediction accuracy.

   • **Confusion Matrix**: Shows how many instances have been assigned to each class.

Here is the classification output on logistic regression for the diabetes database:

```
=== Run information ===

Scheme: weka.classifiers.functions.Logistic -R 1.0E-8 -M -1 -num-
decimal-places 4
Relation: pima_diabetes
Instances: 768
Attributes: 9
                preg
                plas
                pres
                skin
                insu
                mass
                pedi
                age
                class
Test mode: split 80.0% train, remainder test

=== Classifier model (full training set) ===

Logistic Regression with ridge parameter of 1.0E-8
Coefficients...
                          Class
Variable tested_negative
=============================
preg -0.1232
plas -0.0352
pres 0.0133
skin -0.0006
insu 0.0012
mass -0.0897
pedi -0.9452
age -0.0149
Intercept 8.4047


Odds Ratios...
                          Class
Variable tested_negative
=============================
preg 0.8841
plas 0.9654
pres 1.0134
skin 0.9994
insu 1.0012
mass 0.9142
```

```
pedi 0.3886
age 0.9852


Time taken to build model: 0.06 seconds

=== Evaluation on test split ===

Time taken to test model on test split: 0 seconds

=== Summary ===

Correctly Classified Instances 125 81.1688 %
Incorrectly Classified Instances 29 18.8312 %
Kappa statistic 0.5384
Mean absolute error 0.2942
Root mean squared error 0.3768
Relative absolute error 65.6566 %
Root relative squared error 80.6233 %
Total Number of Instances 154

=== Detailed Accuracy By Class ===

                TP Rate FP Rate Precision Recall F-Measure MCC ROC
Area PRC Area Class
                0.914 0.408 0.828 0.914 0.869 0.547 0.836 0.884
tested_negative
                0.592 0.086 0.763 0.592 0.667 0.547 0.836 0.773
tested_positive
Weighted Avg. 0.812 0.306 0.807 0.812 0.804 0.547 0.836 0.849

=== Confusion Matrix ===

  a b <-- classified as
 96 9 | a = tested_negative
 20 29 | b = tested_positive
```

5. **Results List**: Once we run multiple tests with different classifiers within a session, the list is available for comparative analysis. Weka provides various options for the visualization of the generated classification models as follows:

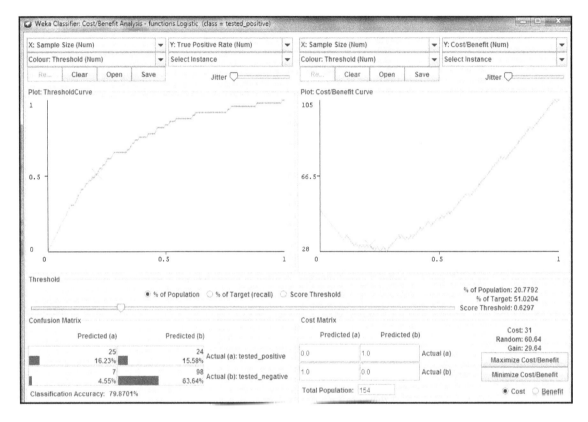

In this section, we have provided a brief introduction to the Weka framework and its intuitive graphical user interface. In the next section, we will use Weka to analyze a genetic algorithm and demonstrate how to use it for attribute search within the datasets.

Attribute search with genetic algorithms in Weka

Once again, let's select the diabetes dataset in the **Preprocess** menu and navigate to the **Select Attributes** menu. In the **Search Method** selection box, select **Genetic Search**. The configuration parameters for the **Genetic Search** can be set by right-clicking the **Search Method** text. As seen earlier in this chapter, we can tune various parameters of the algorithm and experiment with optimum performance. Here is a screenshot representing **Genetic Search** with Weka:.

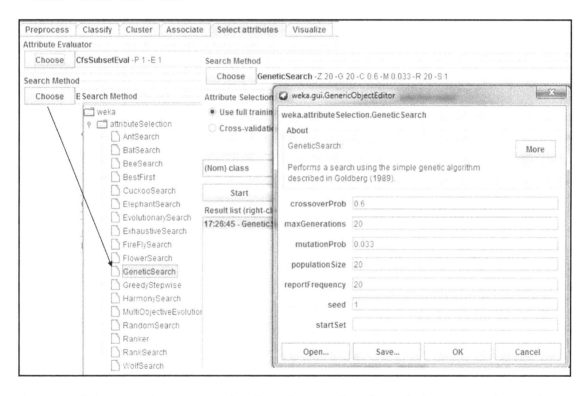

Once we click on the **Start** button, the algorithm searches through the training data and selects the relevant attributes with GA. Here is the output from the GA execution on the diabetes dataset:

```
=== Run information ===

Evaluator: weka.attributeSelection.CfsSubsetEval -P 1 -E 1
Search: weka.attributeSelection.GeneticSearch -Z 20 -G 20 -C 0.6 -M 0.033 -
```

```
R 20 -S 1
Relation: pima_diabetes
Instances: 768
Attributes: 9
                preg
                plas
                pres
                skin
                insu
                mass
                pedi
                age
                class
Evaluation mode: evaluate on all training data



=== Attribute Selection on all input data ===

Search Method:
  Genetic search.
  Start set: no attributes
  Population size: 20
  Number of generations: 20
  Probability of crossover: 0.6
  Probability of mutation: 0.033
  Report frequency: 20
  Random number seed: 1

Initial population
merit   scaled  subset
 0.0147 0 3
 0.07313 0.06963 4 8
 0.13 0.1374 2 3 6
 0.04869 0.04051 5
 0.1413 0.15086 1 2 3 6 7 8
 0.14492 0.15517 2 3 5 6 7 8
 0.08319 0.08162 6
 0.03167 0.02022 3 4
 0.02242 0.0092 7
 0.12448 0.13082 2 3 5 7 8
 0.07653 0.07368 1 8
 0.10614 0.10896 2 4 7
 0.11629 0.12106 5 6 8
 0.0147 0 3
 0.1258 0.13239 1 2
 0.13042 0.1379 1 2 4 5 8
 0.08771 0.087 5 6 7
```

```
 0.13219 0.14001 2 4 5 6
 0.10947 0.11294 2 7
 0.11407 0.11842 1 2 4 7

Generation: 20
merit   scaled  subset
 0.16427 0.18138 2 6 8
 0.16427 0.18138 2 6 8
 0.16108 0.17237 2 5 6 8
 0.15585 0.1576 1 2 6 8
 0.16427 0.18138 2 6 8
 0.14809 0.13569 2 4 5 6 8
 0.16427 0.18138 2 6 8
 0.14851 0.13688 2 3 5 6 8
 0.16427 0.18138 2 6 8
 0.10004 0 1 3 6 8
 0.14851 0.13688 2 3 5 6 8
 0.16427 0.18138 2 6 8
 0.1465 0.13119 2 5 6
 0.16108 0.17237 2 5 6 8
 0.16108 0.17237 2 5 6 8
 0.14851 0.13688 2 3 5 6 8
 0.14851 0.13688 2 3 5 6 8
 0.16427 0.18138 2 6 8
 0.15585 0.1576 1 2 6 8
 0.16427 0.18138 2 6 8

Attribute Subset Evaluator (supervised, Class (nominal): 9 class):
  CFS Subset Evaluator
  Including locally predictive attributes

Selected attributes: 2,6,7,8 : 4
                      plas
                      mass
                      pedi
                      age
```

As we can see, it is very easy to extend Weka and use it to deploy genetic algorithms and experiment with various parameters.

Frequently asked questions

Q: What is the significance of genetic algorithms to data mining?
A: With a growing number of data sources and hence an increase in volume, it is difficult to derive actionable insights from these data assets in reasonable time, despite exponentially growing computation power. We need smart algorithms to search through the solution space. Nature provides inspiration with the evolution of life on Earth. With the use of genetic algorithms we can greatly optimize the search and other data mining activities.
Q: What are the basic components of a GA?
A: Population initialization, fitness assignment, selection, crossover, mutation, and survivor selection are the basic components of a GA. We need to tune the parameter values for these components in order to find the solution in an optimized manner.

Summary

In this chapter, we have introduced the concept of genetic algorithms (GAs) and programming constructs related to GAs. These algorithms derive inspiration from the natural process of evolution. Living species evolve by inheritance, variation in partner selection, and hence attributes of the offspring and occasional (random) mutation in the genetic code (DNA structure). The same concepts are applied in the GAs in order to search the best possible solution from a vast space of possible options. The algorithm is best applied to problems where brute force is insufficient and cannot reach a solution within a reasonable time.

We have seen the structure of GAs in general and implemented a solution for a simple problem in Java. We have reviewed some of the features of the KEEL framework and how it is very easy to translate data into knowledge. KEEL is a Java-based desktop application that facilitates the analysis of the behavior of evolutionary learning in different areas of learning and preprocessing tasks, making the management of these tasks easy for the user.

We have also briefly seen the Encog framework and the API structure, and how it is very easy to extend the framework. We have also explored the Weka framework and the GUI for comparing various algorithms. Weka provides an easy-to-use and rich user interface and comes packaged with sample datasets. In the end, we realized a quick attribute search using genetic algorithms with Weka.

In the next chapter, we are once again going to seek further inspiration from nature, from the intelligent behavior of living creatures, and how some of their concepts can be used to create intelligent machines of the future.

Swarm Intelligence

9

At some point in time, all of you must have observed the behavior of ants. The way they move in a coordinated line one behind another, the way they collect and carry foods (larger than their size) to their nests, the way they form bridges to cover larger gaps. All these behaviors are remarkable considering the fact that the brains in these small creatures are nowhere close to the human brain in terms of number of neurons and hence the connections. This type of ordering is inherent to the natural processes and governed remarkably. One important point to note here is that these insects are very small and it is not in their individual capacity to achieve such larger goals. However, when they work as a group they are able to achieve such bigger goals. In light of that, these insects are also called **social insects**.

Social insects have certain prominent characteristics. They live in colonies, they have division of labor, they have strong group interactions (direct or indirect), and they are flexible. All these behaviors together are applied to achieve collective intelligence of the group. This type of phenomena has prompted researchers to work on a new way of achieving **artificial intelligence** (**AI**) named as **swarm intelligence** (**SI**). The term SI was first coined by Gerardo Beni and Jing Wang in the year 1989, in the context of cellular robotic systems. It is the field of AI that is inspired by natural behavior and coordinated functioning of smaller insects, such as ants, bees, and termites. For any SI system, there would be a colony of simple agents (same as an individual ant in an ant colony), which are also called **boids**. Each of these boids would be interacting with their neighbor and their environments (contexts) to achieve their individual goals. Together they achieve one larger goal of solving the problem at hand.

The idea of SI has appealed to researchers and they are exploring it more for applying it in solving real-world problems. In today's world, where an influx of information is uncontrollable, handling such information diligently is no longer within the capacity of a single human brain or single centralized system due to ever increasing volume of data. You are always limited by individual capacity of human race or machine hardware. SI is emerging as an alternative where information processing is distributed, autonomous, and naturally controlled. In the next few sections, you will have more clarity on how SI is solving some real-world complex problems.

We will be covering the following topics in this chapter:

- Overview of swarm intelligence
- Police swarm optimization model
- Ant colony optimization model
- Mason library
- Opt4J library
- Applications in big data analytics
- Handling dynamical data
- Multi-objective optimization

Swarm intelligence

Swarm intelligence is inspired by group behavior of species such as ants, termites, and bees. In these species, behavior of a group to achieve common bigger goals is beyond the capability of individuals who are part of the group. However, each individual in their limited capacity as per their capability helps in achieving common behavior of the group. As a group, these species behave intelligently without any excessive centralized authority or governance. In the computer science field, SI is a collection of algorithms and concepts which model and formalize such intelligent group behavior.

At a very high level, SI can be seen as a system that focuses on achieving useful smart behavior that is the outcome of the cooperative efforts of individuals who are part of a group (also called *swarm*). These individuals are called **agents**. Each of these agents is homogeneous in nature. They work asynchronously and in parallel without any centralized control or excessive governance. Overall these agents cooperate with each other either knowingly or unknowingly to achieve some specific goal that defines intelligent behavior of a group. From the perspective of AI or computer science, we can give the following definition to swarm intelligence:

> *Swarm intelligence is a collection of intelligent systems inspired by the collective intelligence of a group. This collective intelligence is achieved through the direct or indirect interactions of agents that are homogeneous in nature, yet co-operate with each other in their local environment without being aware of global context or pattern.*

While building any SI-based system there are three fundamental concepts or properties that a proposed system should at minimum comply with. These three basic properties are **self-organization** (**SO**), stigmergy, and division of labor. Let us now look into these properties one by one.

Self-organization

This is one of the most important characteristics of SI systems. SO is the property of SI systems that determines the underlying cooperation among SI agents to achieve a desired collective behavior. SO is one global behavior or phenomena that is achieved by interactions among its lower level agents or bots. These interactions are dependent on a set of rules that are incorporated based on local context or environment in which agents are functioning. These agents are not aware of any global patterns or behavior. However, the global behavior is emergent out of individual functioning of agents. The key is there is no external governing body controlling the agents' local behavior. In a nutshell, global group behavior in any SI system is achieved by the self-organizing capabilities of individual agents whose functional scope is limited to local environment. There are four basic aspects of SO. They are:

- Positive feedback
- Negative feedback
- Random behavioral fluctuations
- Multiple interactions among agents

Positive feedback is certain rules that help in building global best behavior of the swarm. For example, bee's recruitment or reinforcement of new team members for collecting better quality food from a better food source is an example of positive feedback. If a bee colony is presented with two food sources that are similar in nature with respect to food quality and are at the same distance then bees would try to collect food from both sources simultaneously. However, if one food source quality is inferior then bees would exploit the better food source first based on positive feedback received on that food source.

The other behavior that can emerge from positive feedback is that suppose a better quality food source is presented to bees in the middle of collecting food from another source, then the bee colony may abandon that food source completely or partially. They would recruit or reinforce more bees to collect food from newly identified or better food sources. This behavior that increases the survival chances for the entire community is a result of SO. Each individual bee type knows its role and responsibilities and performs actions that lead to completion of their given set of tasks.

A similar behavior of SO is also observed in ants. The ant colony as a whole is always striving to construct a nest that is safe from harsh environments and organize individual ant activities so as to locate the source of food that is nearest among all the available food sources. The ants apply a very unique and smart algorithm for locating the nearest and most abundant food source. Once the shelter (colony) is established, the most important aspect for the colony's survival is to find the nearest and most abundant source of food.

The worker ants (on their own and in a self-organized) manner, start moving out in multiple batches in independent directions. While exploring various places, they secrete a chemical called **pheromones**. While they are still exploring the food source, the quantity of pheromones is constant and is an indication that the search is still going on. As soon as a source is found, the ant traverses the path back to the colony. However, this time it secretes a varied amount of pheromones. The greater the amount of pheromone, the bigger and abundant the source of food. This signal is sufficient for other ants in the colony to start traversing the same path immediately (once again in a self-organized manner). There is no central command and control mechanism that keeps track of all the ants that are out on a specific path. However, the overall goal achievement (finding food in this case) is not dependent on the central command as far as the ants who are self-organizing. If the food source vanishes all of a sudden, the ants have a fallback plan based on the secondary food sources found by another set of ants and based on the level of pheromone on the alternate path.

As is evident, SO for fulfilling the individual responsibility is the key to survival for ants. The AI systems take a lot of inspiration from these examples and should be built with self-organizing agents with a specific job responsibility within the context of the applications environment. The important aspect though is that the individual agents operate without a leader or a centralized control based on a simple rule for its actions within the environment. These simple rules, when operating in harmony, result in intelligent behavior that is way beyond the combined sum of all individual agents' capabilities.

Stigmergy

The rules need to be reactive to the changes in the environmental state and the agent should be able to adapt to the changes autonomously and continue to perform its function. This behavior is called **stigmergy**. Without this property, the agent cannot be self-organizing and will require a centralized controlling agent. With stigmergy, the agent is made aware of the context within which it is operating even if the environment changes from the agents' previous interaction with it.

Take, for example, an ant moving on a path to the food source and there is some water poured on the path. As soon as the ant encounters water on the way, it starts looking for an alternate path based on the pheromone signal. It may also traverse its way back to the colony and then start over again on another path autonomously (without any central control). At the same time, the ant leaves traces for other ants to know that on a particular path to the food source, there is trouble on the way. Other ants immediately adapt to the change in environment based on the previous ants' experience and modify their trajectories based on the simple rules. The ants interact with each other without any explicit communication, but only with the modifications in the environmental state.

At this point, the ants apply laws of reinforcement learning that we explored in the previous chapter. On the way to the food source and back, the ant is constantly adapting to the environment based on the reward for each individual action and state of the environment. The goal for the individual agent (an ant, in this case) is to maximize the reward (locate the food source or fetch food back to the colony) autonomously.

Division of labor

This is the most fundamental aspect of SI. The individual agent within the swarm is extremely limited in its capability to achieve the goal for the entire swarm. The natural system applies division of labor with individual agents performing a set of very specific responsibilities that contribute to the overall success of the swarm.

For example, all the bees in a hive are not doing the same thing. There is a clear division of labor within the bee hive based on the type of the bee. The Queen bee is responsible for laying eggs, the male drones are responsible for reproduction, and the worker bees build the hive and work to get food for the entire population. They also take care of the Queen bee and the drones by feeding them. In AI systems each individual agent needs to be programmed to have its own rules based on the environmental context to perform a specific set of duties. With the division of labor, the parallel processing systems can efficiently work and distribute the work loads without missing the sight of the overall reward and the goal.

With this background with SI, let us look at some of the advantages of collective intelligence for maximizing the rewards.

Advantages of collective intelligent systems

Collective intelligent systems have the following advantages:

- **Flexibility**: The agents have their individual rules for operation within the context of its environment. The agent responds to changes in the environment and then the entire population demonstrates flexibility in order to adapt to the change in environment.
- **Robustness**: Since the agents are individually a very small unit within the whole, even if one agent fails, the community does not suffer and the overall goal can possibly be achieved.
- **Scalability**: Since the individual agents are small units of independent work, it is possible to scale from hundreds to thousands to millions of such intelligent agents based on the use case and achieve exponentially higher returns and cumulative intelligence.
- **De-centralization**: Since there is no central control in the colony, the agents can be deployed onto the edge of the computation (realistic scenario in case of IoT use cases). Unlike a distributed computing framework where a central node server needs to be incrementally powerful, in the case of SI, there is no need for a centralized control since the agents work based on rules within the environment.
- **Self-organization**: The possible solutions that deploy algorithms based on SI can evolve and adapt to the changes in the environment and emerge without being predefined.

- **Adaptation**: The agents and system as a whole can adapt and adjust to the predefined environment along with the new changes in the environment. The adaptation is also a unique feature of the individual agent instead of being centrally controlled.
- **Agility and speed**: The intelligence system based on swarm algorithms demonstrate agility and improved speed with every interaction with the environment.

While designing the systems based on SI, there are certain guiding principles that need to be followed for developing self-sufficient systems.

Design principles for developing SI systems

The design principles to be taken into consideration for developing SI systems are as follows:

- **Proximity principle**: The individual agents within the swarm should be able to communicate back to the population center in a reasonable time while exploring the search space individually. For example, an ant in search of food should be able to report back to the colony, as soon as a food source is found. This reporting needs to happen in a time-sensitive manner for the food source to be relevant. The proximity principle defines an implicit demographic boundary for the members.
- **Quality principle**: While the independent agents get to a solution independently within the search space, the swarm should be able to determine the quality of the solution and move in that direction. Once again, if multiple ants find a food source each they come back with different levels of pheromones on the way in proportion to the quality and quantity of the food source. This helps the group as a whole to decide which food source to go to. However, there is no central command that determines the quality standard and decides the path. On the other hand, the agents communicate and collaborate to reach the right source of food.

- **Diverse response principle**: While the agents are solving a common problem, they should not be focused on a small region within the overall search space. They must be enabled for exploration while exploiting the previously understood patterns. The swarm should look to diversify with a certain threshold that defines the survival boundary of an individual agent.
- **Adaptability principle**: The swarm as a whole should be able to adapt to the changes in environment. The agents should organize themselves in tune with the changing environment.

With the basic understanding of the SI fundamentals, let us understand two of the algorithms that can be used for building artificial agents that work in a size-able group to perform collectively large tasks.

The particle swarm optimization model

The **particle swarm optimization** (**PSO**) model is inspired by flocking of birds and the schooling movement of fish. The goal of the PSO model is to find an optimum solution (food source or a place to live) within a dynamic space. The swarm starts at a random location and a random velocity and is based on the collective behavior by exploring and exploiting the search space. The unique feature of PSO is that the agents operate in a formation that optimizes the search and also minimizes the collective effort in converging to an optimum solution. The agents within a swarm that follows the PSO model follow some of the guideline principles:

- **Separation**: Each individual agent is programmed in a way that it is able to keep a sufficient distance with the flock-mates so that they do not run into each other and at the same time, maintain a separate existence space for itself to be part of a formation in search of an optimum solution. The agent follows the nearest neighbor in order to adjust its position and velocity in order to ensure the right level of separation.
- **Alignment**: Each individual agent aligns with the swarm's overall pattern formation and the average group velocity within the search space.

As a general principle, each member in the swarm that follows the PCO model communicates its experience continuously to the group as a whole and to the nearest neighbors in particular. The agent has a view of the nearest members and their behavior and learning pattern. The agent either influences the movement (position and velocity) of the neighboring agents based on the observations and suitability of its experience within the search space for local optimal solution or adjusts its movement based on a better experience for the nearest members. The core principle is alignment with nearest neighbors and hence the entire swarm as a whole in the interest of the larger goal. Originally, the PSO was proposed as an optimization algorithm within real-value continuous search space and it is now expanded to also deal with binary or discrete search use cases. The core algorithm is defined by the velocity and position equations as follows:

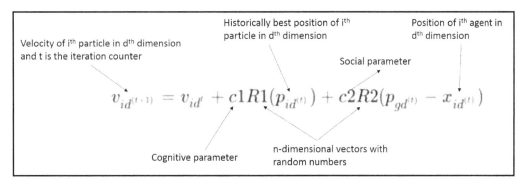

Figure 9.1 Velocity function in PSO

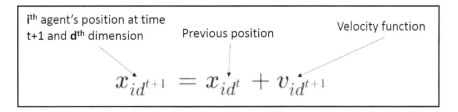

Figure 9.2 Position function in PSO

In order to define the velocity (rate of change of location for an individual agent) two parameters play a major role. The best position across a timeline for the individual agent is represented by $P_{id^{(t)}}$ and $P_{gd^{(t)}}$, which represent the position of the best agent within a swarm's global position within the environmental context. When these two parameters contribute to overall velocity of the swarm, it is the optimum velocity for searching the solution within the space provided that the environment is deterministic.

However, in case of a stochastic environment the factors *R1* and *R2* play a role for adjusting to the changes in the state of the environment. These parameters introduce the required randomness in the swarm in order to explore the search space in an efficient manner. c1 and c2 are the cognitive and social parameters that represent relative importance of a particular agent with respect to the best position of the swarm. The relative values of these parameters constantly move an individual agent to the best position within the swarm even if the environment undergoes a change. The effect of relative difference between c1 and c2 can be represented as follows:

c1	c2	Exploration level
High	High	High exploration in distant regions
Small	Small	Refined search and lower level of exploration
High	Small	Bias towards a particular agent's global best position
Small	High	Bias towards a swarm's global best position

The velocity function has three distinct components:

- **Inertia** (v_{id}^t): Inertia is the resistance of any physical object to any change in its state of motion. This includes changes to the object's speed, direction, or state of rest.

  The velocity in time *t+1* is a function of time *t*. Which means the swarm is not allowed to change the velocity abruptly. Instead, there is a gradual change in velocity depending on the environmental change or if the swarm needs to change the velocity in order to navigate effectively through the search space. Due to this inertia, we observe that the swarm of birds continue in the same direction most of the time and move in a formation since velocity of the agent in time *t+1* is dependent on velocity of the agent at time *t*. This term is also very important for changing the global best agent within the swarm. When an agents' fitness function is more optimum compared to a swarm's global fitness, the agent takes the position as global best agent within the swarm. During the transition, ($p_i = x_i = p_g$) the social expression in the equation becomes zero ($p_{id(t)} - x_{id(t)} = p_{ig(t)} - x_{id(t)} = 0$). At this point the new agent becomes the global best particle by moving with the new velocity and hence changing the position within the swarm.

- **Self-knowledge** ($p_{id^{(t)}} - x_{id^{(t)}}$): This component of the velocity function defines an agents' individuality within the swarm. This translates into the level of attraction for a particle to its own global best value that optimizes the search through the solution space.
- **Social-knowledge** ($p_{gd^{(t)}} - x_{id^{(t)}}$): This component of the velocity function defines adaption to the social behavior among all the agents. With this expression, grade of group learning and experience sharing between the individual members is defined.

The PSO model can be represented as follows:

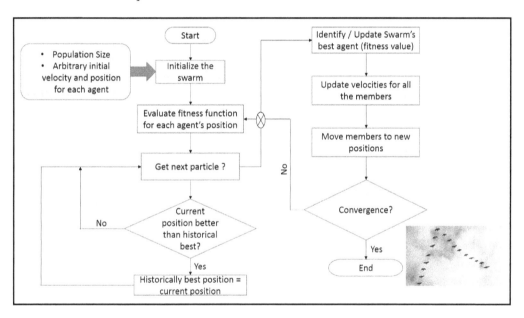

Figure 9.3 PSO model

PSO implementation considerations

We need to have the following PSO implementation considerations:

- PSO stores an agent's best position in a considerable and relevant timeline along with the global best position for the swarm. With this, the agent with a maximum fitness score has an influence on the overall behavior of the swarm and the convergence is fast.

- PSO is a simple algorithm to implement since the mathematical equations for velocity and position are easy to implement due to inherent simplicity.
- PSO can adapt to the changes in environment very efficiently by adjusting the velocity and positions of the members quickly through each iteration.

Ant colony optimization model

The **ant colony optimization** (**ACO**) is another widely used and adapted variation of the SI algorithms. At its minimum, the objective of the ant colony or the artificial agent swarms is to set out in search for an asset (food in case of ants and a package in case of a robot colony in a retailer warehouse) in an optimum way so as to traverse minimum distance to and from the asset and the base location. This model is useful with surveillance drones, autonomous car route planning, and so on.

Let us understand some of the operating principles in an ant colony and get introduced to the terminologies so that those can be applied in designing artificial swarms based on the ACO model. Here is a figure of an **Ant colony** and a **Food source**:

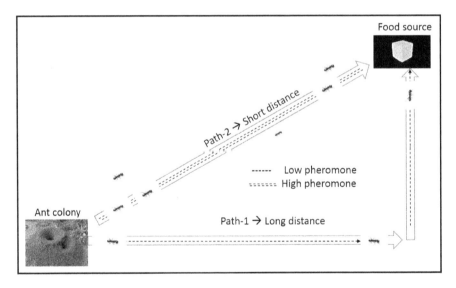

Figure 9.4 Ant colony representation and terms

In this example, there is food source in the vicinity of the ant colony. There are two paths to the food. **Path-1** is a long distance to the **Food source** and **Path-2** is the shortest distance. The ants begin exploration of the search space independently. Each ant that sets out has a task to find the food source. A few ants take the long route and find the food source and on the way secrete a pheromone trail. As the ants return to the colony, other ants get a signal that the food source is found and they start traversing the path. Meanwhile, the ants on the shorter path return faster than the ones on the long path and more ants start traversing the short path since the effective time is less. Over a period of time, the ants on the short distance accumulate more pheromone on the way, which signals to the colony that the food source is more optimum in terms of distance as well as the quality. With time, the pheromone on the long distance path evaporates and the path ceases to exist. Eventually, the ants stop traversing the long path to the food source and the collective behavior of the colony is fully optimized.

When we imitate the concepts of natural ants and their optimization techniques for designing artificial agents, the concepts can be enhanced and further optimized based on the environment. For example, the natural ants do not have any memory. They operate within the set of rules that define their movement and the overall behavior (pheromone secretion). The artificial ants (agents) can have limited memory that stores the rewards based on the past actions and hence the intelligent behavior can be enhanced. The natural ants are subject to ecological modifications and constraints. For example, water drops on the way to the food source. The artificial agents are not subject to the ecological modifications and normally run within a controlled and predictable environment. The artificial agents simulate the patterns from the natural ants by depositing the pheromone on the way in order to reinforce the behavior onto the other agents.

The artificial agents also traverse the path with more pheromone concentration and supplement it with the memory component for optimum behavior. In the case of artificial ants, the pheromone is evaporated quickly in order for the colony to explore further optimizations. This is unlike the real ants that are at work with survival as the basic instinct. The core intuition while developing the ACO-based agents is based on a fitness function that defines the actions for the agents that return maximum pheromone levels on the way. It is also seen as a cost optimization problem that reduces the cumulative cost for the colony to reach the target within the search space.

At the algorithm level, the individual agent works based on a probability rule that helps to select components (sequential steps) that utilize the pheromone levels on the way and the environmental variations. While the artificial ants move through the solution space based on the probability function, it needs to also determine the amount of pheromone for it to deposit. The probability rule is called the **state transition rule**:

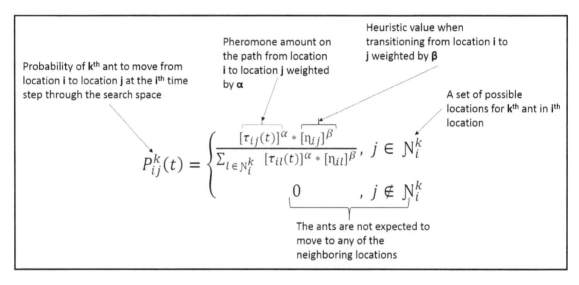

Figure 9.5 Mathematical representation of ACO

In the following equation, α and β are the parameters that control the overall impact of pheromone and heuristic approach in deriving the probability function. This is similar to `c1` and `c2` values in PSO. The effect of relative difference between α and β can be represented as follows:

α	β	Effect on convergence
High	Low	Pheromone information is important. For an agent, there is a higher possibility of choosing the actions and positions that are previously taken by other agents. This may lead to saturation of many agents in the same region and hence reducing the swarm's potential to explore the search space and hence obtaining sub-optimum results.
Low	High	The algorithm behaves as a stochastic multi-greedy algorithm with the individual members of the colony seemingly in charge of finding the optima on their own with low level of co-operation and limited learning from each other's path traversal.

Zero	High	In this case, the algorithm operates as a stochastic greedy algorithm with individual members in charge and with zero learning from others' path traversal. The node with minimum cost will get a preference and there is no weight-age given to the pheromone level on the path.
High	Zero	In this case, the algorithm operates same as the natural ants where the guiding principle is pheromone only and there is no heuristic information utilized in searching through the problem space.

MASON Library

Multi-Agent Simulation Of Neighborhoods or **Networks** (**MASON**) is a Java-based multi-agent simulation library that has a generic API library in order to easily simulate SI algorithms in particular and any general algorithm that explores the search space with the use of independent agents in general. This library is created by George Mason at the University's Center for Social Complexity and Department of Computer Science. It provides a fast and portable core written in Java programming language and is supported by visualization framework for hypothesis testing and visualization. It is a handy framework for modeling new architectures and algorithms. The design goals for the MASON library are:

- Provide a large number of simulations and configurable experiments. The library is very easy to extend for additional simulations and use cases.
- High Degree of modularity and flexibility—the framework is built as a layered architecture and it deploys object oriented fundamentals for keeping the responsibilities of the individual building blocks loosely coupled.
- Separate visualization tools—the framework has a visualization layer that is separate from the code engine and can also be extended based on the use case and the context of the application hypothesis that is being tested.

MASON is a multi-purpose event simulator that runs as a single process that efficiently supports a large number of agents. The applications of MASON are as diverse as modeling social complexity, physical modeling of the search space, and agent interactions with the environment, independent and abstract agents that can be programmed to follow basic rules, and operate as a member of a swarm. The framework is handy for AI and ML research and simulations.

MASON Layered Architecture

MASON has implemented a layered architecture with distinct components that are loosely coupled and integrated with a generic interface. The following figure shows various components within the layered architecture:

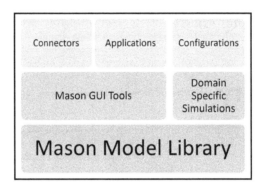

Figure 9.6 Mason library components

Primarily, the MASON library contains two main components, the model library and the visualization framework. The visualization support 2D as well 2D rendering. The model and the visualizations are totally separated and the models can be independently executed and results returned to the console or the output files. The UI is loosely coupled and works based on the current states of the objects within the model objects.

Instead of taking a top-down approach that starts with user interface and initiates the model, the MASON framework keeps the model and visualization components fully independent. This approach gives flexibility to create different visualizations (Java based or if required, web based) as required. One of the core features implemented by Mason is checkpointing. The model can be serialized to the disk and can be invoked on an entirely different platform at a different time and it is initialized to the same state. This facilitates a great deal of interoperability and collaboration among research teams. Here is another representation of the MASON architecture:

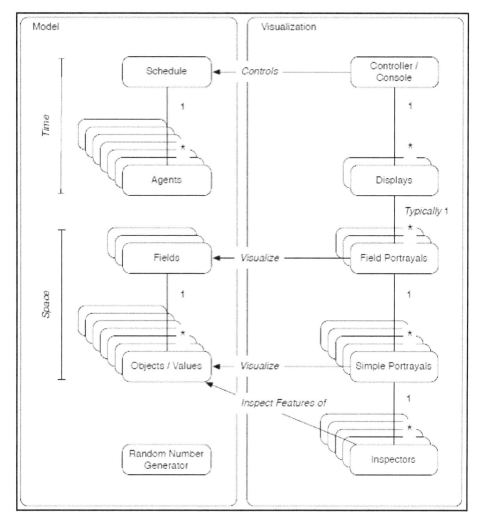

Figure 9.7 MASON Architecture (Source: Mason official manual)

The MASON library provides a simple API to create new simulations. In order to create a new agent object, it needs to extend the `sim.engine.SimState` class. The simplest skeleton implementation is as follows:

```
import sim.engine.*;

public class SWARMAgent extends SimState{

   public SWARMAgent(long seed){
      super(seed);
```

```
    }
    // method used for initialization of the model including the
  configurations and the UI
    public void start(){
       super.start();
    }
    public static void main(String[] args){
       doLoop(SWARMAgent.class, args);
       System.exit(0);
    }
  }
```

MASON creates a global state of the simulation instance as a subclass of `SimState`. The `SimState` encapsulates an event scheduler (`sim.engine.Schedule`). The agents are scheduled with the instance of the `sim.engine.Schedule` class to be stepped. The scheduler is the representation of time for the simulator.

The Mason library contains a set of pre-built simulations. Let us look at the ant colony optimization simulation in the MASON library. This is an implementation of the simple scenario we have seen in figure 9.4, *Ant colony representation and terms*. The search space contains two obstacles, a food source and the colony location. Various parameters such as number of ants and others are configurable as follows:

Figure 9.8 Ant Foraging configuration

Once the simulation starts, the ants get onto a random path individually and deposit a pheromone trail on the way. The high value of evaporation constant ensures that the ants explore the search space instead of gravitating to the already explored paths. As soon as the first ant finds the food source, it starts traversing back and forth between the food source and the base location once again leaving a pheromone trail both ways. The ants are programmed to follow the pheromone trail and eventually the model converges and the ants get on the optimized shortest path. The following figure shows the ACO simulation:

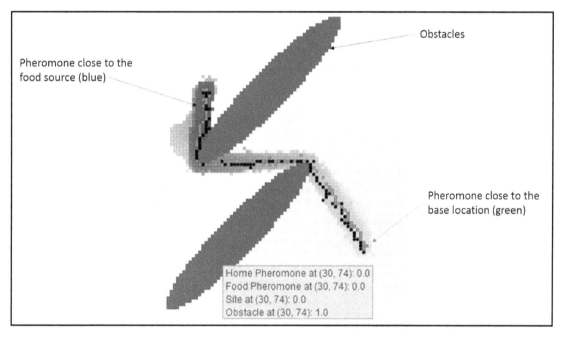

Figure 9.9 ACO Simulation in MASON

MASON library has many more simulations pre-built into the package and we can explore these and experiment with various options. The API can be used for extending the scope of the application with minimum code and leveraging the framework capabilities and the visualization layer. In the next section, we will briefly review another framework, Opt4J, which is primarily built for evolutionary computing and can also be used for experimenting with SI algorithms.

Opt4J library

Opt4J is a modular framework for meta-heuristic optimization that can be applied to a range of evolutionary algorithms. In the context of this chapter, we are looking at implementing SI algorithms such as ACO and PSO using the library. The libraries that deal with optimization problems have three primary components at abstract level. Creator, decoder, and evaluator. The creator provides random genotypes (please refer to `Chapter 8`, *Genetic Programming*, for details on genotype and phenotypes) from the search space. They represent agents in case of SI algorithms. The agents are created by the *creator object*.

The Opt4J library provides an `org.opt4j.optimizers.mopso.Particle` class that works as a creator. The agents within the swarm are the instances of this class that are actually created by a factory class' `org.opt4j.optimizers.mopso.ParticleFactory`. The decoder transforms a genotype to a phenotype. The decoder converts the abstract characteristics into tangible objects and associate behavior patterns with those. Based on the phenotype, the evaluator defines the quality of the current agent in case of the PSO algorithm, the evaluator function returns the velocity and position for the agent and determines if it is the best position and velocity within the swarm. Once the core components are defined, the framework can handle the optimization problem. The architectural components of the Opt4J libraries are as follows (Source: *Opt4J documentation*):

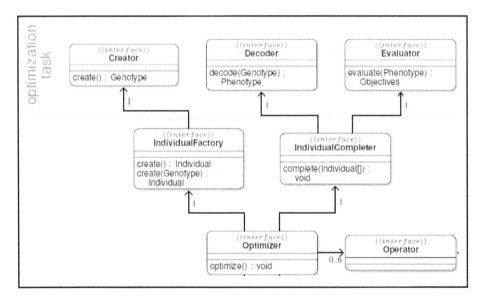

Figure 9.10 Architectural Components of Opt4J (Source: Opt4J documentation)

Opt4J provides a simple and intuitive UI for loading the models and also visualizing in a limited manner:

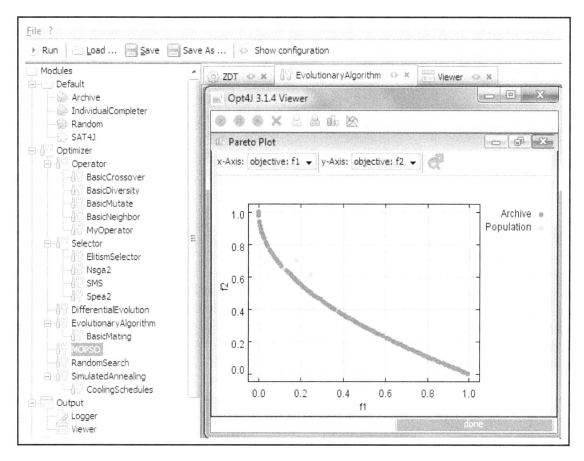

Figure 9.11 Model Visualization with Opt4J

We are at the verge of a data revolution and the data volumes from heterogeneous sources are increasing day by day. Even though the parallel processing frameworks along with cloud computing are getting better at processing more data, the brute force technique will not be able to cope with the growth in data volume. We will need to apply smart techniques inspired by nature such as genetic programming, reinforcement learning, and SI to deal with big data. In the next section, we will look at some possible use cases in dealing with big data and underlying computational assets.

Applications in big data analytics

Every passing minute, we are gathering more data across the globe and we now have computing power to store and process the data assets. Let us briefly understand the fundamental architecture of big data systems. In the current form, the big data computing framework is an enormous collection of computation nodes that are distributed across the globe. There are two primary distinctions within the deployments. The systems can be deployed on-premise for the enterprises and there is a paradigm shift towards cloud computing where the compute infrastructure is virtualized and it is geographically distributed in various regions.

The independent units of compute are termed as **nodes**. The nodes are interconnected and controlled by a centralized computation unit that keeps track of all the nodes and various operations on these nodes. There is a similarity between the natural swarms and the big data nodes in that the nodes are independent work units. However, the similarity ends there. The nodes in a big data deployment are governed by one or more master nodes and worker nodes work in synchronization based on the instructions from the master node. As we have seen in this chapter, the natural swarms (ant colonies, and fleet of birds, and so on) do not have a central command and the individual members (agents) work in an autonomous manner based on the rules and the agents are able to adjust themselves based on the stochastic nature of the environment in which they operate. The concepts of SI can be applied in securing the big data infrastructure as well as ensuring that the nodes are fully balanced. In the mainstream approach, a computation job is first submitted to the master node and it in turn breaks it down into multiple chunks to be performed by the data or compute nodes.

At this point, the jobs are executed independently by the slave nodes. Based on the resource available with the slave nodes, the jobs finish at different times and require varied degrees of computation and storage. Eventually it may happen that the core compute load is not evenly distributed across nodes. Based on some of the concepts we have learned in this chapter, here is a generic (ACO) algorithm based on SI that can be deployed in the distributed computing environment. With this algorithm the general process be:

- **Reproduction**: This is a process by which new artificial ants are generated. The controller checks the platform periodically and generates ants based on the load on the cluster nodes. If the nodes are overloaded or underloaded, new ants are generated for carrying the message across.

- **Exploration**: In this process, the agents are independently in charge of finding the nodes that are overloaded. They can trace through the network and check the operating parameters and on the way leave a trial of simulated pheromone (incremental counter) for the other members of the swarm to get notified about the overloaded or underloaded node(s).

The ants in this swarm move forward and backward (same as the natural ants that move from the colony to the food source in both directions). For the sake of simplicity in the load balancing algorithm, two distinct types of ants move in each direction with independent tasks at hand. The forward moving ant is responsible for finding a node that is overloaded or underloaded. This agent starts from the same position (node) at which it was born and starts exploring the space. The agent that moves backwards carries a signal (quantifiable pheromone) and creates a trail on the way that notifies that a particular node is overloaded or underloaded. For simplicity, in our model, the agent that moves backwards is generated only when a target node (which requires load balancing) is encountered. A forward moving agent is generated within the process of the target node when the threshold of node activity is reached (high as well as low).

With this background and the basic understanding about the approach, the load balancing flow for the distributed computing environment can be broken down into the following steps:

- The agents calculate and quantify the load (under and over) on the node at which it is currently connected.
- Start in the direction of a random new node to calculate its suitability for load balancing.
- The backward ant is generated when a candidate node is found. This agent updates the pheromone information in order to leave a trail of target nodes.
- Calculate the collective requirement for load balancing based on the candidate nodes found by the agents.
- Balance the load on the cluster.

The load balancing algorithm can be depicted as follows:

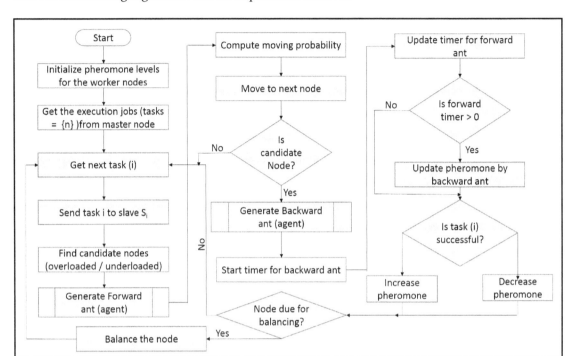

Figure 9.12 Load Balancing Algorithm flowchart

The applicability of SI is even greater in the case of IoT where the computation is moving towards the edge and the sensors that collect data can be treated as the members of the swarm and perform independent operations for the overall benefit of the system by operating based on fuzzy rules instead of hardcoded functions. The edge devices can be programmed with capabilities to explore and exploit within their working environment in order to collectively achieve some of the predefined goals.

We have so far seen the optimization of big data processing in regards to the volume and distributed computing. However, there are two more important aspects of big data, which are variety and velocity of the data. Variety and velocity of the data requires dealing with the big data multi-dimensional problem. In the next section, we will briefly review handling of dynamical data and multi-objective optimization when there is more than one objective (as in the case of real scenarios) for the data processing system.

Handling dynamical data

With increasing sources of data, there is a quest of finding meaning from it and utilizing it for better decision making and deriving autonomous actions. However, as the number of dimensions and input variables increase, the search through the solution space becomes computationally intensive and application of simply the brute force and distributed computing is not sufficient. We can leverage SI algorithms in order to tag the important dimensions with higher weights impacting the overall outcome. In this particular scenario, the velocity of the data generation adds a level of complexity due to the variation in the data that is received.

Some of the challenges that need to be solved when designing the swarm of artificial agents are related to the dynamic target space, the state of the environment changes very rapidly (even after an optimization is performed and the pheromone level is decided by the intelligent agent). Once the swarm finds global optima, the actual value may change dynamically. This requires a different set of rules to be built into the agents, which address the dynamism of the environment. At this point, the algorithm needs to evolve to consider the increased cost of optimization within the dynamic search space and trade it off with the quality of the solution that is obtained. The artificial agents require a level of fuzziness built in its objective function in order to effectively deal with dynamical data.

Multi-objective optimization

So far in this chapter, we have taken the examples of the problem with one objective (finding a food source for an ant colony). However, in real-world scenarios, often there is more than one objective that needs to be met by the individual agents as well as the swarm. For example, in the case of honey bees they need to look for the food source, gather the food, and find a safe and viable place for the beehive. One objective is fulfilled at the cost of another objective. The agent should be programmed to consider the trade-off in the larger interest of the swarm.

As far as possible, the optimization function for the agent should bring optimum solution for more than one objective, but it is not feasible to mutual exclusivity. In such cases, the agent should be able to operate without a central control and decide the objective weightage based on the environmental context and should favor the objective that will fulfill the swarm's overall objective for an elongated period instead of deciding based on a short-term strategy. The goal of the optimization as a whole is to reach Pareto Optimality for the swarm:

Pareto optimality is a formally defined concept used to determine when an allocation is optimal. An allocation is not Pareto optimal if there is an alternative allocation where improvements can be made to at least one participant's well-being without reducing any other participant's well-being. If there is a transfer that satisfies this condition, the reallocation is called a Pareto improvement. When no further Pareto improvements are possible, the allocation is a Pareto optimum.

Frequently asked questions

Q: What is the difference between distributed computing paradigm and swarm intelligence? In the case of distributed computing, we also divide the work units in chunks that are processed by individual nodes.

A: The basic difference between these two types of systems is that the distributed computing systems are centrally controlled. There is a master node or processing unit that keeps track of all the worker nodes and allocated work units based on their availability. The frameworks also maintain a level of redundancy so that the system is reliable in case of failure of one of the worker nodes. In case of intelligent swarm behavior demonstrated by social creatures, there is not centralized control and all the agents operate independently within their operating principles. The agents are self-organizing and collaborate intuitively and implicitly instead of an explicit collaboration managed by a central controlling unit.

Q: How do systems based on SI algorithms mimic the natural phenomenon such as pheromone generation?

A: Pheromone is a chemical that is secreted by ants on their way to and from the food source, which signals to other ants that there is a food source around. This chemical is the primary mechanism in which the ants communicate with each other and varying concentration of pheromone indicates different things to the ants. In case of artificial agents, the agent maintains a quantification of pheromone as a numeric value that is incremented to indicate additional pheromones and there is also a process for evaporation that is based on a time parameter. In a way, the behavior is simulated to match the natural phenomenon.

Q: What are some of the use cases and the real applications of artificial swarm intelligence?

A: The principles of SI can be applied to a diverse set of problems and use cases across industries. We have already seen a use case in distributed computing for balancing the load of the nodes. We can also deploy SI algorithms in logistic planning and supply chain optimization, network and communication routers, intelligent traffic and fleet control, optimizing factory operations, and workforce optimization in customer services operations.

Summary

In this chapter, we have seen an interesting aspect in building AI. Nature has the best algorithm when it comes to harmoniously managing an extremely complex ecosystem that has a massive scale. We take inspiration from nature and some of the smallest creatures that have tiny brains and hence a very small number of neurons compared to human beings. However, these small creatures are able to collectively achieve feats that are far bigger than the sum of their individual capabilities. The operating principles of these community creatures cannot be ignored when we are on a quest to build AI systems that complement and augment human capabilities.

In this chapter, we have seen some of the fundamental concepts of natural swarm intelligence and some of the principles we need to consider while developing modern systems based on SI. We have tried to represent the collective behaviors in a mathematical form and derive some of the patterns in developing the algorithmic behavior for the artificial agents with PSO and ACO algorithms. In this chapter, we have reviewed two computational frameworks and libraries, MASON and Opt4J, which can be easily leveraged for various experiments and advanced analysis. These libraries provide effective visualization layers. We have covered a use case for load balancing the servers in a distributed computing environment.

In the next chapter, we will once again derive inspiration from nature and look at an important algorithm called **reinforcement learning**. Unlike supervised learning, reinforcement learning leverages reward and punishment as the inputs for learning behavior for the artificial agents.

10
Reinforcement Learning

In `Chapter 3`, *Learning from Big Data*, we were introduced to two fundamental types of machine learning techniques: supervised learning and unsupervised learning. In case of the supervised learning, a model is trained based on the historical data (observations) for predicting the outcomes based on the new data inputs. In the case of unsupervised learning, the model tries to derive patterns within the datasets and define logical grouping boundaries in order to separate the solution space. There is a third type of machine learning algorithm that is equally important for the evolution of artificial intelligence.

Remember the process of learning to ride a bicycle. We observe another person who is riding a bicycle, create a mental model on how to do it, and attempt it ourselves. It is not possible to just get the balancing and movement on a bicycle right in the first attempt. We (actor) try for the first time (action) on the road (environment) and may fall down (reward). We try over and over again with different balance on the left and right side with different speed and strategy to pedal and this time may go some more distance (higher reward) and finally get the cycling right (goal!). This process when repeated a number of times reinforces the right set of actions based on the environmental conditions at a particular point in time in order to maximize the reward.

The process we have just visualized is called reinforcement learning. This is the third fundamental category of machine learning algorithms, which we are going to study in this chapter. In this chapter, we will understand:

- The concept of reinforcement learning algorithms
- Q-learning
- SARSA learning
- Deep reinforcement learning

Reinforcement learning algorithms concept

Let's create a simplistic model for reinforcement learning with an introduction of the basic terminologies:

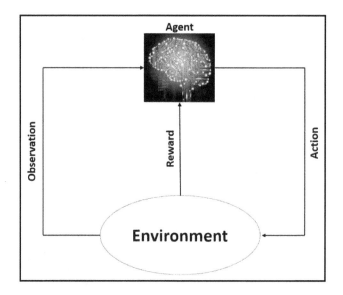

At each step and time (t), the agent:

- Executes action a_t
- Receives observation o_t
- Receives a reward r_t

At each step and time (t), the environment:

- Receives action a_t
- Generates observation $ot+1$
- Generates scalar reward r_{t+1}

The environment is considered to be non-deterministic (action a_t based on o_t will receive reward r_t and the same action in the same state may result in different rewards).

The agent (intelligent machine) is connected to the environmental context with its observation and action. The agent perceives the environment in a unique-to-itself manner and decides the action based on some of the popular and evolving techniques. At each step in time, the agent receives signals that represent the state of the environment.

The agent responds with an action that is one among several possible options at that point in time. The action generates an output that changes the state of the environment. Remember the results pyramid from the first chapter? If the agent needs better results it has to take the right actions based on the environment and overall goal for its existence. The change in state of the environment due to an agent's action is communicated back to the agent with a reinforcement signal r. The overall result is a combination of discrete actions that the agent needs to choose to maximize or increase the sum of reward (reinforcement signal). This is learned over a period of time based on trial and error strategies supported by some of the evolutionary algorithms.

With this background, we can clearly see that there are two distinct ways in which reinforcement learning can be achieved:

- **Use genetic algorithm and programming**: In this approach, the agent searches within the space of possible pathways to the optimal solution or action based on the environmental context. While use of a genetic algorithm model tends to eliminate dependence on the brute-force for achieving an agent's overall goal of maximizing rewards, this approach at time yields sub-optimized actions for the agent.
- **Use statistical techniques and dynamic programming model**: This is the approach taken by modern computational paradigm of distributed computing and parallel processing in development of the agents that outperform human intelligence at some challenging tasks (games such as Chess and Go).

There is a fundamental difference between reinforcement learning and supervised learning models. In the case of supervised learning, we have access to historical data that maps the independent variables to the output variable(s). This historical data is used as input for training the supervised learning model. The model is then able to predict the output value for a new set of input datasets. In the case of reinforcement learning, the agent needs to search within the available solution space and does not have access to a historical set of actions that have resulted in maximum reward. A hybrid approach in which the starting point for the agent is a trained model that eliminates some of the search space and the agent can reach the goal (maximizing reward) for a set of environmental transitions in a more optimized manner seems to be the preference for building machine intelligence.

The state transition for the environment based on the agent's actions can be visualized as follows:

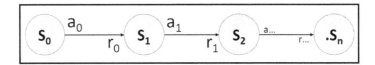

The overall goal for the reinforcement learning algorithm is to derive a policy P to maximize the sum of reward for all the actions combined:

$$\mathbb{P} = Max(\sum_{t=0}^{n} r(t))$$

There are two primary strategies that an algorithm needs to apply for reinforcement learning. Imagine reinforcement learning as navigating through a maze in which we get positive and negative rewards along the way. We derive the navigation policy with exploration and trace the path back if the rewards are decreased over multiple actions. This technique is called exploration with focus on rewards. However, simply following a path of maximum reward within the limited visibility into the maze, we cannot reach the end state of finding the optimum path out.

We need to exploit unknown territories at random to venture into new directions. This is formally termed as exploitation of the search space. A combination of exploration and exploitation steps leads to the overall goal of reinforcement learning. While the agent applies exploration and exploitation to meet an overall objective of maximizing the rewards, there needs to be a consideration for optimum behavior. There are three distinct modes in which the agent can optimize the search through the solution space within the visible environment:

- **Finite horizon model**: At any given point in time the agent cannot have visibility of the entire search space. The agent breaks the search for maximum reward for the next *m* steps:

$$\mathbb{P} = Max(\sum_{t=0}^{m} r(t))$$

The agent does not worry about the steps beyond the mth step in future. In this approach, the agent has a **non-stationary policy** that may be subject to change depending on the state of the environment that is encountered. At this point the agent takes *m*-step optimal action, which is the best sequence of actions for *m* steps in reinforcement. On the next step, the agent optimizes for *m-1* steps and so on to the end of the limited search space.

- **Infinite horizon model**: The notable difference in this model is that the search space and the state transitions are considered to be infinite. The model is trained with long-term reward maximization in mind over the entire search space. The rewards are discounted in the geometric proportion as per a discount factor β with a value range between 0 and 1:

$$\mathbb{P} = Max(\sum_{t=0}^{\infty} \beta^t r(t))$$

- **Average reward model**: In this case, the agent takes actions based on optimum value of average reward across action steps. This is a limiting case of the infinite horizon model and it is considered to be more conservative in terms of digression to an un-optimized solution in the interim.

When the algorithm follows one of the models, the performance is measured with three basic criteria:

- **Slow and eventual convergence to optimal**: The agent that initiates the learning slowly and eventually converges to optimum state with action steps for maximum reward are less preferred compared to the ones that converge to 90% optimal behavior quickly.
- **Measure of speed of convergence to optimal**: Since the state of optimal is uncertain, the speed of convergence needs to be a relative and subjective measure and a function of acceptable differential from global optima or near-optimality. We can also measure level of performance after a given amount of time or action steps. There is normally a period of time during which mistakes do not occur and hence the minimum time needs to be carefully selected within the context of the environment in which the agent is operating. At times, it becomes an inappropriate measure if the agent operates within the environment for an elongated amount of time. It is also possible that the agent pays a high penalty during the overall learning period. A model that converges quickly to the threshold performance and accuracy can be selected with this measure.

Reinforcement learning techniques

With this background in reinforcement learning, in the next few sections we are going to look at some of the formal techniques for exploration into the search space with the goal of maximizing the rewards in an optimal way.

Markov decision processes

In order to understand the **Markov decision processes** (**MDPs**), let us define two environment types:

- **A deterministic environment**: In a deterministic environment, an action taken within a particular state of the environment determines a certain outcome. For example, in the game of chess out of all the possible moves at the beginning of the game, when we move a pawn from e4 to e5, the immediate next step is certain and does not differ across various games. There is also a level of certainty of reward in a deterministic environment along with the next possible state(s).
- **A stochastic environment**: In the case of a stochastic environment, there is always a level of randomness and uncertainty in terms of next state of the environment based on the agent's action in the previous state.

As you can sense, most of the real-world environments that the agents are going to be part of when building intelligent systems are going to be stochastic in nature. MDPs provide a framework that facilitates decision making in a stochastic environment with the overall goal of the agent being to find a policy to reach the final intended state based on a series of actions within the context. MDPs deviate from simple planning in the sense that the actions are determined and adjusted based on the environmental conditions. MDPs provide a formal quantification model for the decision making process for the agent in the stochastic environment.

The agent takes a step (action **a**) from a set of all the available actions at time t within its current state s. The environment moves to new state s' while on the way giving a reward to the agent $\mathbf{R_a(s,s')}$. Due to the stochastic nature of the environment, transition from state **s** to a particular state **s'** cannot be guaranteed with certainty. This transition is possible with a probability value $\mathbf{P_a(s,s')}$. Each action step within state s is independent of previous states and actions and satisfies Markov property.

A stochastic process has the Markov property if the conditional probability distribution of future states of the process (conditional on both past and present states) depends only upon the present state, not on the sequence of events that preceded it. A process with this property is called a **Markov process**.

The stochastic nature of the environment with state transitions due to a series of actions can be visualized as follows:

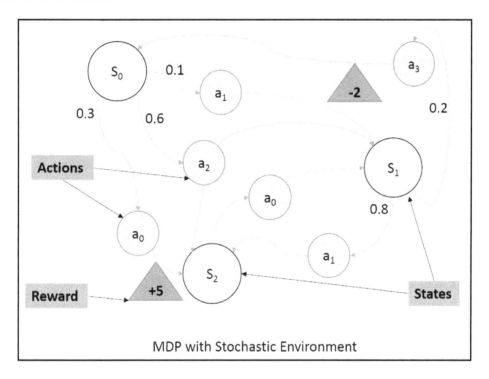

MDP with Stochastic Environment

The MDP has five basic components:

- **S**: A set of all the possible states of the environment.
- **A**: A set of all possible actions for the agent. A_s represents the set of possible actions at state **s**.

- **$P_a(s,s')$**: Probability that the action **a** in state **s** leads to state **s'**. In the previous diagram, there is a **0.6** probability that action a_2 at state s_1 will transition the environment state to s_1.

- **$R_a(s,s')$**: This represents the reward as a result of action **a** when the environment transitions from state **s** to **s'** as a result of action **a**. In the previous diagram, the agent receives reward of **-2** for action a_3 at state s_1 and transitioning to state $s_{0x'}$.

- **$\Upsilon \in [0,1]$**: This represents a discount factor, which is the difference between future rewards and the current reward for a state transition based on a specific action.

The MDP attempts to find a policy that maximizes the cumulative reward for all the actions within a finite set of states. The goal can be achieved with the help of a dynamic programming framework.

Dynamic programming and reinforcement learning

Within the context of reinforcement learning, the dynamic programming approach deals with the interactions between a controller or the agent that needs to take actions and the process within the environment. This interaction takes place with three types of distinct signals:

- **State signal**: Describes state of the process
- **Action signal**: With this, the agent (controller) influences the process
- **Reward Signal**: Provides feedback to the controller based on its most recent action

The agent moves through the solution space with repetitive iterations of a state-action-reward-state cycle. A policy defines the overall behavior of the agent. The policy can be dynamically aligned based on the nature of the environment (deterministic or stochastic). For dynamic programming, the overall goal for the agent is to figure out an optimal policy that maximizes the cumulative reward (return) over the course of the agent's existence. We will consider the return over infinite-horizon, which leads to a stationary optimal policy in which for a given state the choice of optimal actions will always be the same. While DP and RL share the same goal over the infinite-horizon, there are some differences between them in terms of their applications and algorithms. Before we take a deep dive into DP and RL, here is a quick comparison between them:

	Dynamic Programming (DP)	Reinforcement Learning (RL)
Area of application	Automatic control	Artificial Intelligence
Application to problem area	Non-linear and stochastic optimal control problems	Adaptive optimal control
Terminologies	Controller / Process	Agent / Environment
Algorithm Type	Model based	Model free

DP and **RL** apply common iterative strategies such as value iteration, policy iteration, as well as search policies in order to achieve their optimization goal.

Let us first consider the **DP** and **RL** algorithms in the context of a deterministic environment setting. In this environment, when an action a_t is taken by the agent in state s_t at time step t, the state changes to s_{t+1} according to the transition function $f: S \times A \rightarrow S$ so that, $s_{t+1} = f(s_t, a_t)$. At this time, the agent receives a scalar reward signal r_{t+1} according to the reward function ρ: $S \times A \rightarrow \mathbb{R}$ so that, $r_{t+1} = \rho(s_t, a_t)$. The agent chooses further actions as per policy $\pi: S \rightarrow A$ using $a_t = \pi(s_t)$. When the transition function f, reward function ρ, current state s_t, and current action a_t are known, the next state s_{t+1} and next reward r_{t+1} can be determined.

Learning in a deterministic environment with policy iteration

Let us understand the agent's learning process based on the dynamic programming model in a deterministic environment depicted in the following diagram. Let us imagine an agent that is learning to play music on a simple keyboard:

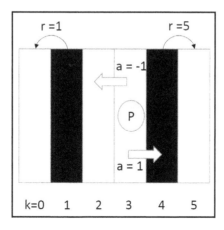

In this diagram, **P** represents the keyboard playing agent and **K** {0,1,2,3,4,5} represents the keys numbered from **0** to **5**. In this simple setup, the agent can move forward and backward represented by **A{-1,1}**. Movement to the right side is denoted by **a = 1** and left side by **a = -1**. Assume that the agent gets a reward for playing a specific note and in this case, when it moves from key number **4** to **5**, the reward is **5** and when it moves from key **1** to key **0**, the reward is **1**. For all the other transitions, the reward is **0**. Assume for simplicity that the keys **0** and **5** are terminal states for the sound note and once the agent reaches there, the agent cannot leave.

In this case, the transition function can be represented as follows:

$$f(k, a) = k + a \quad \text{if } 1 \leq k < 4$$

$$f(k, a) = k \quad \text{if } k = 0 \text{ or } k=5$$

The reward function is represented as follows:

$$\rho\,(s, a) = \begin{cases} 5 & \text{If s = 4 and a = 1} \\ 1 & \text{If s = 1 and a = -1} \\ 0 & \text{For other state transitions} \end{cases}$$

With this context, the goal of the agent is to gain the highest cumulative reward based on the transitions on the keyboard based on any starting position k_x. The infinite horizon reward is formulated as follows:

$$R(k_x) = \sum_{k=0}^{\infty} \gamma^k r_{(}k + 1_{)} = \sum_{k=0}^{\infty} \gamma^k \rho(s_k, f(x_k))$$

In this case, $\gamma \in [0,1]$ is the discount factor that represents the delayed gratitude acceptance for the agent in regards to the rewards. With this, the cumulative reward is bounded if the individual action rewards are bounded. The agent only uses feedback from each action step in order to maximize overall cumulative reward.

The current action step in this case does not provide any indication of the overall reward for the agent. It is imperative to select the right value for γ, which sets a trade-off between quality of the solution in maximizing the reward and the convergence rate. In order to derive an optimal policy for the agent, value functions are used. There are two types of value functions denoted as Q-functions and V-functions. Q-functions are state-action value functions and V-functions are state value functions.

The Q-function Q^p: $S \times A \rightarrow \mathbb{R}$ of a policy $\mathbb{P}$ gives a return when starting from a given state s and the given action a and following policy $\mathbb{P}$. As a result $Q^p(s,a) = \rho(s,a) + \gamma \mathbb{R}^p(f(s,a))$. Here, $\mathbb{R}^p(f(s,a))$ is the return from the next step $f(s,a)$. The Q-function can also be represented as a discounted sum of rewards by taking a in s and then following the policy $\mathbb{P}$:

$$Q^p(s,a) = \sum_{k=0}^{\infty} \gamma^k \rho(s_k, a_k)$$

When $(s_0,a_0) = (s,a)$, $s_{k+1} = f(s_k, a_k)$ for k = 0, and $a_k = \mathbb{P}(s_k)$ for $k \geq 1$, the first term can be separated from the cumulative value function.

$$Q^p(s,a) = \mathbb{P}(s,a) + \sum_{k=1}^{\infty} \gamma^k \mathbb{P}(s_k, a_k)$$

$$= \mathbb{P}(s,a) + \gamma \sum_{k=1}^{\infty} \gamma^{k-1} \mathbb{P}(s_k, \mathbb{P}(s_k))$$

$$= \mathbb{P}(s,a) + \gamma \mathbb{R}^p(f(s,a))$$

The optimal Q-function is the one that gives maximum Q-value over various transitions of the agent to the search space.

$$Q^*(s, a) = max_p Q^p(s, a)$$

The V-function V^p: S → ℝ of a policy p is obtained by starting from a particular key and following p. This V-function can be derived from the Q-function of policy p:
$V^p(s) = R^p(s) = Q^p(s, \rho(s))$. Again, the optimal V-function is the one that gives maximum V-value over various transitions and can be computed from optimum Q-function.

When learning in a stochastic environment, the agent cannot move to a state $s+1$ with a certainty when it takes action $a+1$. In that case, the Q-value and V-value are obtained as a probability of the transition that is learned by the agent over multiple iterations through the search space.

In the next section, we will explore one of the popular model-free Q-learning algorithms.

Q-Learning

Q-learning is a model-free learning algorithm that is useful in situations when the agent knows all the possible states and the actions, which leads to these states within the search space. Q-learning is able to choose between immediate reward and the long-term reward, which enables optimization for reaching the goal of maximizing rewards accumulated over the set of actions.

Let us explain this with a simple example. Consider a maze with six locations (*L*∈ {0,1,2,3,4,5}) within it and when the agent comes to location number 5, it finds treasure (the end state or the agent's goal). The maze has the following structure. The bi-directional arrows indicate possible state transitions and the numbers indicate the reward:

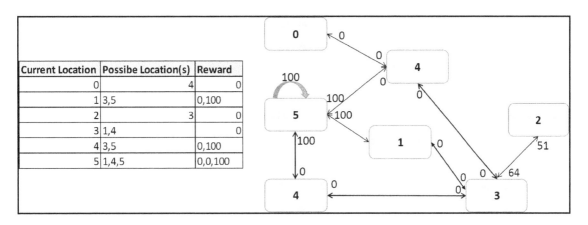

Current Location	Possibe Location(s)	Reward
0	4	0
1	3,5	0,100
2	3	0
3	1,4	0
4	3,5	0,100
5	1,4,5	0,0,100

The state transitions are represented in a standardized manner in Q-learning as a matrix where the rows indicate state and the columns indicate actions. **-1** indicates that the action **a** is not possible or blocked in a specific state, **100** indicates the reward of **100** points for a state transition. For all the other transitions the reward is **0**.

$$R = \begin{array}{c} \text{State} \\ \begin{array}{c} 0 \\ 1 \\ 2 \\ 3 \\ 4 \\ 5 \end{array} \end{array} \begin{array}{cccccc} 0 & 1 & 2 & 3 & 4 & 5 \\ \left[\begin{array}{cccccc} -1 & -1 & -1 & -1 & 0 & -1 \\ -1 & -1 & -1 & 0 & -1 & 100 \\ -1 & -1 & -1 & 0 & -1 & -1 \\ -1 & 0 & 0 & -1 & 0 & -1 \\ 0 & -1 & -1 & 0 & -1 & 100 \\ -1 & 0 & -1 & -1 & 0 & 100 \end{array}\right] \end{array}$$

The agent now needs to build a Q matrix that stores all the learning that the agent does with a series of actions and corresponding state transitions. In the Q matrix also, the rows represent current state and the columns represent possible actions that lead to the next stage. The initial state of the Q matrix is when the agent does not know anything about the environment and hence the matrix contains all zero values. In our example, let us assume that the agent is aware that there are six possible states of the environment. However, in real scenarios, the agent will not have knowledge of all the states and needs to explore the search space. In that case, the Q learning algorithm adds columns to the Q matrix as a new state is encountered. The transition rule for Q learning is represented as

$Q(s, a) = R(s, a) + \gamma * Max[Q(s + 1, a_{0,n})]$.

A value assigned within the Q matrix represents a sum of corresponding values in R matrix and learning parameter γ multiplied by maximum value of Q for all possible actions in the next state. As the agent transitions from start position to the goal state, it updates the Q matrix and this transition is called one episode. With this context, the Q learning algorithm is represented as follows:

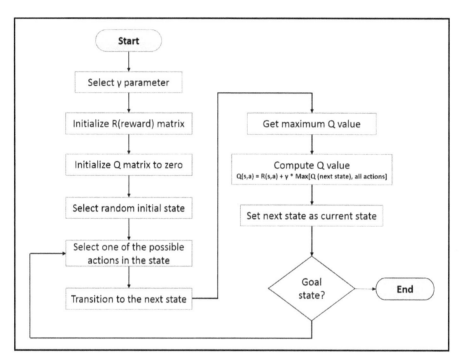

With this algorithm, the agent's memory is enriched with each episode and it stores more information about the state transition rewards. When trained over a reasonable number of episodes, the agent can quickly derive the optimal path through the search space. The γ parameter ranges between 0 and 1. When this parameter is closer to zero, the agent prioritizes the rewards during initial episodes. When γ is closer to 1, the agent considers future rewards with greater weights willing to delay the reward in the interest of cumulative gain.

Let us use the algorithm for a couple of episodes based on the maze example we have seen previously. Here is the initial state of Reward matrix R and Q-matrix Q:

$$R = \begin{array}{c} \\ \text{State} \\ 0 \\ 1 \\ 2 \\ 3 \\ 4 \\ 5 \end{array} \overset{\text{Action}}{\begin{array}{cccccc} 0 & 1 & 2 & 3 & 4 & 5 \\ \left[\begin{array}{cccccc} -1 & -1 & -1 & -1 & 0 & -1 \\ -1 & -1 & -1 & 0 & -1 & 100 \\ -1 & -1 & -1 & 0 & -1 & -1 \\ -1 & 0 & 0 & -1 & 0 & -1 \\ 0 & -1 & -1 & 0 & -1 & 100 \\ -1 & 0 & -1 & -1 & 0 & 100 \end{array}\right] \end{array}} \qquad Q = \begin{array}{c} \\ 0 \\ 1 \\ 2 \\ 3 \\ 4 \\ 5 \end{array} \begin{array}{cccccc} 0 & 1 & 2 & 3 & 4 & 5 \\ \left[\begin{array}{cccccc} 0 & 0 & 0 & 0 & 0 & 0 \\ 0 & 0 & 0 & 0 & 0 & 0 \\ 0 & 0 & 0 & 0 & 0 & 0 \\ 0 & 0 & 0 & 0 & 0 & 0 \\ 0 & 0 & 0 & 0 & 0 & 0 \\ 0 & 0 & 0 & 0 & 0 & 0 \end{array}\right] \end{array}$$

Initial State for the Reward and Q matrix

Let us consider that the agent's initial state is *1* and we use an arbitrary value of γ as *0.8*. As we know, from state *1*, the possible states to which the agent can go are *3* and *5* and at this point let us consider that the agent randomly goes to state *5*. In stage *5*, the agent has three possible state choices: *1, 4,* and *5*. Let us apply the Q learning equation:

$$Q(s, a) = R(s, a) + \gamma * Max[Q(s+1, a_{0,n})]$$

$Q(1,5) = R(1,5) + 0.8 * Max[Q(5,1), Q(5,4), Q(5,5)]$

    $= 100 + 0.8 * Max[0,0,0]$

     $= 100 + 0.8 * 0$ (Remember the Q matrix is initialized to a zero)

     $= 100$

Since *5* is the goal state, we have finished one episode with a new version of the Q matrix as follows:

$$Q = \begin{array}{c} \\ 0 \\ 1 \\ 2 \\ 3 \\ 4 \\ 5 \end{array} \begin{array}{cccccc} 0 & 1 & 2 & 3 & 4 & 5 \\ \left[\begin{array}{cccccc} 0 & 0 & 0 & 0 & 0 & 0 \\ 0 & 0 & 0 & 0 & 0 & 100 \\ 0 & 0 & 0 & 0 & 0 & 0 \\ 0 & 0 & 0 & 0 & 0 & 0 \\ 0 & 0 & 0 & 0 & 0 & 0 \\ 0 & 0 & 0 & 0 & 0 & 0 \end{array}\right] \end{array}$$

Q matrix after episode 1

For the next episode, the agent gets into the initial state of 3. Refer to the R matrix, at stage 3, there are three possible actions: 1, 2, and 4. The agent decides to take action 1, which lands it into state 1. Now imagine that the agent is in state 1. At this point the agent can go to states 3 and 5. Let us compute the Q value for this route:

$$Q(s, a) = R(s, a) + \gamma * Max[Q(s + 1, a_{0,n})]$$

Q(3,1) = R(3,1) + 0.8 * Max[Q(1,3), Q(1,5)]

　　　= 0 + 0.8 * Max[0,100]

　　= 0+ 0.8 * 100

　= 80

At this point, the agent is in state 1, which is not the terminal or goal state and hence the loop iterates to the goal state (5 in this case). Let us assume that the agent randomly goes to state 5 from state 1, which is the goal state and hence **episode 2** is concluded. The following is the Q matrix at the end of **episode 2**:

Q =	0	1	2	3	4	5
0	0	0	0	0	0	0
1	0	0	0	0	0	100
2	0	0	0	0	0	0
3	0	80	0	0	0	0
4	0	0	0	0	0	0
5	0	0	0	0	0	0

Q matrix after episode 1

Q =	0	1	2	3	4	5
0	0	0	0	0	400	0
1	0	0	0	320	0	500
2	0	0	0	320	0	0
3	0	400	256	0	400	0
4	320	0	0	320	0	500
5	0	400	0	0	400	500

Q matrix after convergence

The matrix can be scaled by dividing all the non-zero numbers with the maximum number and multiplying by 100. With normalization, the final converged Q matrix is as follows:

Q =	0	1	2	3	4	5
0	0	0	0	0	80	0
1	0	0	0	64	0	100
2	0	0	0	64	0	0
3	0	80	51	0	80	0
4	64	0	0	64	0	100
5	0	80	0	0	80	100

Normalized Q matrix

Once the converged and normalized *Q* matrix is obtained, the agent has memorized and learned the optimal actions for state transitions in order to reach the goal state (5 in this case). The state transition diagram with *Q* matrix values is as follows:

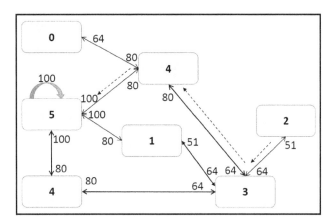

Once this transition matrix is defined, the agent can navigate through the search space in an optimal way by choosing an action at each step with maximum *Q* value, as indicated by the dotted arrow in the previous diagram.

Here is a code snippet that implements the Q-learning algorithm with the same example that we have seen previously:

```
package com.aibd.rl;

import java.util.Random;

public class QLearner {

        private static final int STATE_COUNT        = 6;
        private static final double GAMMA            = 0.8;
        private static final int MAX_ITERATIONS      = 10;
        private static final int INITIAL_STATES[]    = new int[] {1, 3, 5, 2,
    4, 0};

        // initialize the R matrix with the state transition combinations
        private static final int R[][] =
            new int[][] {{-1, -1, -1, -1,  0, -1},
                         {-1, -1, -1,  0, -1, 100},
                         {-1, -1, -1,  0, -1, -1},
                         {-1,  0,  0, -1,  0, -1},
                         { 0, -1, -1,  0, -1, 100},
                         {-1,  0, -1, -1,  0, 100}};
```

```
private static int q[][] = new int[STATE_COUNT][STATE_COUNT];
private static int currentState = 0;
public static void main(String[] args) {
    train();
    test();
    return;
}
private static void train() {
  // initialize the Q matrix to zero values
  initialize();

    // Perform training, starting at all initial states.
    for(int j = 0; j < MAX_ITERATIONS; j++){
        for(int i = 0; i < STATE_COUNT; i++) {
            episode(INITIAL_STATES[i]);
        }
    }
    System.out.println("Q Matrix:");
    for(int i = 0; i < STATE_COUNT; i++) {
        for(int j = 0; j < STATE_COUNT; j++){
            System.out.print(q[i][j] + ",\t");
        }
        System.out.print("\n");
    }
    System.out.print("\n");
    return;
}
private static void test() {
    // Perform tests, starting at all initial states.
    System.out.println("Shortest routes from initial states:");
    for(int i = 0; i < STATE_COUNT; i++) {
        currentState = INITIAL_STATES[i];
        int newState = 0;
        do {
            newState = maximum(currentState, true);
            System.out.print(currentState + " --> ");
            currentState = newState;
        }while(currentState < 5);
        System.out.print("5\n");
    }
    return;
}
private static void episode(final int initialState) {
    currentState = initialState;
    do {
        chooseAnAction();
    }while(currentState == 5);
```

```
                for(int i = 0; i < STATE_COUNT; i++){
                    chooseAnAction();
                }
                return;
        }
        private static void chooseAnAction() {
            int possibleAction = 0;

            // Randomly choose a possible action connected to the current
    state.
            possibleAction = getRandomAction(STATE_COUNT);

            if(R[currentState][possibleAction] >= 0){
                q[currentState][possibleAction] = reward(possibleAction);
                currentState = possibleAction;
            }
            return;
        }
        private static int getRandomAction(final int upperBound) {
            int action = 0;
            boolean choiceIsValid = false;

            // Randomly choose a possible action connected to the current
    state.
            while(choiceIsValid == false) {
                // Get a random value between 0(inclusive) and 6(exclusive).
                action = new Random().nextInt(upperBound);
                if(R[currentState][action] > -1){
                    choiceIsValid = true;
                }
            }

            return action;
        }
        private static void initialize() {
            for(int i = 0; i < STATE_COUNT; i++)
            {
                for(int j = 0; j < STATE_COUNT; j++)
                {
                    q[i][j] = 0;
                } // j
            } // i
            return;
        }
        private static int maximum(final int State, final boolean
    ReturnIndexOnly) {
                // If ReturnIndexOnly = True, the Q matrix index is returned.
                // If ReturnIndexOnly = False, the Q matrix value is returned.
```

```
        int winner = 0;
        boolean foundNewWinner = false;
        boolean done = false;

        while(!done) {
            foundNewWinner = false;
            for(int i = 0; i < STATE_COUNT; i++)
            {
                if(i != winner){ // Avoid self-comparison.
                    if(q[State][i] > q[State][winner]){
                        winner = i;
                        foundNewWinner = true;
                    }
                }
            }

            if(foundNewWinner == false){
                done = true;
            }
        }

        if(ReturnIndexOnly == true){
            return winner;
        }else{
            return q[State][winner];
        }
    }
    private static int reward(final int Action) {
        return (int)(R[currentState][Action] + (GAMMA * maximum(Action,
false)));
    }

}
```

This program produces the following output:

```
Q Matrix:
0, 0, 0, 0, 396, 0,
0, 0, 0, 316, 0, 496,
0, 0, 0, 316, 0, 0,
0, 396, 252, 0, 396, 0,
316, 0, 0, 316, 0, 496,
0, 396, 0, 0, 396, 496,

Shortest routes from initial states:
1 --> 5
3 --> 1 --> 5
5 --> 5
2 --> 3 --> 1 --> 5
4 --> 5
0 --> 4 --> 5
```

As we have seen, Q-learning is a method for optimizing discounted rewards, generally making the future rewards less prioritized compared to near-term rewards. In the next section, we will look at a variation of Q-learning algorithms called **SARSA learning**.

SARSA learning

State-Action-Reward-State-Action (**SARSA**) is an on-policy algorithm where the same policy that generated previous actions can generate the next action. This is unlike the Q-learning where the algorithm is off-policy and only considers current state and rewards along with available next actions without any consideration to the ongoing policy.

At each step within SARSA, the agent's action is evaluated and improved by improving Q-function estimates. The Q-value is updated as a result of the error and adjusted by a factor of learning rate termed as α. In this case, the Q-values represent potential reward from the next state transition as a result of action a_t+1 in state s plus the discounted (γ) future reward received from the next state-action observation. The algorithm can be mathematically represented as follows:

$$Q(s_t, a_t) \leftarrow Q(s_t, a_t) + \alpha [r_t + \gamma Q(s_{t+1}, a_{t+1}) - Q(s_t, a_t)]$$

The first deviation from Q-learning is that in the case of SARSA learning, the agent is learning action-value functions rather than state-value functions. The agent needs to estimate $Q^{\wp}(s,a)$ for the current alignment with policy $\mathbb{P}$ for all the states s and actions a. The agent needs to consider the transitions from one state-action pair to another state-action pair and learn the value of state-action pairs. The updates are done after transition from s_t where it is a non-terminal state. If s_{t+1} is the terminal state, then $Q(s_{t+1}, a_{t+1})$ is defined as 0. SARSA utilizes all the elements in decision making *(st, at, rt+1, st+1, at+1)* on transition from one state to the next. Similar to Q-learning, SARSA is also an iterative algorithm that can be represented as follows:

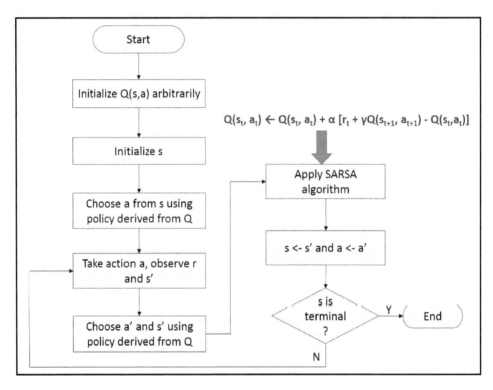

Another method that is less popularly used in reinforcement learning is R-learning, which tries to optimize average rewards for the agent. It considers future and near-term rewards equally in deciding the optimal policy.

Deep reinforcement learning

In order for the reinforcement learning algorithm to be deployed in real-world use cases and scenarios, we need to leverage the power of deep neural networks, which can infer the information from the environments in a human-like manner. One of the goals of AI is to augment human capabilities by creating autonomous agents that interact with the environment in which they operate, learn optimal behaviors that improve over time, and learn from mistakes.

For example, the signals from the video camera can be interpreted using a deep neural network. Once this signal is interpreted, the objects and patterns observed by the camera can be analyzed with the help of a deep neural network, as we have seen in the chapters on **artificial neural networks (ANNs)**. These deep neural networks can then be used for application of reinforcement learning algorithms for creating a navigation system that learns over a period of time based on the training feeds.

Fundamentally, a combination of deep neural networks and reinforcement learning algorithms are poised to achieve near-human performance with object detection, self-driving cars, video games, natural language processing, and so on. In this section, we will review various approaches and techniques for DRL.

As we know, the **deep neural networks (DNNs)** can deduce low dimensional representations of the high dimensional datasets such as audio/video signals. On the other hand, the reinforcement learning model reduces dependence on training data and relies on the reward/punishment paradigm for the agent to navigate through the stochastic environments and improve over a period of time. Deep learning enables the reinforcement learning to a new level towards near-human performance and for some of the activities that require brute-force the autonomous agent is able to outperform human capabilities.

While a lot of pioneering work is done with use of DRLs, the initial breakthrough was achieved with training the algorithm to master the Atari 2600 video games and achieve superhuman level of expertise just by feeding the pixel data. The agent was trained purely based on the reward signal in conjunction with the pixel map that represented the stochastic environment. Another prominent success was with the intelligent agent, AlphaGo, which beat the Go world champion based on the use of neural networks that were trained using a combination of supervised and reinforcement learning along with a self-learning algorithm.

DRLs are found to be useful in the area of robotics where the video signal is interpreted with an ANN that activates the controllers that perform mission critical tasks such as operating CNC machines as well as attempt to do surgeries. The push is towards making the agents that can meta-learn, meaning learning to learn. This is also possible with DRLs. It is imperative that the DRL agents will evolve to fully complement human capabilities in the near future. The DRLs have been successful due to the ability to extrapolate low dimensional learning techniques to high-dimensional, unstructured datasets.

The neural networks are good at approximation and learning based on the high-dimensional data. With this, the DRLs can deal with the curse of dimensionality and train models for various stochastic environments in high dimension space. The **convolution neural networks** (**CNNs**) can be used as building blocks for the DRLs, which enables learning directly from the real-life raw data assets that are high dimensional in nature. The DRLs enable training a deep neural network to come up with optimal policy through state transitions along with optimal value functions, **V**, **Q**, and **A**. While the possibilities with a combination of neural networks and reinforcement learning are enormous, we will evaluate the application of deep neural networks as function approximators in policy search methods within DRL. One of the most popular algorithms is **deep Q-network** (**DQN**).

Frequently asked questions

Q: What is the difference between supervised learning and reinforcement learning?

A: In the case of supervised learning algorithms, the model is trained based on historical data which describes the trend for the data historically and establishes a correlation between the event data and resultant output. In that case, the supervised learning model is a curve fitting exercise that maps the data points (independent variables) to a set of output variables (dependent variables). Availability of the historical data is essential for supervised learning. In case of reinforcement learning, the agent is modeled based on the rewards it receives based on the action(s) it takes within the context of the environment in which it is operating. There is no historical data available to the agent to train itself. However, a hybrid approach often works great where the agent is aware of the historical trends as well as applies exploration and exploitation strategies in order to maximize the reward as it transitions through the search space towards its goal.

Q: What are the basic components of **Reinforcement Learning** ?

A: The Reinforcement Learning happens within the context of an environment. The environment defines all the external factors that impact the performance of an agent, which is the second component of RL. The agent transitions through the solution space within multiple states with a goal to achieve the terminal state and maximizing the reward on the way. Every action the agent performs generates a reward or punishment and a makes a corresponding change in the environment state.

Q: What are the types of environment that an intelligent agent encounters?

A: An intelligent agent encounters a deterministic or a stochastic environment. The deterministic environment has a level of certainty based on the environment stater and the latest action by the agent. In this type of environment, an action a_t at time step t when the environment is in state s_t results in a deterministic state and reward. However, in case of a stochastic environment, there is a level of uncertainty in terms of state of environment as well as reward for the same action within the same environment state.

Summary

In this chapter, we have explored one of the most important machine learning techniques, RL. We understood the difference between RL and supervised learning. Learning based on behavioral reinforcement for the agent is extremely critical in modeling the intelligent machines that will bridge the gap between human capabilities and the intelligent machines. We have seen the basic concepts of the RL algorithm along with the participating components. We have also tried to establish mathematical equations for a generic RL algorithm where the overall goal is to maximize cumulative rewards for the agent as it transitions through various states with every action.

We have briefly tried to understand the MDPs in a deterministic and stochastic environment. We also explored dynamic programming concepts in brief along with Q-learning and SARSA learning algorithms. In the end, we briefly discussed deep reinforcement learning DRL as a combination of deep neural networks and the reinforcement learning paradigm. The use cases that can be derived are enormous and with this chapter we have established a foundation to explore our creativity.

In the next chapter, we are going to explore one of the most important aspects of data management, security. Cyber security is extremely critical with growing volumes of data. We will explore the basic concepts of infrastructure protection along with some of the frameworks available for Stream processing and real-time threat detection.

11
Cyber Security

During the course of this book, we have established one thing. In order to realize AI, we need access to large volumes of data. Data plays a central role in building capabilities for intelligent machines which complement and augment human capabilities. The applications we develop based on machine learning architectures and algorithms are only as good as the underlying data. As our dependence on data increases and we start seeing data as an asset for mission-critical systems such as medical equipment, aviation, banking systems, and so on, maintaining the integrity of the data assets is one of the most important priorities and key ingredients for successful widespread adoption of AI-based systems. Protection of critical infrastructure from data breaches is generally known as **cyber security**.

In this chapter, we are going to see how we can leverage various data governance frameworks to protect the critical data assets and utilize our understanding of Big Data management and machine learning frameworks to keep our most important asset (data) secure. We will cover the following topics in this chapter:

- How we can leverage Big Data to protect critical infrastructure
- General concepts of stream processing
- Security information and event management
- Web server access log file structure and strategies to utilize it for cyber security
- Splunk as an enterprise application for implementing cyber security
- ArcSight as an enterprise security management platform

Big Data for critical infrastructure protection

Critical infrastructure (**CI**) is a term used by enterprises and government agencies to define the assets and working models that need to function at their optimal level in order for a seamless and harmonious experience for the stakeholders who directly or indirectly benefit from or are impacted by these systems. Examples include the power grid, water supply, transportation, law enforcement, and many such systems that need to work seamlessly around the clock. Over the last few decades, most of the CI has become digitized and is generating more and more data from heterogeneous sources. These additional data assets result in continuous improvement and elimination of the need for human intervention and thereby reduce error.

The data generated by these systems is used as an asset for descriptive and predictive analytics in order to schedule preventive maintenance and prevent failures. With a data-driven approach for core functioning of the CI, we have seen tremendous improvements in efficiency and overall reliability of the CI. However, there are enormous incidents in which attackers with malicious intentions to disrupt the CI have been successful in breaching into the CI and creating disruption. For example, Stuxnet, which was found in 2010, targeted **SCADA** (**Supervisory Control and Data Acquisition**) systems and caused damage to fuel enrichment plans in Iran by interfacing with the **Programmable Logic Controllers** (**PLCs**). There are many such incidents and attempts which disturb CI and cause perpetual damage.

One of the most important aspects of preventing cyber security attacks on the CI is the availability of data from the CI which is generated in a working environment. This data needs to be available for analysis and potential actions as close to the event time as possible. Along with the data from core CI components, the data from other heterogeneous systems which are indirectly linked to the CI needs to be utilized for building a robust defense mechanism against cyber attacks. That means we need data **volume**, **velocity**, and **variety** in order to effectively protect the CI. These three Vs along with value as fourth V which is derived from the data together constitute Big Data. In other words, Big Data is a critical asset for effective strategies against cyber attacks. We require a constantly evolving, data-driven framework and processes for protection of CI, leveraging Big Data analytics for effective security monitoring and protection.

This data-driven framework has three main components, as depicted in the following diagram:

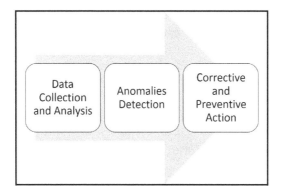

Figure 11.1 Components of a data-driven framework for critical infrastructure protection

Data collection and analysis

The core systems that constitute CIs generate data assets in the form of event logs. The data collection component needs to gather these logs from all the components (software and hardware). Apart from the core systems, the process should also gather data from the contextual environment of the CI systems. The heterogeneous logs help with holistic analysis and more accurate and timeline resolution. Along with the running logs, the system should also have the ability to store and access the historical data for the CI systems.

The historical data provides insights based on pattern similarity with past events. If the past mitigations have resulted in quick correction and resolution of the critical event, then supervised learning can be deployed in order to take similar actions based on experience. Historical data also greatly helps in preventing future attacks based on similar system vulnerabilities.

The data (log) generated by the CI components and related environmental context can be categorized into three types:

- **Structured data**: In the case of structured format, the individual elements (attributes) of an entity are represented in a predefined and consistent manner across time periods. For example, the logs generated by the web servers (HTTP log) represent fields such as the IP address, the time the server finished processing the request, the HTTP method, status code, and so on. All these attributes of a web request are represented consistently across requests. The structured data is relatively easy to process and does not require complex parsing and pre-processing before it is available for analysis. With structured data, processing is fast and efficient.

- **Unstructured data**: This is a free-flowing application log format that does not follow any predefined structural rules. These logs are typically generated by the applications and are meant to be consumed by someone who is troubleshooting the issues. The intention is to log the events without an explicit goal of making the logs machine readable. These logs require extensive preprocessing, parsing, and some form of natural language processing before those are available for analysis.

- **Semi-structured data**: This is a combination of structured and unstructured data where some of the attributes within structured format are represented in an unstructured manner. The information is organized into fields which can be easily parsed but the individual fields need additional preprocessing before being used in analysis.

Anomaly detection

As we start gathering data from heterogeneous systems, there is a pattern that is established in terms of data volume, structure, information content, and velocity of the data. This pattern remains consistent during standard operating conditions and there can be expected surges or changes in the patterns. For example, an online retailer can expect more orders during the holiday season and this event does not count as an anomaly. When there is an unanticipated change in the regular pattern of data in terms of volume, velocity, and variety, the anomaly detection component triggers an alert and notification. One of the important characteristics of a greatly evolved and reliable anomaly detection component is that it is able to generate the alert as soon as the event occurs, with minimum lag between event time and the alert/notification time.

The following diagram depicts the ideal, reliable, and unreliable anomaly detection components based on the time difference between the event and alert time:

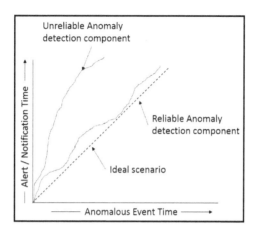

Figure 11.2 Anomaly detection reliability based on Event Time and Alert/Notification Time

Corrective and preventive actions

When the suspicious activity is detected by the anomaly detection component, there are two ways to respond. In the first case, the alert/notification requires manual intervention in order to trigger the corrective action. In the second case, the system itself takes some corrective action based on the context and the acceptable threshold of the error margin.

For example, if a hack into the thermostat circuitry starts increasing the temperature of the cold storage in an unanticipated manner, the system can switch the control to an alternate thermostat and ensure that the temperature is back to normal and maintained at normal levels. This component can use supervised learning as well as reinforcement learning algorithms for triggering the corrective actions on their own based on historical data or the reward function. When the correction is applied and the CI state is restored to normal, the system needs to analyze the root cause and train itself to take preventive actions (application of a patch, changes to the security model, implementing new access controls, and so on).

Conceptual Data Flow

In typical Big Data environments, a layered architecture is implemented. Layers within the data processing pipeline help in decoupling various stages through which the data passes to protect the critical infrastructure. The data flows through ingestion, storage, processing, and an actionize cycle, which is depicted in the following figure along with popular frameworks used for implementing the workflow:

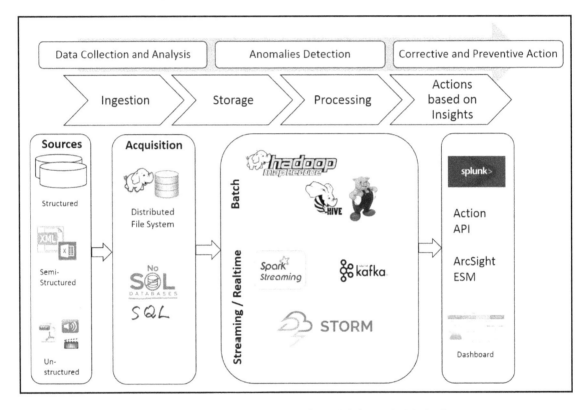

Figure 11.3 Conceptual Data Flow along with popular frameworks for implementing Cyber Security

Most of the components used in this figure are open source and a result of collaborative efforts from a large community. A detailed discussion of all these components is out of the scope of this chapter. However, let us understand these components at a high level within the context of cyber security.

Components overview

For successful implementation of CI protection strategy, it is imperative to collect data from heterogeneous sources beyond the obvious sources like server logs. As more data sources are identified and integrated, the storage requirement increases. Considering the volume and velocity of data, it is not possible to accommodate the data using traditional file systems. Instead, the modern architectures utilizes distributed file systems.

Hadoop Distributed File System

The **Hadoop Distributed File System** (**HDFS**) is one of the most popular implementations of a distributed file system. It is at the core of Hadoop which is a distributed computing platform. HDFS was designed and has evolved with the following goals in mind, which complement the storage requirements for the protection of the CI:

- **Hardware failure:** HDFS replicates each file block on three (default) nodes. The core idea of using distributed computing is to be able to leverage commodity hardware and hence the cluster consists of a large number of relatively small-size nodes. With large numbers of nodes, the probability of failure of a node increases. Detection and recovery from these hardware failures without any data loss is one of the primary goals of HDFS. The CI protection systems also needs the same level of reliability and fault tolerance in order to detect cyber security threats.

- **Large datasets:** The applications that utilize HDFS as underlying data stores are assumed to be dealing with large datasets in the range of multiple gigabytes to terabytes and more. HDFS is inherently built to support large data files. CI protection systems also generate and deal with large data volumes. A good example is the central governing authority of a country which monitors the internet backbone of the country and deals with hundreds of gigabytes of data per second.

- **Simple Coherency Model**: The CI applications generate log files which need to be written once and read multiple times. The coherence model is also one of the primary design goals of HDFS. A file, once created and written, does not need to be changed with this model. This goal also complements the cyber security applications.

- **Portability across heterogeneous hardware and software platforms**: HDFS is easy to port across various platforms. This goal also complements the core requirement of the cyber security systems. The cyber security systems are deployed on a variety of different platforms and the portability of HDFS as an underlying file system can be an added advantage.

NoSQL databases

NoSQL (**Not only SQL**) is a paradigm in which the data is stored in the form of entities instead of the typical RDBMS type tabular relational format. One of the primary goals for NoSQL databases is horizontal scaling and high availability. Based on the underlying data structure of the NoSQL databases, they are categorized into:

- **Document databases:** Each key in the database is mapped to a document. A document can be a binary file or a nested structure like XML or JSON. The examples of document databases are MongoDB, CouchDB, Couchbase, and so on.
- **Graph databases**: These are useful with the data which is in the form of connected graphs like social media connections. The examples of graph databases are Neo4j, OrientDB, Apache Giraph, and so on.
- **Columnar databases**: These databases represent the data by storing column data together instead of rows. They are optimized for distributed storage and fast query access over very large databases. The examples of columnar databases are Cassandra, HBase, and so on.

The NoSQL databases can be effectively used in implementations of cyber security applications since they can easily handle large volumes of structures and semi-structured and unstructured data which is gathered from heterogeneous sources surrounding the CI. The NoSQL databases also support geographically distributed architecture which can be scaled out on demand without impacting the already persisted data. This feature is handy in case of incremental growth in CI infrastructure, such as the telecommunication services in the remote areas which are incrementally built.

MapReduce

MapReduce (**MR**) is a programming paradigm at the core of Hadoop. It can scale the processing of data to massively high volumes. The data and processing can be distributed to hundreds and thousands of nodes for horizontal scalability. As the name suggests, the MR jobs contain two phases:

- The map phase
- The reduce phase

In the map phase, the dataset is divided into chunks and sent to an independent process to gather the result. These parallel mapper processes work independently on various available nodes in the cluster. Once their processing is completed (map task), the results are shuffled and sorted before initiating the reduce tasks. The reduce tasks once again run independently on the available nodes and the entire computation is completed as a whole. The intermediate results are stored on the file system (HDFS) and involve IO operations. Due to these IO operations, the MR paradigm is suitable for batch-oriented workloads where very large volumes of datasets are to be processed. In the context of cyber security, the MR framework can be used for processing the historical data originating from the CI and the surrounding application and environmental context. The data can be aggregated for reporting and can be used as the training data for supervised learning-based cyber security implementation.

Apache Pig

HDFS and MR are storage and compute engines at the core of Hadoop. The raw implementation of parallel processing applications is complex and error prone. Apache Pig provides a wrapper around the parallel processing jobs on Hadoop. Pig makes it easy to process large datasets by providing a simple programming interface and API. The tasks and actions written with Pig are inherently parallelized on the underlying Hadoop cluster. In the context of cyber security, Pig can be used for the implementation of complex parallel data aggregation and anomaly detection tasks along with preparation of the training data for supervised learning in case the CI protection application is leveraging machine learning algorithms.

Hive

Apache Hive is the data warehouse built on top of Hadoop. Hive provides an SQL-like interface for the data residing on HDFS. The queries are executed as MR, Tez, or Spark jobs on the Hadoop cluster. Hive supports indexing for fast queries along with compressed storage types like ORC. In the context of cyber security, Hive can be used for storing the aggregate views of various logs which are generated by the CI applications.

While the batch processing frameworks like MR on Hadoop are useful in processing very large volumes of data in an efficient manner, they are not suitable for providing security to mission CIs. Such CI systems require real-time (at least near real-time) processing of the streaming or micro-batch data for quick alerts, notifications, and timely actions. Stream processing architecture requires more focus in the context of cyber security and protection of CIs.

Understanding stream processing

The software applications that are deployed in the enterprise have two basic components:

- The infrastructure
- The applications

The infrastructure includes the physical hardware and the network that connects different systems together. The security implementation for infrastructure and applications have different considerations due to which the frameworks and processes for protecting the CI are also different.

The security systems need to operate across the peripheries of the infrastructure and within the applications. There are various events through which the data (network and application) flows. The events take place at a point in time and the corresponding data is available for analysis and action immediately after the event occurs.

For example, a client application such as a web browser requests access to a website over the HTTP protocol. The sequence of events are initiated right after the URL is entered through the browser. The related analysis based on the request needs to happen as close to the event time as possible in order to protect the web application from malicious attacks. The capability to process the data as a stream for detection of anomalies is a key consideration for an effective cyber security implementation. The key considerations for stream processing are unbounded data, unbounded data processing and low latency-based analysis:

- **Unbounded data**: This term refers to virtually unlimited datasets. For example, the network packets which flow from one physical system to another. These packets contain information that keeps generating as a continuous stream.
- **Unbounded data processing**: The processing needs to happen while the data is in motion. The network packets or the application data needs to be accessed and processed as they are getting generated, unlike a batch processing engine where the data lands into persistent storage before getting processed.
- **Low latency analysis**: The analysis based on the unbounded data needs to happen as close to event time as possible in the case of streaming use cases. Cyber security is a critical use case which requires low latency analysis and actions for it to be effective. As we have seen in *figure 11.2*, anomaly detection is reliable when the event time and alert/notification time is separated by a minimum skew. This differential is variable and depends on multiple conditions such as network congestion, latency introduced to processing overhead in a distributed environment, and so on.

Stream processing semantics

As the events are triggered in a system, there are messages (data packets) which are generated at source and processed within the processing engines. There are three distinct semantics for the stream processing systems, at least once, at most once, and exactly once:

- **At least once**: In this case, the message may be sent by the source more than once. However, the processing engine needs to guarantee that one message is processed at least once out of multiple transmissions of the same message. It is possible that the message is processed more than once and may be acceptable in certain use cases. The end application may need to run a de-duplication check on the semantics.

- **At most once**: The stream processing application guarantees that the message is processed only once. Even if there are multiple transmissions of the same message, the processing engine needs to guarantee that the message is not processed more than once. It may happen in this case that a particular package is not processed at all but it cannot be processed more than once. This semantic is critical in the applications where the end result of the transaction leads itself into an inconsistent state if the message is processed more than once. For example, a banking transaction with a fund transfer needs to strictly follow at most once semantic.

- **Exactly once**: Even if the source system delivers the message more than once, it is consumed and processed exactly once. This is the most ideal semantic for the cyber security systems. A critical message processed only once guarantees timely and right action which can prevent potential attacks on the network and application infrastructure. However, this semantic of exactly once is the most difficult to implement since it requires close collaboration between the source and the target systems. Strong consistency is a primary requirement for the exactly once semantic.

The exactly once semantic of streaming data processing is supported by some of the open source frameworks such as Spark Streaming, Apache Kafka, and Apache Storm. Let us understand these frameworks at a high level before looking at the high-level architecture of the cyber security system that leverages these frameworks.

Spark Streaming

Spark is a general purpose, in-memory, distributed computation engine. The Spark Streaming API is an extension of the core Spark library which was designed with scalability, high throughput, and fault tolerance for streaming (unbounded) data goals in mind. Spark Streaming integrates with a variety of data sources such as TCP network sockets, HTTP server logs, kafka producers, social media streams, and so on.

The streams and complex events are processed with generic operations such as MapReduce, join, and windowing. The data in motion can be analysed, aggregated, filtered, and sent to downstream applications, persistent storage, or live dashboards. Machine learning and graph processing algorithms and APIs can be applied to the unbounded data with Spark Streaming. Spark Streaming breaks down the streaming data into batches based on time-based windowing.

The stream is chunked at specific (predefined and configurable) time intervals and processed as discretized stream as a low-level abstraction of a processing unit. This is called a DStream. DStreams can be created from the input streaming data (network or application logs) or can be consumed from the streaming systems such as Flume, Storm, or Kafka. The Spark Streaming pipeline can be seen conceptually as follows:

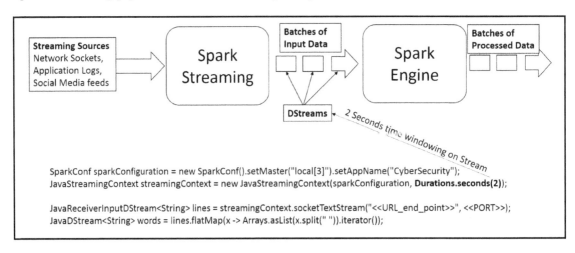

Figure 11.4 Conceptual view of Spark Streaming pipeline

Spark Streaming provides exactly once semantics on the streaming data as a reliable receiver when the streaming source is enabled for acknowledgement processing (for example, Kafka).

Kafka

Kafka acts as a write-ahead log that records messages to a persistent store and allows subscribers to read and apply these changes to their own stores in a system-appropriate timeframe. Common subscribers include live services that do message aggregation or other processing of these streams, as well as Hadoop and data warehousing pipelines, which load virtually all feeds for batch-oriented processing. Overall, Kafka was built with the following goals in mind:

- Loose coupling between message producers and message consumers
- Persistence of message data for different consumers and failure handling
- Maximize end-to-end throughput with low latency components
- Managing diverse data formats and types
- Scaling servers linearly without affecting existing setup

In Kafka, every message is an array of bytes. Producers are the applications or processes that want to store information into Kafka queues. They send messages to Kafka topics, which stores messages of all types. Each topic is divided into one or more partitions. Each partition is an ordered write-ahead log of messages. There are only two operations the system performs:

- To append to the end of the log
- To fetch messages from a given partition beginning from a message ID

Physically, each topic is spread over different Kafka brokers, which host one or two partitions of each topic. Ideally, Kafka pipelines should have a uniform number of partitions per broker and all topics on each machine. Consumers are applications or processes that subscribe to a topic or receive messages from these topics.

The following visual lays out the simplified conceptual layout of a Kafka cluster:

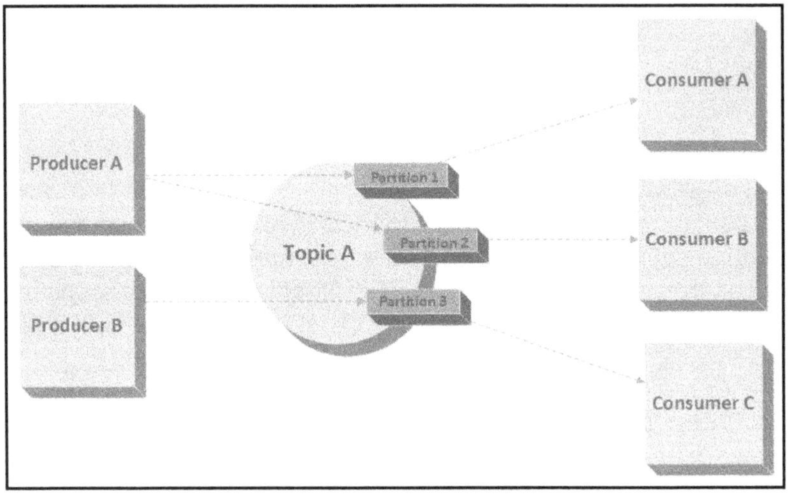

Figure 11.5 Conceptual layout of a Kafka cluster

In messaging systems, messages need to be stored somewhere. In Kafka, we store messages in Topics. Each topic belongs to a category, which means you may have one topic storing items information and another may store sales information. A producer who wants to send a message may send it to a a category of its choosing. A consumer who wants to read those messages will simply subscribe to the category of topics he is interested in and will consume it. Here are few terms that we need to know in terms of publish and subscribe architectures:

- **Retention period**. The messages in the topic need to be stored for a defined period of time to save space irrespective of throughput. We can configure a retention period which is by default 7 days to day of our choice. Kafka will keep messages for the configured period of time and then will delete them.
- **Space retention policy**: We can also configure a Kafka topic to clear messages when the size reaches the threshold mentioned in the configuration. However, this scenario may occur if you haven't done enough capacity planning before deploying Kafka into your organization.
- **Offset**: Each message in Kafka is assigned a number called an **offset**. Topics consist of many partitions; each partition stores messages in the sequence in which they arrived. Consumers acknowledge the message with the offset; this means all the messages before that message offset are received by consumer.

- **Partition**: Each Kafka topic consists of a defined number of partitions. We need to configure the number of partitions while creating topics. Partitions are distributed and help in achieving high throughput.
- **Compaction**: Topic Compaction was introduced in Kafka's 0.8 release. There is no way to change over to previous messages in Kafka, message gets deleted when the retention period is over. Sometimes you may get new Kafka messages with the same key which includes a few changes and on the consumer side you only want to process the latest data. Compaction helps you achieve this goal by compacting all messages with the same key and creates a map offset for **key: offset.** It helps in removing duplicates from large numbers of messages.
- **Leader**: Partitions are replicated across Kafka clusters based on the replication factor specified. Each partition has a leader broker and followers, and all the read and write requests to the partition will go through the leader only. If the leader fails another leader will get elected and the process will resume.
- **Buffering**: Kafka buffers messages both at the producer and consumer side to increase throughput and to reduce IO.

A combination of Spark Streaming and Kafka produces a comprehensive architecture for the implementation of cyber security applications. These applications are fault tolerant, ensure low latency, and are capable of handling large numbers of events per second. Here is a reference architecture for cyber security applications using the Big Data ecosystem:

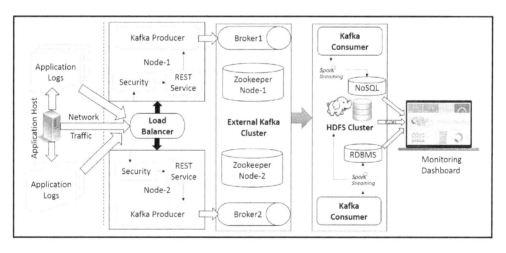

Figure 11.6 Cyber security application - reference architecture

Let's now understand some of the common types of cyber security attacks and general strategies to deal with those.

Cyber security attack types

"One of the main cyber-risks is to think they don't exist. The other is to try to treat all potential risks. (Fix the basics, protect first what matters for your business and be ready to react properly to pertinent threats. Think data, but also business services integrity, awareness, customer experience, compliance, and reputation)."

– Stephane Nappo

As more and more systems and CIs are getting digitized, the number of security breaches is also growing. The attackers utilize novel techniques to exploit the vulnerabilities within the applications to get access to unauthorized information and administrative privileges. In this section, we will list some of the common attack types and generic resolutions to those.

Phishing

This is one of the most common and successful (from an attacker's perspective) attacks on the applications. Most of the time, the attacker sends an email or some kind of familiar communication to the user to trick him/her into following the URL and providing the credentials. The idea is to make the user believe that the message is genuine. The attacker, at times, creates a dummy but identical web page which the user is familiar with and finds no reason to suspect the genuineness. Once the user clicks the URL, some malicious software gets downloaded to the machine and starts accessing information over the connected networks.

 These attacks can be prevented by using machine learning algorithms. The user's email headers and content can be used as the training data and can train the model to understand the common patterns. This learning can help in detecting the phishing attempt based on the behavioral trends in the historical emails.

Lateral movement

When an attacker gets access to the network of an enterprise, he/she tries to exploit vulnerabilities on a given network node. While doing this, the attacker moves from one network endpoint to another while gaining access to more services and the administration of the network and application infrastructure. This movement leaves traces within the network logs.

Machine learning algorithms can be trained with lateral movements to trace data and detect the suspicious user movements. If these movements are tracked by streaming the live network logs through the processing systems, the intrusion can potentially be detected in near real time.

Injection attacks

The malicious code is supplied into the target application via form fields or other input mechanisms. SQL injection is a special case of injection attack where the SQL statements are pushed into the system via field inputs and the SQL commands can get the dump of the sensitive data outside of the network. The attacker can get access to the authentication details if they reside in the database. Despite all the field validations and filtering at the web server layer, the injection attacks are frequent and one of the leading types of attack. The database logs can be used to train machine learning models based on statistical user profiles which can be built over a period of time as the users interacts with the databases.

The abnormalities in the access pattern can be called out as anomalies and the alerts can be generated. Apart from SQL injection, the attackers at times run scripts that impersonate the actual application user and execute business functional actions on behalf of the actual user. For example, if the attacker can get access to the e-commerce platform and starts placing orders on behalf of the actual users or performs similar operations such as changing the address. In this case, the machine learning models need to be trained to learn the individual user behavior and these models should be utilized to identify the suspicious changes in the user navigation and action pattern in the web application.

AI-based defense

"With AI and machine learning we can do inference and pattern-based monitoring and alerting, but the real opportunity is the predictive restoration."

– Rob Stroud

As the AI becomes democratized, the attackers will also have access to tools and techniques to leverage AI for attacking the CIs. The defense mechanism for such attacks also needs to upgrade itself to use the power of data and computation to quickly build AI-based models in order to defend the CI and other applications.

As a general principle, the following diagram shows the stages of AI-based defense mechanisms against cyber security attacks:

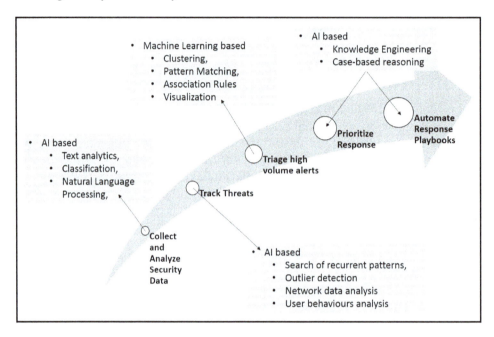

Figure 11.7 Stages of AI-based defence against cyber security attacks

Various machine learning algorithms can be used for detection and prevention of cyber attacks. While each application is different in terms of its network and security configuration, a general guideline for the prevention of cyber attacks by different machine learning algorithms is depicted in the following diagram:

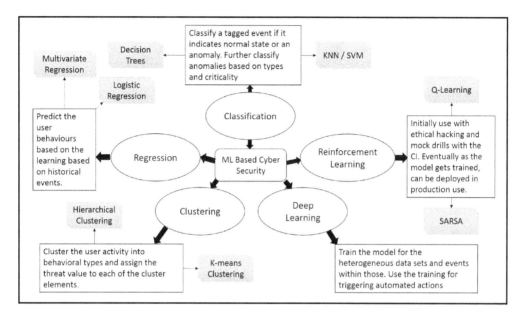

Figure 11.8 Prevention of cyber security attacks with Machine Learning algorithms

Understanding SIEM

Security Incident and Event Management (**SIEM**) is a process that helps cyber security implementation by gathering security-related information (network and application logs for example) at a centralized location or tags those information assets at the edge (the location where the data is generated in the case of IoT) and uses this information for identification of anomalies which indicates breaches to the security infrastructure of an enterprise.

The SIEM also facilitates continuous monitoring of the security infrastructure by providing intuitive visualization dashboards. SIEM as a process is implemented as a suite of software which is governed by enterprise security with role-based access control. The common characteristic features of the SIEM system are depicted in the following diagram:

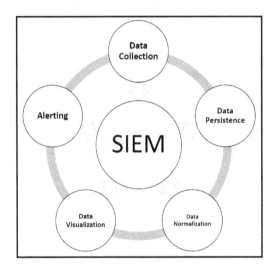

Figure 11.9 Features of the SIEM system

The SIEM software application needs to support the basic building blocks as follows:

- **Data Collection**: The SIEM software should support a variety of network communication protocols in order to connect to heterogeneous systems within the organization's boundary. The raw data is available in the form of logs from the enterprise applications, network traffic packets, and hardware controllers. These raw data assets need to be collected in a seamless and secure manner. Each individual system should be identified and added to the data collection stack for the successful implementation of the SIEM. The collected data from across systems can have a variety of formats such as text, XML, JSON, binary, and so on. The SIEM system needs to support a diverse variety of data formats.
- **Data Persistence**: Depending on the data volumes, the SIEM software can use the local and network drives or utilize distributed file systems like HDFS for data persistence. As soon as the data from the applications and appliances is available to SIEM, it needs to parse the data depending on the format, index it, and make it available for ad hoc searching by the human user or by an integrated application. The historical and rolling logs are an ongoing and ever-increasing asset and hence the indexing function of the SIEM system needs to be advanced and efficient.

- **Data Normalization**: This is one of the most important aspects of SIEM software. Once the data is sourced and persisted, it needs to be modeled and normalized. The purpose of normalization is to make it easy for the visualization component to display critical information on the dashboard. The normalization module can also utilize the data assets to build machine learning models based on historical trends. The SIEM systems that leverage the data to train the machine learning models and provide predictive analytics will be more in demand compared to the SIEM systems which perform descriptive analytics and provide rules-based alerts.

- **Data Visualization**: The visualization is the window for the personnel in charge of enterprise security as well as management, which may require a high-level view of overall system status. Since the decisions and actions are based on what is visually seen on the dashboard, the SIEM systems need to deploy a thoughtful and thorough process for defining visualizations. Since every enterprise and the use case is unique, one visualization cannot fit all. The SIEM tool needs to provide easy customizations to the visualization component. A generic set of features of visualization are depicted in the following diagram:

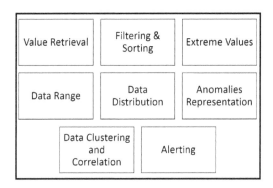

Figure 11.10 Features of the visualization component within SIEM

Visualization attributes and features

The visualization attributes and features are as follows:

- **Value retrieval**: The SIEM software should support retrieval of any attribute values across the data assets. In an ideal scenario, the SIEM software will support the SQL-like query language to fetch data based on multiple datasets based on some join condition.

- **Filtering and sorting**: The SIEM software should support intuitive filtering and sorting on the basis of one or multiple key columns desired by the end user.
- **Extreme values**: The SIEM software should support highlighting the extreme values for the attributes with color coding so that the user can quickly take action based on critical conditions.
- **Data range**: For the key attributes, the SIEM should provide a feature to highlight the range values so as to identify anomalies, if any.
- **Data distribution**: The SIEM software should have a feature to show the data distribution for key attributes based on a set of criteria. It can answer questions like: what is the distribution of various types of cyber security attacks? The support team can tackle the top reasons to safeguard the CI efficiently.
- **Anomalies representation**: The anomalies should be represented in such a way that they attract attention and provide enough information for mitigating the risks immediately.
- **Data clustering and correlation**: The data related to CI security infrastructure applications should be visualized in clusters or groups of correlated entities. The application should be able to support some operations (filtering, sorting, and so on) on the clusters.
- **Alerting**: The SIEM software should support mechanisms to generate alerts on critical events. The user needs to have the capability to configure alert thresholds and configure new alerts as required. In case of commonly used logs like web server access logs, the application should have predefined alerts which can be quickly set up by configuring threshold values. The software should also make use of historical data to train machine learning models which generate preventive alerts based on the past trends.

We are going to review two SIEM software packages in this chapter. Splunk and ArcSight ESM are two of the most popular SIEM applications which are widely deployed for some of the mission CIs.

Splunk

Splunk is one of the most popular and time-tested SIEM solutions on the market at the time of writing. It is trusted by more than 15,000 customers worldwide for the protection of CIs. In this section, we will review some of the features Splunk supports for security monitoring and alerting.

A high-level overview of the Splunk platform is depicted in the following visual:

Figure 11.11 Overview of the Splunk platform

Splunk as a platform provides a range of sub-products which cater to specific organizational needs. In the context of this chapter, let us review the high-level features of **Splunk Enterprise Security** and **Splunk Light**.

Splunk Enterprise Security

This is a comprehensive suite which takes a holistic view of enterprise security by improving security operations with reduced action time, making machine data available for end-to-end visualization with interactive dashboards, and leveraging machine learning and AI to train predictive models for preventive security measures.

Splunk Light

Splunk Light is a specific product feature that deals with enterprise-wide logs. The logs contain loads of information which can be leveraged for corrective and preventive cyber security. Splunk Light enables enterprises to collect and index all the log files irrespective of their structure and other semantics.

The data input layer is flexible enough to accept logs in any format. There is an intuitive user interface that reads logs from the configured location and drives the user through various runtime configurations which makes it easy to index the contents of the log files. The forwarder component can collect the logs from the systems which are not directly accessible to Splunk due to network limits.

The forwarder can connect to external sources with numerous supported protocols and fetches the data into Splunk Light for preprocessing and indexing. Splunk supports the schemaless writes paradigm of Big Data frameworks. The schema is defined at the read time and there can be multiple interpretations of the data assets based on context and the use case.

Another handy feature is the support for chronology inference. Splunk can determine the event sequence based on the timestamp and the messages where the timestamp is missing; it can also infer the timestamp based on context. All the logs are available at a centralized location and can be accessed in a consistent manner irrespective of source and format. The logs are continuously indexed in the background and are available for analysis, filtering, sorting, and aggregation.

Splunk supports **Splunk Search Processing Language** (**SPL**) as a simple SQL-like query interface into the log files. It also supports analytical and visualization commands which makes it easy to detect anomalies based on distinct patterns and outliers. The search is agnostic with respect to pre-processed and indexed logs or the streaming logs. There is a common interface for searching the logs which enables real-time query into the logs.

The search results can be visualized with an interactive dashboard. The visualization provides slice and dice capabilities out of the box and can be easily customized based on the enterprise requirements. Here is a screenshot of Search Processing Language query execution:

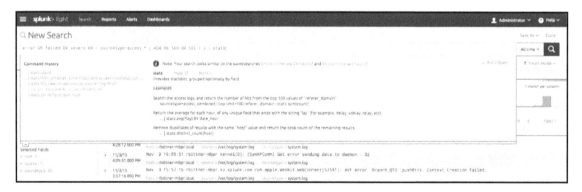

Figure 11.12 Search Processing Language in Splunk

For an SIEM to be effective, the event data from multiple discrete sources needs to be available for analysis at a centralized place; Splunk enables the correlation of complex events across various systems. This enables monitoring of the lineage of the event as it originates from the source and its correlation with the events from other source systems. This facilitates out-of-the-box investigation for the security team with improved chances of finding the root cause of anomalies.

Splunk Light can detect changes in pattern automatically without requiring any user intervention. For example, a particular web application host receives n requests on day d of a week, if there is a significant change. Splunk can highlight the change in pattern which can be quickly investigated. Splunk Light allows the configuration of alerts based on common searches performed by the administration teams. The alerts queries can be set to run with a predefined frequency or in real time as per the use case context, as seen in the following screenshot:

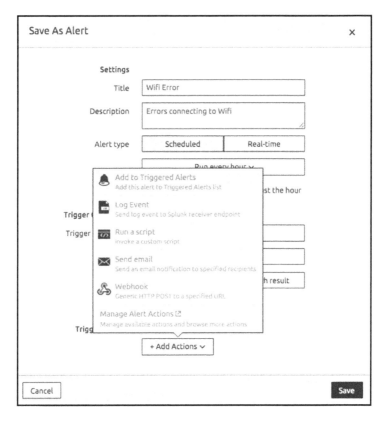

Figure 11.13 Configuration of alerts based on queries in Splunk (source: splunk.com)

ArcSight ESM

ArcSight ESM is an HP SIEM product which provides premiere security event management solutions. ArcSight analyzes and correlates every event and makes it available for anomaly detection. The product greatly complements efforts in compliance and risk management. It helps the network operations teams. Key features of ArcSight are as follows:

- Regulatory compliance
- Automated log collection and archiving
- Fraud detection
- Real-time threat detection
- Business KPI to IT assets mapping and monitoring
- Business impact analysis of the threats and automated prioritization

Frequently asked questions

Let us have a small recap.

Q: What is the significance of Big Data in cyber security?

A: Big data and cyber security complement each other and play a vital role in each other's relevance and utility. As more and more devices are getting digitally connected, they are generating more data (volume); the data generated by these connected devices needs to be processed in neartime (velocity) and it follows a variety of forms such as structured, unstructured, and semi-structured (variety). These three Vs constitute Big Data in general which lead to Value as fourth V. The cyber security systems require that the Big Data is processed in its entirety in order to provide actionable insights into the security infrastructure of an enterprise and to help in detecting anomalies and preventing attacks on an organization's computing assets.

Q: What is the meaning of **critical infrastructure** (**CI**)? What are the key components for protection of the CI?

A: Critical Infrastructure is a term used by enterprises and government agencies to define the assets and working models that need to function at their optimal level in order for a seamless and harmonious experience for the stakeholders who directly or indirectly benefit from or are impacted by these systems. A country's power grid is a good example of CI.

Most of the CI systems are now digitized and hence controlled with computer programs with minimum human supervision. The criticality of these systems functioning round the clock also makes them vulnerable to cyber attacks. The systems that protect the CI against the attacks are also critically important from a defense perspective. The CI systems generate large volumes of log data and other operational data. This data is the most important asset in protecting the CIs. Apart from data, we need systems that are able to consume and process these data assets in a timely manner for detecting anomalies in system behaviors and generate alerts which trigger human or automated actions.

Q: How can machine learning and AI be leveraged for effective protection of CI?

A: Rules-based alerts and monitoring systems are not sufficient to deal with the cyber security attacks and for protecting CIs. The machine learning models need to be trained based on the historical data (supervised learning) in order to predict the occurrence of malicious activities in advance or in near real time when the intrusion is in progress. The machine learning and AI transitions the cyber security systems to predictive analysis which helps in preventing the attacks.

Q: Is it possible that the attackers also leverage AI for breaching security infrastructure? How do we protect against it?

A:Yes, AI and machine learning is already leveraged by attackers in breaching security infrastructure. It is a race to get the better of the attackers and protect the systems. Data is the advantage with the systems which protect the CI. The data across heterogeneous sources needs to be leveraged in near real time to stay ahead and protect the CIs.

Q: What is the significance of Stream Processing in cyber security?

A: Big data assets can be processed in batch and real-time modes. Batch mode processing is suitable for large volumes of data and when the processes are not time sensitive (do not need to be real time). However, the CI systems constantly generate data as an unbounded source of information. The ingestion, processing, and analysis needs to happen as close to the event time as possible in order to stand a chance of protecting the CIs. Stream processing is an architectural paradigm that deals with unbounded data which is consumed as a stream and processed even while it is in motion. This comes handy with performing anomaly detection even while the intrusion is in progress and helps in preventing potential attacks on CI.

Summary

In this chapter, we have studied the basic concepts of cyber security and the significance of Big Data in dealing with threats to the security of critical applications. Big data processing has two fundamental types, batch processing and real-time processing, for streaming data sources. We have studied the fundamental concepts and frameworks in batch and real-time processing.

Real-time stream-based processing is important in dealing with cyber security threats. We have seen the different types of common security threats and vulnerabilities exploited by the attackers. Machine learning and AI are largely democratized and leveraged by attackers for sophisticated attacks on the CIs. This makes utilization of machine learning and AI a critical consideration while building the systems which deal with cyber security attacks. We have reviewed the basic building blocks of the SIEM systems and a couple of examples, Splunk and ArcSight SEM, as two of the most popular SIEM frameworks. The field of cyber security is of prime importance and more research needs to happen in order to protect data assets. The protection of data assets is even more significant with ever-increasing dependence of CI and other systems on the availability of accurate and reliable data.

In the next and final chapter of this book, we will study cognitive computing. Cognitive intelligence takes the machines as close to human intelligence as possible. It is an exciting field of research and we will review some of the fundamental concepts and tools available for experimenting with and realizing cognitive intelligence in smart machines which will complement and augment human capabilities.

12
Cognitive Computing

So far in this book, we have studied the general principles of **machine learning** (**ML**) and **artificial intelligence** (**AI**). This is a good foundation and a starting point for creating intelligent machines that can complement and augment human capabilities. This is possible with the ever increasing computational power along with the availability of ever growing volumes of data. However, in order to build artificial machines that can potentially match (or inch closer to) the human brain, we need to develop our understanding of human cognition.

While a tremendous amount of research and thinking has happened for so many decades (or centuries), we are far from fully decoding nature's program when it comes to human cognition. In this chapter, we will initiate the reader on cognitive science and introduce some of the frameworks that are available to take the research forward. During the course of this final chapter, we will introduce you to the following:

- General principles of cognitive science
- Cognitive Systems
- Application of cognitive intelligence in big data analytics
- An introduction of IBM Watson as one of the most advanced cognitive computing frameworks
- Developing an IBM Watson application in Java

Cognitive science

In our quest to build intelligent machines, we are attempting to build capabilities that match and for the most part mimic the human brain and the sensory organs. There are five senses and primary organs corresponding to each through which we perceive this world. The goal of cognitive science is to build these sensory capabilities in intelligent machines so that the interactions with them are natural and seamless:

- **Vision**: To see the objects, understand their position in three primary dimensions, and also their movement along with time as the fourth dimension. While we use our eyes as an external interface for vision, everything else happens within the brain. By deploying principles of cognitive science, we are able to build intelligent systems that can see the objects and their movements with video cameras and create a mathematical model for converting the visual signal into a knowledge.
- **Audition**: With this sense, we hear various audio signals. The external interface to this in the human body is ears, and once again the audio processing takes place in the brain. We can identify the person via voice, understand the meaning of the signal all due to the brain's capacity to process the signal in real time, and use memory to put the audio signal in context and trigger necessary actions. The AI systems can also be modeled to perceive audio signals and process those with NLP and translate them into knowledge and also trigger actions.
- **Gustation**: With this sense, we can perceive taste of an object (food). The external interface is the tongue and the taste signal is processed within the brain.
- **Olfaction**: With this sense, we can smell various objects. The external interface is the nose and the signals are all processed within the brain.
- **Somatosensation**: With this sense, we can feel various objects. The external interface is the skin and once again the entire processing of temperature, texture, and all the other tangible aspects of an object are processed and understood by the brain.

During the course of this book in previous chapters, we have seen theories, mathematical models, tools, and frameworks for creating intelligent machines that mimic human intelligence with these five senses. The manifestations of these senses are tangible and can be physically modeled. However, there is a sixth organ and corresponding sense that governs human life within a larger context and it is called the **mind**.

The **human mind** is the closest manifestation of universal consciousness and it is believed to control all the other five senses. The mind is in play when we talk about willpower, emotions, determination, and all other things intangible, but it is the most important aspect when it comes to building intelligent machines or fully creating AI that is going to complement and augment human capabilities in a larger sense.

While it is important to study and eventually mimic the human mind, at the same time, it is difficult. This is because the human mind is not easy to observe, measure, or manipulate and sometimes it is termed as the most complex entity (that is intangible too) in the universe. Cognitive science is a branch of science that performs interdisciplinary study of the mind. While the individual disciplines are independent of each other in their research space and domain, they have a common string connected to the study of the mind. Some of the primary fields that coincide with study of the mind are depicted in the following diagram:

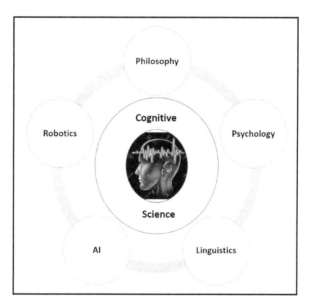

Figure 12.1: Cognitive science as an interdisciplinary study of mind

While the functioning of the mind is still an unexplored area of research to a large extent, for the sake of simplicity, we can treat the mind as a central information processing unit and relate it to a computer that gathers inputs, processes those based on predefined and fuzzy rules, and transforms them into outputs that serve a larger purpose. The human mind can also represent the information and translates it into knowledge and actions. The inputs are received from the perceptive organs that we have listed earlier.

However, there is a fundamental difference between the digital computers and primarily analog human mind and its representation in the brain. When we think about building intelligent machines, the larger goal of AI when it comes to cognitive computing is to use computing infrastructure and knowledge assets (database) to solve real-world problems that complement and augment human capabilities. The deeper-level goal is to ultimately decode the meta-knowledge and human intelligence to have a chance at building machines with cognitive abilities (emotional and spiritual intelligence). With the deeper goal in perspective, the AI can be divided into three stages, as depicted in the following diagram:

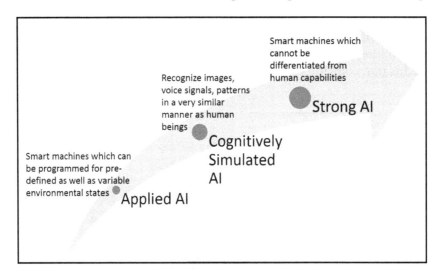

Figure 12.2: Stages of AI

They are as follows:

- **Applied AI**: We have had applied AI in mainstream use for quite some time now. The household appliances that work on fuzzy logic (washing machines, air conditioners, and so on), the smart navigation systems that can predict the driving time based on real-time traffic situations, the industrial robots that perform predefined tasks within a level of variation in the environmental state are some of the examples of applied AI. The applied AI leverages machine learning models and the data assets to implement supervised, unsupervised, and reinforcement learning algorithms to develop smart machines.

- **Cognitively Simulated AI**: With this, the machines are enabled with natural language processing, interpreting video and other sensory inputs from the environment, and react based on the context and truly augment human capabilities. The intelligent assistants that we have on our phones simulate cognitive intelligence for a seamless interaction with the smart machines. In order to realize cognitively simulated AI, we require a higher level of computation power along with data. With big data systems in the mainstream, we have already realized the applications based on cognitively simulated AI.

- **Strong AI**: In this stage, the field of AI gets as close to human intelligence as it can be and with the brute force as an additional advantage with the computers, the systems based on strong AI can potentially surpass human intelligence and create a paradigm shift in our experience of the world. At this level, the AI is based on high-level cognition and can perform multi-stage reasoning, fully understand the "meaning" of the natural language, and can potentially generate artifacts without being instructed to do so.

"The goal of strong AI is nothing less than to build a machine on the model of a man, a robot that is to have its childhood, to learn language as a child does, to gain its knowledge of the world by sensing the world through its own organs, and ultimately to contemplate the whole domain of human thought."

–Weizenbaum (MIT AI Laboratory)

While applied AI and cognitively simulated AI are already well adopted for various use cases and have become mainstream, the Cognitive science is a quest toward Strong AI. That means, some of the very basic activities which human beings can perform naturally without any external training like use of language, logical reasoning, plan future activities and strategies are some of the most difficult abilities to be replicated in intelligent machines. These behaviors are the core cognitive competencies which we are planning to incorporate in machines within the scope of study of Cognitive science and developing strong AI.

In the next section, let us review some of the characteristics of the Cognitive Systems which can possibly be built with the goal to achieve Strong AI.

Cognitive Systems

One of the key characteristics of **Cognitive Systems** (**CS**) is that they have the ability to interact and interface with human beings with natural language in a similar as possible manner to human interactions. The systems are capable of learning and thinking from the stochastic environmental context as well as historical data inputs. The systems should be able to quickly evolve from dependency on the structured data inputs (traditional computing) to semi-structured and unstructured data inputs very similar to the human interface.

We have already seen in the chapter on fuzzy systems that the systems based on AI should be trainable to accept fuzzy inputs in a natural format without any cleansing or harmonizing. Since Cognitive Systems interact with human beings in a natural way, they can extend and amplify human capabilities with an added advantage of brute-force and a virtually unlimited amount of data storage capabilities.

As we have seen in the introductory section in this chapter, the development of CS is a multidisciplinary effort and requires a great deal of collaboration and knowledge sharing in order to progress in the direction of realizing a truly Cognitive System that cannot be differentiated from human capabilities in terms of intelligent behavior. The multidisciplinary nature of Cognitive Systems can be depicted as follows:

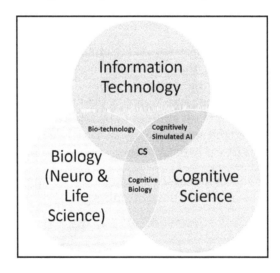

Figure 12.3: Cognitive Systems (CS) as a multidisciplinary effort

As we can see, Cognitive Systems can be built with combined efforts from **information technology** (**IT**), Biology (Neuro and Life Science), and Cognitive science. IT provides the backbone for the CS with data storage and data processing capabilities. With the advent of cloud-based distributed computing, we have potentially unlimited storage and computing power at our disposal. IT systems also translate the high-level natural inputs into low-level digital forms that are interoperable and a means of communication between multiple Cognitive Systems. Biological knowledge, specifically in the area of neurology and physiological study of the brain and the nervous system, helps in emulating some of the tangible patterns in Cognitive Systems. The nervous system is the most complex system and is far from being fully understood at this time. However, Cognitive Systems can draw a lot of inspiration from neurological studies.

Cognitive science incorporates the knowledge of psychology, mind, and its interface with physiology, linguistics, and so on. These three fields combined together have the potential to develop a true Cognitive System that resembles human behavior and complements and augments its capabilities.

Let's look at how far CS has evolved at this point.

A brief history of Cognitive Systems

Cognitive Systems have greatly evolved at this point in time even though we are far from making a truly Cognitive System that matches human abilities.

Here is a brief timeline of the evolution of Cognitive Systems:

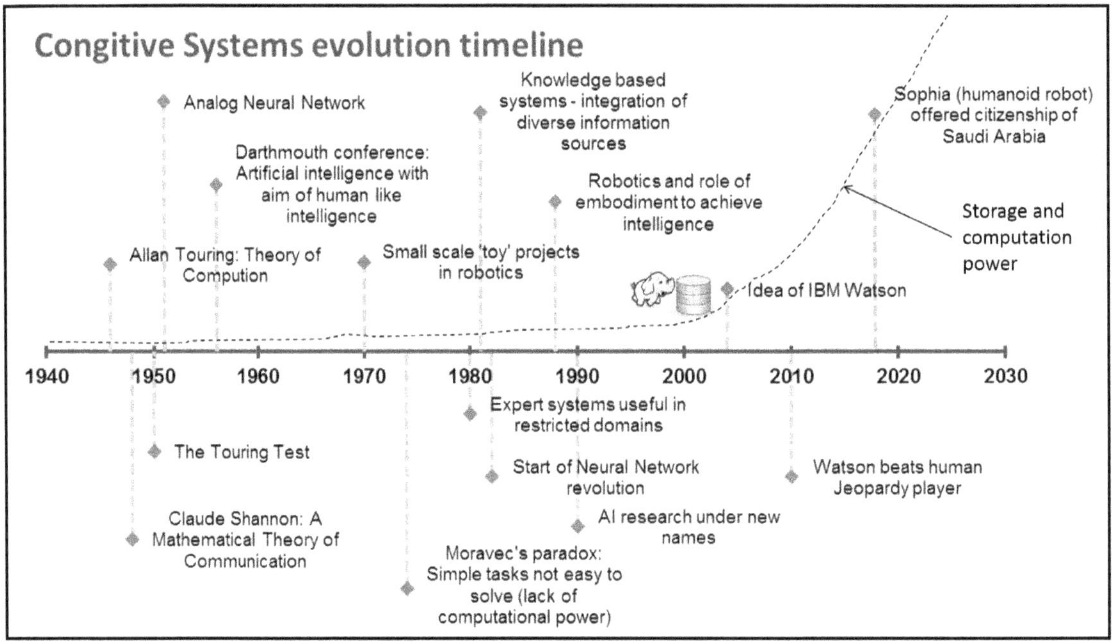

Figure 12.4: Cognitive Systems evolution timeline

As you can see in this figure, the general theories and science behind realization of Cognitive Systems have existed for decades, but the acceleration in the evolution process is a result of availability of big data analytics frameworks that are based on distributed computing architectures that started becoming mainstream around the year 2000. With exponential growth in the digital data assets along with the computation power, the systems are poised to evolve at a faster rate every passing day. A significant feat was achieved in 2010 when IBM's Watson engine, which is based on cognitive intelligence, beat a world champion in a game of Jeopardy.

With this background, let us look at some of the goals for Cognitive Systems.

Goals of Cognitive Systems

The primary goal for Cognitive Systems is to complement human capabilities and augment those for overall benefit and betterment of human society by helping to solve some of the problems (effective and accurate diagnosis of some diseases, autonomous and self-driving cars, decoding human DNA, and so on) that are faced by the human race. When we design Cognitive Systems, there are certain generic capabilities that contribute to achieving overall goals for the CS. These capabilities are as follows:

- **Exploration**: The CS should be able to autonomously explore the environmental context and infer meaning from it. This exploration can go beyond the immediate or close context into the vast amounts of digital data that is available for converting into information and finally into knowledge assets. The architecture of Cognitive Systems should facilitate unbounded exploration within and outside of the context.

- **Retrieval**: Once the data is available as knowledge assets in logically and cognitively connected entities, the architecture should enable effective and timely retrieval of the knowledge assets as and when required for the system to drive effective and accurate actions.

- **Semantic Search**: This is a generic extension of the retrieval capabilities. Whenever a human interface or another Cognitive System needs some information based on cognitive inputs, the CS should be able to search the knowledge assets in a timely manner and feed the extracted information to the entity that has requested the information based on the context. At this point, the keywords should have semantic context associated with them instead of being just plain text. This is based on the ontological mapping as we have seen in `Chapter 2`, *Ontology for Big Data*.

- **Physical activity and state manipulation**: The Cognitive System should have tangible components that are capable of physical activities. For example, a robotic arm that can perform a delicate surgery. The system should also be able to manipulate the state of the environment based on the context and the optimal behavior of the intended Cognitive System. For example, the system should be able to turn ON the music for a person in a room based on the mood, time of the day, and so many other personalized parameters.

- **Information enrichment**: This is a very important aspect of a Cognitive System. Based on the historical data, current environmental context, and the learning, the CS should be able to enrich the knowledge assets in an implicit and seamless manner without having to explicitly perform data entry operations. It should be an automated closed control loop that draws and commits information into the knowledge base in order to enrich it with every interaction.

- **Navigation and Control**: The Cognitive Systems should be capable of navigating physical objects within the problem space considering the environmental context. The well known example is the self-driving cars, traffic control systems, and smart-home systems that can control various operating parameters of the system in real time.

- **Decision Support**: The Cognitive Systems should facilitate effective decision making in day-to-day as well as mission critical applications. For example, a medical decision to operate a particular condition in a patient or to treat it with available medicine based on the patient's history, symptoms, and various reports can be taken by the Cognitive System based on the following:

    - **Model**: In this type of **decision support system** (**DSS**), the decision is made based on well-established models and theories in the specific field of consideration. The Cognitive System should be able to interpret and infer from the model in a consistent manner.

    - **Data**: In this type of DSS, the decision is made based on the historical data. This is an example of supervised learning algorithms that the CS can deploy for decision making.

    - **Communication**: The Cognitive System should be able to communicate in real time with various other human and non-human Cognitive Systems in order to derive decisions in a particular situation.

    - **Document**: Document-driven decision is based on large volumes of unstructured data that is digitized as scanned documents and audio-video files. The Cognitive Systems should be enabled to search into these knowledge assets and provide context sensitive decision support in a timely and efficient manner.

    - **Knowledge**. These are specialized types of Cognitive Systems that operate on domain-specific data assets and ontologies. These are meant for special purposes with a very limited context. These systems also leverage the machine learning models based on the historical data assets and past decisions. These systems constantly add to the data assets, build semantic relationships within the domain, and provide decisions similar to the natural human interfaces in which management seeks some of the reports and projects from the teams. The decision support systems based on domain-specific knowledge assets within the enterprise can potentially improve operational efficiencies multifold.

- **Natural language interface**: Cognitive Systems support natural language as a means for data input and generate outputs in natural language that resemble human interactions. These systems should also be enabled to interact with the other Cognitive Systems in a standardized and natural format. This facilitates seamless knowledge exchange and system improvisations with time.

With these goals and expected capabilities within Cognitive Systems, let us look at some of the entities that enable realization of Cognitive Systems.

Cognitive Systems enablers

In order to build Cognitive Systems that resemble human intellectual behavior, we need the following core ingredients:

- **Data**: As depicted in the previous diagram, the Cognitive Systems evolution accelerated after the mainstream availability of large volumes of data in digital format. The theories and algorithms that were prescribed decades ago, could not be evaluated to lack of substantial amounts of data. Data is one of the biggest enablers for Cognitive Systems.
- **Computation**: In order to process the data and apply the theories and algorithms, we need ever increasing computational power. Once again, as soon as the distributed computing power was mainstream, the evolution of Cognitive Systems has accelerated.
- **Connectivity**: Cognitive Systems need data from heterogeneous sources for cross referencing the entities and derive meaning from those in order to create a knowledge base. The connectivity of all the data sources as well as the entities within the data sources is extremely critical for development of efficient and accurate Cognitive Systems.
- **Sensors**: There has been a recent advance in Internet of things (IoT) where the sensing devices generate data that can be mission critical in many applications. Cognitive Systems also deploy various sensors that emulate human sensory systems in order to facilitate natural language conversations and interactions with human beings as well as other Cognitive Systems.
- **Theories in understanding human brain**: In order to propel the research in the right direction, we need to understand the functioning of the human brain in more detail. We are still far from fully understanding how the human brain works. In order for Cognitive Systems to really come close to human intelligence levels, we need to also study the mind. Mind research is complex due to the intangible nature of the mind.

- **Nature**: Cognitive Systems need to derive inspiration from nature and how various creatures interact with each other with the basic survival instincts. All the natural creatures have the level of intelligence to interact within their environmental context as well as survive effectively. As we have seen in the chapter on swarm intelligence, the natural behaviors for the creatures can help in building Cognitive Systems.

Application in Big Data analytics

Frequently, the terms big data and Cognitive Intelligence are used together. Let us understand the relationship between these two concepts. During the course of this book, we have already seen primary aspects and details of big data, such as Volume, Velocity, and Variety. The data volumes are growing exponentially with more devices and systems producing data across business domains and platforms.

As a simple example, a person living in any urban area across the world, is producing at least a few megabytes of data every day with the use of smartphones, televisions, various electronic gadgets, and even cars. These personalized datasets along with industrial and enterprise data assets are adding to the volume of data everyday. This data is generated and stored at an ever increasing velocity into centralized servers on the premise or within the cloud. In order for the data assets to be of value, the analysis and actionable insights should be generated as close to the event time as possible. That means the velocity of data processing is another key aspect of big data.

Most of the data assets we have talked about in this section do not have a standardized format. They are generated in a large variety of formats and are mostly unstructured in nature. There is also an increasing volume of structured and semistructured data that is constantly getting generated. The variety is the third dimension of big data. The computational models that can store and process this big data is very well established in the form of distributed computing frameworks such as Hadoop and others. The growth of big data analytics is also fueled and accelerated with the availability of these **platforms as a service** (**PAAS**) onto cloud. The entire cluster of analytics platform can be spawned within minutes and it can be auto-scaled as per the data volume and compute requirements.

These big data analytics platforms are the foundation on which cognitive intelligence can be built. As we have seen earlier in this chapter, underlying technologies that facilitate big data, are the core components that are required for building artificial intelligence. The key components are the ability to store massive amounts of data and massive amount of computation power.

Despite growing volumes of data that is available in digital format, we still have more than 80% of data that is in rudimentary format. For example, the ancient scriptures, century-old official documents in paper format, handwritten books, and so on. Some of these knowledge assets are digitized, but they are still in unstructured raw format. This large data is extremely critical and a significant portion of our knowledge assets. This data as a whole is called dark data. One of the core objectives and possibilities with the use of big data and Cognitive Intelligence together is to be able to tap into the dark data.

Using cognitive intelligence, we can create a semantic view of the dark data that can be brought into mainstream data assets can be part of the evolution of Cognitive Systems. It is impossible to fully understand and use the dark data with manual processes. We need big data technology tools along with the algorithmic approach of cognitive intelligence in order to utilize the dark data. The cognitive image and document processing techniques such as advanced imaging, optical character recognition, natural language processing, and various machine learning algorithms for text classification. Once the knowledge assets are digitized, they are semantically organized along with the relationships at the ontological entity level.

Within the traditional big data systems that are collectively referred to as **Enterprise Data Hub (EDH)** or Data Lake, one of the key components is data modeling. This is an exercise that maps the source systems to the target data structure into the data lake. The data modeling is a largely manual process, which requires understanding the significance of the data attributes (columns) in the source systems that are domain specific structures and map those to the fields in the data lake. With the use of cognitive intelligence, it is possible to fully eliminate the data modeling process. In this new paradigm, the Cognitive System parses and semantically understands the source database and generates a connected prototype of the target structure, which is efficient in search and exploration and fully available for advanced analytics. Essentially with a combination of big data technologies along with the cognitive intelligence, the data management systems are poised to be autonomous, more efficient, and accurate. Since the manual intervention is minimum, the data analysis and hence actionable insights are available faster.

With the use of cognitive intelligence, it is possible to seamlessly interact with the data platform. In the traditional big data analytics world, we are using visualization and reporting tools for generating and showing trends in the data and doing prescriptive analytics on the data. The data assets are also made available for machine learning models for performing predictive analytics. If we introduce cognitive intelligence in these systems, we can interact with the data platform in a more natural manner.

This is very similar to human interaction where we can ask domain and context specific questions to the platform in natural language and by tapping into the underlying data assets and application of various machine learning algorithms, the answers are presented to the user in a natural form. This capability opens up a whole new world of how human-machine interfaces can evolve to the extent where it will be difficult to tell if we are interacting with a machine or a human being.

Cognitive intelligence as a service

The field of cognitive intelligence is vast and exciting since we are trying to follow an intangible entity, the human mind. As our understanding of how human cognition works, we can implement similar behaviors in Cognitive Systems. At a high level, the cognitive intelligence based human decision process has four basic components as follows:

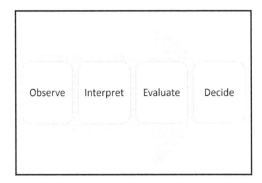

Figure 12.5: Basic components of cognitive intelligence based human decision process

We observe the environment and the various inputs simultaneously through the sensory organs. The inputs are interpreted within the context of environmental state. During the interpretation stage, we refer to the historical data as well as the intended goal for the process. Once the interpretation is done, various options based on the past experiences and future rewards are evaluated and the best option is selected, which maximizes the overall gain. The decision making is also based on a reinforcement learning process, which we have seen in Chapter 10, *Reinforcement Learning*. Any platform that facilitates the decision making processes based on cognitive intelligence needs to implement the four building blocks at the core.

While the research is ongoing and it will accelerate in the near future, companies like IBM, Microsoft, and Google are some of the pioneers in the field. They have already invested in AI research in general and cognitive computing related research and application development in particular. The success of IBM's Watson in the game of Jeopardy has encouraged the community to make the application using cognitive intelligence commercially available. There is also a commitment from the front runners to democratize the knowledge as well as create layers of abstraction for wider and easy adoption. As a result, the community of data scientists and enthusiasts have access to storage and computing power with minimum boot time as well as minimum cost to explore and experiment. Let us explore some of the frameworks, APIs, and tools that are available for running experiments and research in cognitive intelligence.

IBM cognitive toolkit based on Watson

IBM initially developed Watson as an engine that could play the game of Jeopardy. In this game, a human moderator asks questions in a somewhat cryptic manner in natural language. The question is heard by all the participants at the same time. The players can press a buzzer to indicate that they are ready with an answer. The first player to press the buzzer gets the chance to answer the question. Watson was successful in outperforming the Jeopardy world champion in year 2010. As we can see, this process also goes through the Observe | Interpret | Evaluate | Decide cycle. Here is the high-level architecture of IBM Watson as an intelligent machine that can answer questions in natural language:

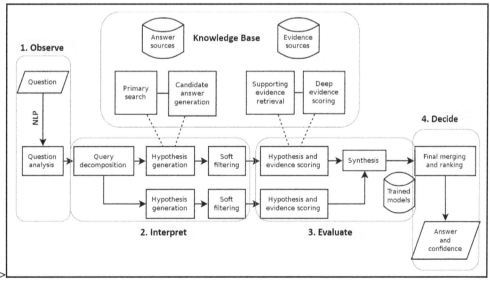

Figure 12.6: High level architecture of IBM Watson as an intelligent machine

"The computer's techniques for unravelling Jeopardy! clues sounded just like mine. That machine zeroes in on keywords in a clue then combs its memory (in Watson's case, a 15-terabyte databank of human knowledge) for clusters of associations with those words. It rigorously checks the top hits against all the contextual information it can muster: the category name; the kind of answer being sought; the time, place, and gender hinted at in the clue; and so on. And when it feels sure enough, it decides to buzz. This is all an instant, intuitive process for a human Jeopardy player, but I felt convinced that under the hood my brain was doing more or less the same thing."

–Ken Jennings (one of the best players in Jeopardy)

After the initial success of Watson as a Jeopardy engine, IBM has evolved Watson into Cognitive Intelligence as a Service and it is available on IBM cloud. The Cognitive System enablers that we have seen earlier in this chapter (Data, Computation, Connectivity, Sensors, Understanding of human brain functioning, Nature, and collective intelligence) are made available with a common interface on the platform.

Watson-based cognitive apps

At the time of writing, IBM supports the following cognitive applications as services on the IBM Cloud platform:

- **Watson assistant**: This application was formally named as "Conversation". This application makes it easy to add a natural language interface to any application. It is easy to train the model for the domain-specific queries and implement customized chatbots.
- **Discovery**: This application enables search into the user's documents as well as a generic cognitive keyword based search on the internet. The service delivers connections, metadata, trends, and sentiment information by default. It is possible to input data from local filesystems, emails, and scanned documents in unstructured format. It is also possible to connect to enterprise storage repository (sharepoint) or a relational database store. It can seamlessly connect to the content on cloud storages.

- **Knowledge Catalog**: The application facilitates organization of data assets for experimenting with various data science algorithms and hypothesis. A data science project in the knowledge catalog contains data, collaborators, notebooks, data flows, and dashboards for visualization. Watson knowledge catalog is a handy and useful application when there are thousands of datasets and hundreds of data scientists who need access to these datasets simultaneously and need to collaborate. The knowledge catalog provides tools to index the data, classify the documents, and control access based on the users and roles. The application supports three user roles. Administrators with full control over the data assets, Editors who can add content to the catalog and grant access to various users, and Viewers who have role-based access to data assets.

- **Language Translator**: This is an easy to use application that is a handy tool that can be easily incorporated within mobile and web applications in order to provide language translation services. This can facilitate development of multilingual applications.

- **Machine Learning**: With this app we can experiment and build various machine learning models in a context sensitive assisted manner within the Watson studio. The models are very easy to build with model builder web application available on IBM cloud. The flow editor provides a graphical user interface to represent the model and this is based on SparkML nodes representation of the DAGs (Directed Acyclic Graphs).

- **Natural Language Understanding**: This is a cognitive application which makes it easy to interpret the natural language based on pre-built trained models. It makes it very easy to integrate within mobile and web applications. The app supports identification of concepts, entities, keywords, categories, sentiment, emotion and most importantly semantic relationship between the natural language text presented as input.

- **Personality Insights**: This application gets as close as possible to cognitive intelligence human beings demonstrate while interacting with each other. We judge a person by the use of specific words in the language, the assertion in making certain statements, pitch, openness to ideas from others, and so on. This application applies linguistic analytics and personality theory using various algorithms and comes up with a Big Five, Needs, and Values score based on the text available in Twitter feeds, blogs, or recorded speeches from a person. The output from the service is delivered in a JSON format that contains percentile scores on various parameters, as seen in the following screenshot:

Figure 12.7: Percentage scores on various parameters

- **Speech to Text and Text to Speech**: These are two services to add the speech recognition capabilities to the enterprise applications. The services transcribe the speech from various languages and a variety of dialects and tones. The services support broadband and narrow-band audio formats. The text transmissions (requests and responses) support JSON format and UTF-8 character set.

- **Tone Analyzer**: This is another cognitive skill that we humans possess. From the tone of a speaker, we can identify the mood and the overall connotation. This determines the overall effectiveness of a specific communication session when it comes to call centers and other customer interactions. The service offerings can be optimized based on the detected tone of the client. This service leverages cognitive linguistic analytics for identification of various types of tones and categorize emotions (anger, joy, and so on), social nature (openness, emotional range, and so on), and language styles (confident and tentative).
- **Visual Recognition**: This services enables applications to recognize images and identify objects and faces that are uploaded to the service. The tagged keywords are generated with confidence scores. The service utilizes deep learning algorithms.
- **Watson Studio**: This service makes it very easy to explore machine learning and cognitive intelligence algorithms and embed the models into the applications. The studio provides data exploration and preparation capabilities and facilitates collaborations among project teams. The data assets and notebooks can be shared and visualization dashboards can be easily created with the Watson Studio interface.

Developing with Watson

Watson provides all the services listed previously along with many more on IBM Cloud infrastructure. There is a consistent web-based user interface for all the services, which enables quick developments of the prototypes and tests. The cognitive services can be easily integrated within the applications since most of those work with REST API calls to the service. The interactions with Watson are secure with encryption and user authentication. Let us develop a language translator using Watson service.

Setting up the prerequisites

In order to leverage IBM Watson services, we require an IBMid:

1. Create an IBMid at `https://console.bluemix.net/registration/?target=%2Fdeveloper%2Fwatson%2Fdashboard`.
2. Log in to IBM Cloud with the login name and password.

3. Browse the Watson services catalog at `https://console.bluemix.net/catalog/?`
   `search=label:litecategory=watson:`

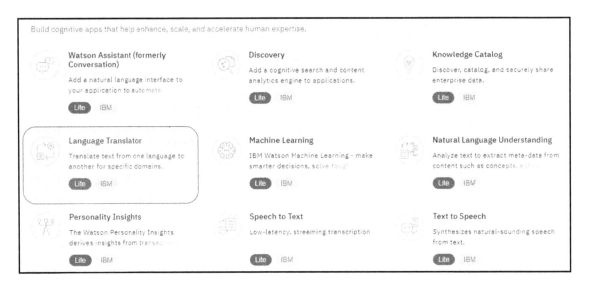

Figure 12.8: IBM services catalog

4. Select **Service Name** (you can use the default name), region/location to deploy
   the service in, and create the service by clicking on the **Create** button.

5. Create the service credentials (username and password) for authenticating the
   requests to your language translation service:

Figure 12.9: Language translator

6. Once we get the service credentials along with URL endpoint, the language translator service is ready to serve the requests for translating text between various supported languages.

Developing a language translator application in Java

We proceed as follows:

1. Create a Maven project and add the following dependency for including Watson libraries:

```
<dependency>
        <groupId>com.ibm.watson.developer_cloud</groupId>
        <artifactId>java-sdk</artifactId>
        <version>5.2.0</version>
</dependency>
```

2. Write the Java code for calling various API methods for LanguageTranslator:

```
package com.aibd;

import com.ibm.watson.developer_cloud.language_translator.v2.*;
import
com.ibm.watson.developer_cloud.language_translator.v2.model.*;

public class WatsonLanguageTranslator {
  public static void main(String[] args) {
    // Initialize the Language Translator object with your
authentication details
    LanguageTranslator languageTranslator = new
LanguageTranslator("{USER_NAME}","{PASSWORD}");
    // Provide the URL end point which is provided along with
service credentials
languageTranslator.setEndPoint("https://gateway.watsonplatform.net/
language-translator/api");
    // Create TranslateOptions object with the builder and adding
the text which needs to be
    // translated
    TranslateOptions translateOptions = new
TranslateOptions.Builder()
                .addText("Artificial Intelligence will soon become
mainstream in everyone's life")
                        .modelId("en-es").build();
    // Call the translation API and collect the result in
TransalationResult object
    TranslationResult result =
```

```
languageTranslator.translate(translateOptions)
                    .execute();
    // Print the JSON formatted result
    System.out.println(result);
    // This is a supporting API to list all the identifiable
languages
    IdentifiableLanguages languages =
languageTranslator.listIdentifiableLanguages()
                        .execute();

    //System.out.println(languages);
    // The API enables identification of the language based on the
entered text.
    IdentifyOptions options = new IdentifyOptions.Builder()
                .text("this is a test for identification of the
language")
                .build();
    // The language identification API returns a JSON object with
level of confidence
    // for all the identifiable languages
    IdentifiedLanguages identifiedLanguages =
languageTranslator.identify(options).execute();
    //System.out.println(identifiedLanguages);
    // API to list the model properties
    GetModelOptions options1 = new
GetModelOptions.Builder().modelId("en-es").build();
    TranslationModel model =
languageTranslator.getModel(options1).execute();
    //System.out.println(model);
  }


}
```

Output # 1: The translation output is returned in JSON format, which contains a number of words that are translated, the character count, and the translated text in the target language based on the model that is selected:

```
{
  "word_count": 9,
  "character_count": 70,
  "translations": [
    {
      "translation": "Inteligencia Artificial pronto será incorporar en la
vida de todos"
    }
  ]
}
```

Output # 2: The `listIdentifiableLanguages` provides the list of languages that are supported in JSON format:

```
{
  "languages": [
    {
      "language": "af",
      "name": "Afrikaans"
    },
    {
      "language": "ar",
      "name": "Arabic"
    },
    {
      "language": "az",
      "name": "Azerbaijani"
    },
    {
      "language": "ba",
      "name": "Bashkir"
    },
    {
      "language": "be",
      "name": "Belarusian"
    },
  . . .
  . . .
```

Output # 3: The service provides API for identifying the language of the text that is provided as input. This is a handy feature for the mobile and web applications where the user can key-in text in any language and the API detects the language and translates into the target language. The output is presented in JSON format with the confidence score for each language. In this case, the service is returning language as English (en) with 0.995921 confidence:

```
{
  "languages": [
    {
      "language": "en",
      "confidence": 0.995921
    },
    {
      "language": "nn",
      "confidence": 0.00240049
    },
    {
      "language": "hu",
```

```
        "confidence": 5.5941E-4
    },
  ..
  ..
```

Output # 4: The model properties can be displayed with the `GetModelOptions` API call:

```
{
  "model_id": "en-es",
  "name": "en-es",
  "source": "en",
  "target": "es",
  "base_model_id": "",
  "domain": "news",
  "customizable": true,
  "default_model": true,
  "owner": "",
  "status": "available"
}
```

Frequently asked questions

Q: What are the various stages of AI and what is the significance of cognitive capabilities?

A: In terms of applicability and its resemblance level with the human brain, AI can be divided into three stages. Applied AI is the application of machine learning algorithms on the data assets in order for the smart machines to define the next course of action. These smart machines operate on the models that can operate within a pre-defined environmental context as well as to a certain degree work within stochastic environments. This level of AI is generally available and is finding use cases and applications in our day to day lives.

Cognitively Simulated AI is the next stage in AI development. In this stage, the intelligent machines are capable of interfacing with human beings in a natural format (with speech, vision, body movements and gestures, and so on). This type of interface between man and machine is seamless and natural and the intelligent machines in this stage can start becoming complementary to human capabilities. The next stage is Strong AI with which we intend to develop intelligence machines that match or exceed human cognitive capabilities. With the availability of large volumes of data along with the machine's brute-force, potentially these intelligent machines can fully augment human capabilities and help us define solutions for some of the most difficult problems and open new frontiers in AI. At that point, it will be difficult to differentiate the intelligent machines from human beings in terms of their cognitive intelligent behavior.

Q: What is the goal of Cognitive Systems and what are the enablers that move the systems towards the goal?

A: The primary goal of developing Cognitive Systems is to create intelligent machines that supplement and augment human capabilities while keeping the interface between man and machine through primary senses. Instead of interacting with keyboard, mouse with the machine, we interface through the five primary senses and mind as the sixth organ and sense. The most important enabler for the development of Cognitive Systems that incorporate strong AI is availability of data and computation power to process the data.

Q: What is the significance of big data in development of Cognitive Systems?

A: The theory of machine learning, various algorithms, and Cognitive Systems has existed for decades. The acceleration in the field has started with the advent of big data. The systems learns from the past patterns that can be searched in the data. The supervised learning and learning models are more accurate with availability of large volumes of data. Big data also allows the systems to have access to heterogeneous data assets that provide key contextual insights within the environment, which makes the intelligent machines more informed and hence enables wholistic decision making. Cognitive Systems also get benefit from the availability of big data assets. The knowledge that is available in unstructured format can be utilized with the use of cognitive intelligence and it opens an entirely new frontier for Cognitive Systems.

Summary

In this chapter, we were introduced to cognitive computing as the next wave in the development of artificial intelligence. By leveraging the five primary human senses along with mind as the sixth sense, the new era of Cognitive Systems can be built. We have seen the stages of AI and the natural progression towards strong AI along with the key enablers for achieving strong AI.

We have also seen the history of Cognitive Systems and observed that the growth is accelerated with availability of big data, which brings large data volumes and the processing power in a distributed computing framework. While the human brain is far from being fully understood, the prospects are looking great with the pioneering work done by some of the large companies that have access to the largest volumes of digital data. The consistent push towards democratizing the AI by enabling AI as a service, these companies are accelerating research for the entire community.

In this book, we have introduced some of the fundamental concepts in Machine Learning and AI and discussed how big data is enabling accelerated research and development in this exciting field. However, just like any new tool or innovation in our hand, as long as we do not lose sight of the overall goal to complement and augment human capabilities, the field is wide open for more research and some of the exciting new use cases that can become mainstream in the near future.

Other Books You May Enjoy

If you enjoyed this book, you may be interested in these other books by Packt:

Artificial Intelligence with Python

Prateek Joshi

ISBN: 9781786464392

- Realize different classification and regression techniques
- Understand the concept of clustering and how to use it to automatically segment data
- See how to build an intelligent recommender system
- Understand logic programming and how to use it
- Build automatic speech recognition systems
- Understand the basics of heuristic search and genetic programming
- Develop games using Artificial Intelligence
- Learn how reinforcement learning works
- Discover how to build intelligent applications centered on images, text, and time series data
- See how to use deep learning algorithms and build applications based on it

MySQL 8 for Big Data
Shabbir Challawala

ISBN: 9781788397186

- Explore the features of MySQL 8 and how they can be leveraged to handle Big Data
- Unlock the new features of MySQL 8 for managing structured and unstructured Big Data
- Integrate MySQL 8 and Hadoop for efficient data processing
- Perform aggregation using MySQL 8 for optimum data utilization
- Explore different kinds of join and union in MySQL 8 to process Big Data efficiently
- Accelerate Big Data processing with Memcached
- Integrate MySQL with the NoSQL API
- Implement replication to build highly available solutions for Big Data

Leave a review - let other readers know what you think

Please share your thoughts on this book with others by leaving a review on the site that you bought it from. If you purchased the book from Amazon, please leave us an honest review on this book's Amazon page. This is vital so that other potential readers can see and use your unbiased opinion to make purchasing decisions, we can understand what our customers think about our products, and our authors can see your feedback on the title that they have worked with Packt to create. It will only take a few minutes of your time, but is valuable to other potential customers, our authors, and Packt. Thank you!

Index